Uttering, Muttering

Collecting, Using and Reporting Talk for Social and Educational Research

Edited by Clem Adelman

CB 17154 £4.95. 11.81

First published in 1981 by
Grant McIntyre Ltd
39 Great Russell Street, London WC1B 3PH

Copyright © Clem Adelman 1981

British Library Cataloguing in Publication Data

Uttering, muttering.
  1. Social sciences – Methodology
  2. Speech of social status – Research
  I. Adelman, Clem
  300.7′2   H61

ISBN 0–86216–042–1
ISBN 0–86216–043–X Pbk

Photoset in 10/12pt Bembo, by V & M Graphics Ltd, Aylesbury, Bucks
Printed and bound in Great Britain at The Pitman Press, Bath

Uttering, Muttering

1 Week Loan

This book is due for return on or before the last date shown below

Contents

CLEM ADELMAN

Introduction

This book discusses ways of inquiry which use as evidence what people say. The contributors have extensive and recent experience of collecting, using and reporting talk. This experience includes case studies of school systems, local education authorities, individual schools and classrooms and teachers. The different papers exemplify the varied ways by which talk may be analysed, and the purposes for which it is used as evidence.

Each contribution contains enough introduction and context to be read separately, although the book would best be read in sequence by those for whom these approaches to inquiry are novel. A technical knowledge of linguistics is not presumed and although the reading and analysis of transcripts may be new, this unfamiliarity should easily be overcome. Some of the papers require a limited acquaintance with the terminology of sociology but even here the expository yet non-prescriptive style should allow the significance of each contribution to be understood.

By the early 1960s there had accumulated evidence in Great Britain and the United States that the intelligence of children, however measured, was not the sole or necessary cause of school failure or achievement.[1] Working class children matched with middle class children of similar intelligence would probably achieve less at school. A variety of factors were suggested as contributing to these social class differences in achievement. Working class children were said by some to be disadvantaged in various ways. For instance, working class children did not use or conceive of language with a complexity that would allow them to perform as well in school, or in other public institutional settings, as a middle class child. This notion of language deficit[2] became linked to the working class and those minority groups whose first language was not English. Government intervention in the form of programmes of compensatory education[3] and educational priority areas[4] placed considerable funds at the disposal of educationalists of various persuasions. In the United States an enormous programme of language enrichment and reinforcement was developed, particularly for younger children. Language was conceived as a human behaviour that could be nurtured and shaped by predominantly psychological techniques. Enhanced language performance would be evaluated by standard tests. The social context of the use of language was not taken as a significant aspect affecting language performance. Even in linguistics, as Roger Shuy points out, 'work has focused on the universals and sought generalities which characterise a language. Only within the past decade, however, have linguists begun to examine the context or the setting in order to understand the variability of language to a fuller extent'.[5]

The deficit model of language competence prevalent during the early 1960s stimulated researchers in the United States and Great Britain to study how language, particularly talk, was used in school classrooms. In the United States a deficit model was presumed by many of the enrichment and compensatory programmes aimed mainly at poor children. Programmes such as 'Head Start' and 'Follow Through' were aimed at improving language comprehension and performance by behaviouristic methods.[6] Major criticism of these attempts at intervention came, not only from some of the evaluations of the programmes, but also from sociolinguists such as Hymes,[7] Cazden[8] and Labov.[9] The book *Functions of Language in the Classroom* (Cazden, John and Hymes, eds, 1972)[10] and Labov's 'The Logic of Non-Standard English'[11] mark the establishment of a socio-cultural perspective on language use in schools.

In Great Britain there was a prolonged and heated debate about the connections between the educational performance of working class and middle class children, and the connection between this performance and what Bernstein termed 'restricted' and 'elaborated' codes,[12] to indicate the structures underlying the manifestations of language. This debate was accompanied by a considerable amount of research and, as in the United States, the most significant work came from those who took into account the social contexts of talk in school classrooms. Although Bernstein made it clear that he did not support a deficit model of language competence,[13] he did not in his own work engage in the explication of his ideas through, for instance, transcript examples of social interaction in classrooms. The work of sociolinguists who have concentrated on social interaction and language form is exemplified by the work of Stubbs,[14] Hammersley[15] and Atkinson.[16] In the field of education this work was first brought together in the book *Explorations in Classroom Observation* which had a delayed publication in 1976 (Stubbs and Delamont, eds).[17] Recently Edwards and Furlong[18] have reviewed and contributed to this work through their book *The Language of Teaching* (1979), whilst in the United States Hugh Mehan's *Learning Lessons* (1979) has an analogous place.[19]

Courteney Cazden has recently been studying bilingual classrooms in association with Fred Ericson.[20] The work of Roger Shuy,[21] Peggy Griffin, Marilyn Merritt[22] and others at the Centre for Applied Linguistics, Washington D.C., has contributed extensively to our understanding of variation, form and social function of talk in school classrooms. A series of projects has been funded by the National Institute of Education in the United States to study the particular communicative activities within classrooms. This funding emerges from a conference convened by the National Institute for Education in 1977 on 'Teaching as a Linguistic Process in a Cultural Setting'. The detail of these studies not only shows the richness of the variety of manifestation of types of communicative competence but also its occurrence at all stages of schooling. From these studies a very convincing picture of the complexities of teaching can be built up which could be used for pre-service and in-service training of teachers. However, unlike category systems used in competency-based programmes of preparation, these communicative events from teaching do retain the meaning and reference and some sense of the social context and appropriateness for the utterance. In these ways teachers on pre- or in-service courses are able to relate these utterances to their own personal identities in the ways in which they cope with the social world through social relationships. This use of transcript and its analysis, rather than categorisation of the talk into behavioural categories such as the category scheme of Flanders,[23] not only allows readers to make connections with their own social actions but also helps them to try to understand the talk from several points of view and several types of analysis.

One problem with using talk lies in its familiarity. To penetrate beyond the 'ordinariness' of talk, to attribute social categories, value judgments and other cultural features requires the researcher to separate out his own knowledge as a member of the culture from the talk being used by a fellow member of that culture. This separating out allows the researcher to sustain a critical inner dialogue, monitoring the researcher's reactions, prejudices and taken-for-granted categorisations when reading the transcript. Such reflexivity comes through attention to what people say, and self-critical analysis of transcripts.

To be capable of using talk as a means of research the researcher has both to maintain rapport with the subject by the ordinary means of conversation (intonation, emphasis, non-verbal gestures) and yet, at the same time, remain uninvolved in terms of empathy with the account that is being given. This critical listening to accounts of others is an essential requisite for those who wish to collect talk as reasearch data. The researcher using talk responds to what is said at two levels. There is the conversational analysis of what is heard in terms of 'when this person says these words they are probably addressing this issue or concern'. At the same time the researcher tests these putative categories against alternatives. This process of re-categorising whilst interviewing, listening to tapes and so on, is dependent on the researcher's reflexive understanding of the culture of the speaker. This ability of the researcher to converse and make sense, whilst at the same time considering his own categories in a self-conscious manner, is something that people in ordinary conversation occasionally do, but unsystematically.

When talk is used as evidence in research, underlying assumptions and systematic inquiry are often revealed. Where the researcher has begun with a hypothesis, the talk is often used to illustrate the presence or absence of some phenomenon. Such positivistic research does not explain or analyse what is distinctive about the talk one considers as evidence. In ethnomethodological parlance the re-searcher does explicate how he used his knowledge as a member of the culture to categorise, clarify and give significance to the talk. Interpretative or naturalistic research uses talk as a means of reconstructing the realities of those being studied – a process that involves the researcher in critical reflection of his own predilections. This is the predominant approach used by the contributors to this book. Talk is not taken merely as a surface illustration but is questioned for meaning, pursued for discrepancies, placed in context over time, compared with other accounts and its intentionality elucidated through triangulation. These are not empty ruminations but an attempt to understand and so more fairly represent the researched.

Given that talk often carries its authorship by its content and idiosyncrasies, the problem arises of how to protect the identity of the researched from being discovered. This protection is usually provided in a closed system or institution by confidentiality agreements and to a wider public by assuring anonymity by the use of pseudonyms.

THE ARRANGEMENT OF THE BOOK

The contributions are grouped by the stages of research that they explore, collection of the talk, analysis of transcripts, negotiation of accounts and the reporting of the stages of research. The papers by Mike Stubbs and Roy Todd, whilst not reporting any particular studies, are essential reading. The reader needs to be acquainted with the ideas and debates they raise as these reflect the competing criteria which need to be clarified before thinking about and practising research can begin.

The contributors have helped establish and develop a range of research perspectives. Not all of these perspectives are represented in this book, and in many cases the papers exemplify more than one of the perspectives. These perspectives may be characterised as:

(a) Talk as a realisation of the relationship between linguistic form and function – discourse analysis for instance in the work of John Sinclair and Malcolm Coulthard.[24]

(b) Talk as a relationship between linguistic form and social function, for instance the contributions by Paul Atkinson and Mary Willes.

(c) Talk as an emulation of cognitive process, for instance the paper by Douglas Barnes and Frankie Todd.

(d) Talk as a realisation of intentionality, for instance the paper by Clem Adelman.

(e) Talk as a realisation of social structure and stratification, as exemplified by the work of Basil Bernstein.

(f) Talk as a manifestation of human expression as distinctive and varied as the language of literature. This perspective is exemplified by some of the work of James Britton, Harold Rosen and Douglas Barnes.[25]

(g) Talk as illustrative of cultural variation as exemplified by ethnographers such as Dell Hymes, John Gumperz and Susan Philips.[26]

(h) Talk as exemplifying different social perspectives, for example, those covered by the symbolic interactionist sociologists such as Anselm Strauss,[27] and Howard Becker,[28] represented in this volume by Peter Woods.

(i) Talk as self-commentary on practice associated with curriculum development and evaluation using case study and naturalistic methods, exemplified by Bob Stake[29] and Barry MacDonald,[30] and in this volume by Helen Simons and Tom Fox.

The process of collecting talk during fieldwork in the school is described by Peter Woods. Some of the talk was used as evidence in the construction of a typology of recurrent interaction significant in the social order of the school. Helen Simons describes entry to a school for the purpose of case study. The problems of access to informants and the rights of the interviewee with regard to the interview data are crucial issues in the collection and reporting of talk. The case study to which the interviews are contributory is not only a format for reporting but also a methodological and ethical approach to the process of educational research.

Mary Willes concentrates on how talk provides the contextual means for the implicit communication of rules of participation to children becoming pupils during their early days in school. Willes acknowledges her attribution of meaning to the utterances – how they are intended to be understood by the pupils. It is very unusual for children of four or five years of age to be able to give accounts of the intention of another's utterance, although they do mention rules of participation and conduct during interaction with their peers.

Douglas Barnes and Frankie Todd reveal the tribulations of attempts to allocate segments of talk to categories in their classification. They explain how talk has not only an intended meaning, but also a guiding influence on social interaction. Strategy is there term for this and the article here reflects Vygotsky's influential ideas about the relationship between thought, language and action.

The interpretation of another's utterance and the intended meanings of one's own generates numerous questions for researchers. The researcher often infers or attributes meaning particularly when he or she has become familiar with the classroom, school or other social setting. However, even with prolonged, intensive and expert fieldwork, the researcher may still make wrong interpretations. Often these interpretations are made during analysis of notes away from the field, but participant observation requires social interaction with those being studied. Fieldworkers, feeling confident that they have a knowledge of the culture that will allow them to participate in the situation, may be woken with a shock. For instance, R. T. Keiser[31] describes how his misinterpretation of a gesture by a member of a street gang other than the one he is studying leads to a knife being drawn on him. K. Stoddart[32] studying the argot of heroin users describes how complicated and delicate the exploration of the term 'pinched' becomes.

In classrooms interpretations of teacher and pupil talk are often made without checking these interpretations with the talkers. Triangulation (which is described in Chapter Five) is a method that resuscitates intended meanings and interpretations allowing the researcher to elucidate the significance of the talk for the talkers.

Although time-consuming, triangulation goes some way towards disclosing the complexities of social interaction from the participants' perspective. Participants' terms of reference, their interpretations and intended meanings are explored by taking a particular section of interaction as the topic. Triangulation is one way of bringing the researcher closer to the emic – the complex of values, beliefs, principles and rules that guide practice. The exploration of the emic demands active research; empathy, enhanced through familiarity, does not necessarily penetrate into the inner world of the participants even if the researcher shares the same ethnicity.

Paul Atkinson explains the ways in which analysis of talk, particularly through the concept of turn taking, contributes to our knowledge and understanding of how conversations are achieved. The relationships between different segments of conversation are complex and this method of analysis brings out the detail of the inherent logic of the coherence of conversation.

Mike Stubbs presents a wide ranging discussion of the integrity of talk. He maintains that talk is often used as evidence for inferring social/psychological phenomena without first analysing the system of talk of which any section is part. This is a very demanding task for those who use talk as evidence and therefore might have objection to the low priority given in Strubbs's paper as to what the talk accomplishes in social situations. Stubbs, however, makes a strong argument against using isolated segments of talk as evidence. The discourse community in which the talk is situated must be defined in order to locate the significance of the talk as reliable evidence for making inferences about other social phenomena. This paper acts as a brake on the over-enthusiastic and impulsive, making for reflection on the practice of research using talk.

Gordon Wells presents a self-contained system for collecting, analysing and theorising about the talk of children with adults. In detailed analysis transcripts he brings out the interpretation of the researcher. By sustaining the research for several years, by codifying the talk, Wells and his associates have emerged with some findings that have been used as critical comments on current knowledge and practice concerning children's language development. In particular, the widely reported work of Joan Tough[33] has been one of the subjects of this critical scrutiny.

Tom Fox gives an account of a method of eliciting teachers' terms of reference and terminology graphically. This article provides in great detail the complexities of endeavours to go beyond the researchers' interpretation. Fox, like other authors in this volume, believes that teachers have complex theories of practice that remain tacit until deliberate research and development curriculum intervention or change are attempted. Rather than taking teachers' accounts as exemplifying 'false consciousness' or 'folk myths', the case-study worker and curriculum researcher try to collect and pursue discrepancies from the widest range of accounts, acknowledging in the reporting the many perspectives in a classroom, school or school system. Fox uses talk as a means to illustrate teachers' beliefs, values, perspectives and rules about their teaching. By eliciting the teachers' and pupils' perspectives, a more sensitive evaluation, closely related to the issues and concerns of teachers and pupils, can be assembled.

Roy Todd reminds researchers that they do their work in a social and ideological context. The different approaches to educational and social research used by their purveyors are in competition with one another for acceptance and applicability.

By using talk in its social context as a main source of information, the emphasis of research is directed towards the quality and variation in educational practice and social interaction in other settings. As all educational research aims to contribute to the improvement of practice, albeit by different criteria, research helps practitioners to become more aware of their practice, and enables them both to initiate and to respond to innovation and change.

The approaches to inquiry offered in this book provide information about quality and variation in talk contributing to our understanding of the complexities of educational and social practice. Researchers, naive and sophisticated, students of education and social science, oral historians and sociolinguists should find this book pertinent to their activities. Teachers inquiring, for instance, into language across the curriculum should find the papers in this volume provide guidance on procedural and methodological practice.

Editor's Note: This book emerges in part from two conferences for which I received funds from the Social Science Research Council in 1975 and 1976. The participants included Paul Atkinson, Douglas Barnes, Deirdre Burton, Irene Bowman, Ian Birkstead, Richard Choat, Jenny Haystead, Martin Hammersley, David Hargreaves, Elisabeth Newson, Frankie Todd, Roy Todd, Peter Trudgill, Maureen Shields, Helen Simons, Mike Stubbs, Irene Robertson, Paul Willis, Rob Walker, Mike Whitehead, Gordon Wells, Peter Woods and Stefan Zaklukiewicz. Two hundred copies of the conference papers were subsequently circulated. This book, while retaining the title of that original set of papers, contains new and revised contributions. In particular, the contributions from Mary Willes, Paul Atkinson, Tom Fox and Roy Todd are new; the authors of the remaining contributions have revised their original papers; and two of the papers in the first *Uttering, Muttering* do not appear here.

NOTES

1 SILVER, H., *Equal Opportunity in Education: a reader in social class and educational opportunity*, Methuen, 1973.
   BOUDON, R., *Education, Opportunity and Social Inequality*, Wiley, 1974.
   GINSBERG, H., *The Myth of the Deprived Child*, Prentice-Hall, 1972.
   DOUGLAS, J. W. B., ROSS, J. M. & SIMPSON, H. R., *All Our Future*, Peter Davies, 1968.

2 BEIREITER, C. & ENGLEMAN, S., *Teaching Disadvantaged Children in the Pre-school*, Prentice-Hall, 1966.

3 This refers to the Elementary and Secondary Act of 1965. For an example of a critical commentary see:
   HOUSE, E. R., GLASS, G. V., McLEAN, L. D. & WALKER, D. F., 'No simple answer; critique of the follow-through evaluation', *Harvard Educational Review*, 48 ii, pp. 128–160, 1978.

4 HALSEY, A. H., *Educational Priority*, Vols 1–4, Department of Education & Science, HMSO, 1972.

5 SHUY, R., 'Toward future study of the effect of school setting on learning', Mimeo, Centre for Applied Linguistics, Washington D.C., June 1978.

6 BEIREITER, C. & ENGLEMAN, S., op. cit.
   BLANK, M., *Teaching Learning in the Pre-school: A Dialogue Approach*, C. Merrill, 1973.

7 HYMES, D., 'Ethnographic monitoring' in H. T. Treuba (ed.) *Studies in Classroom Ethnography*, Rowley, 1980.

8 CAZDEN, C., 'The situation; A neglected source of social class differences in language use' in J. P. Pride & J. Holmes, (eds.) *Sociolinguistics*, Penguin, 1972.

9 LABOV, W., 'The logic of non-standard English' in F. Williams (ed.) *Language and Poverty*, Markham, 1970.

10 CAZDEN, C., JOHN, V. & HYMES, D., *Functions of Language in the Classroom*, Teachers College Press, New York, 1972.

11 LABOV, W., op. cit.

12 BERNSTEIN, B., *Class Codes and Control*, Vol. 1, Routledge and Kegan Paul, 1971.

13 BERNSTEIN, B., 'Education cannot compensate for society', in

R. Dale *et al*. (eds), *School and Society*, Open University, 1971.
BERNSTEIN, B., Response to W. LABOV, *Class Codes and Control Vol. 1.,* op. cit.

14 STUBBS, M., *Language, Schools and Classrooms*, Methuen, 1976.

15 HAMMERSLEY, M., 'School learning; the cultural resources required by pupils to answer a teacher's question', in P. Woods & M. Hammersley (eds) *School Experience*, Croom Helm, 1977.

16 ATKINSON, P. & DELAMONT, S., 'Mock-ups and cock-ups', in *School Experience*, ibid.

17 STUBBS, M. & DELAMONT, S., *Explorations in Classroom Observation*, Wiley, 1976.

18 EDWARDS, A. & FURLONG, V., *The Language of Teaching*, Heinemann, 1979.

19 MEHAN, H., *Learning Lessons*, Harvard University Press, 1979.

20 ERICSON, F., CAZDEN, C., CARRASCO, R. & VERA, A., *Social and Cultural Organisation of Interaction in Classrooms of Bi-lingual Children*, Harvard University School of Education, June 1980.

21 SHUY, R., For instance 'Bi-lingualism and language variety', in J. Alatis (ed.), *International Dimensions of Bi-lingual Education*, Georgetown University, Washington D.C., 1978.
GRIFFIN, P. & SHUY, R., *Children's Functional Language and Education in the Early Years*; final report to the Carnegie Corporation of New York, Centre for Applied Linguistics, Washington, D.C., 1978.

22 MERRITT, M. & HUMPHREY, F., 'Service-like events during individual worktime and their contribution to the nature of rules for classroom interaction', Centre for Applied Linguistics, Washington D.C., 1980.

23 FLANDERS, N., *Analysing Teaching Behaviour*, Addison Wesley, 1970.
WALKER, R. & ADELMAN, C., 'Interaction analysis in informal classrooms: a critical comment on the Flanders System', *British Journal of Educational Psychology*, 45, 1975.

24 SINCLAIR, J. & COULTHARD, M., *Towards an Analysis of Discourse*, Oxford University Press, 1977.

25 BRITTON, J., ROSEN, H. & BARNES, D., *Language, the Learner and the School*, Penguin, Revised Edition, 1971.

26 PHILIPS, S., 'Participant structures and communicative competence', in Cazden, John, & Hymes, op. cit.

27 STRAUSS, A., *Mirrors and Masks: The search for identity*, Martin Robertson, 1977.

28 BECKER, H. S., 'On becoming a Marijuana user', in *School and Society*, Open University, 1971.

29 STAKE, R., 'Responsive evaluation', in *Evaluating the Arts in Education*, C. Merrill, 1975.

30 MACDONALD, B., *The Experience of Innovation*, Centre for Applied Research in Education, University of East Anglia, Occasional Publication, No. 6.

31 KEISER, R. T., 'Fieldwork amongst the vice lords of Chicago', in G. Spindler, *Being an Anthropologist*, Holt, Reinhart & Winston, 1970.

32 STODDART, K., 'Pinched: notes on the ethnographic location of argot', in R. Turner, *Ethnomethodology*, Penguin, 1974.

33 WELLS, G., 'Language use and educational success: an empirical response to Joan Tough's "The Development of Meaning"', *Research in Education* No. 18, November 1977.

PETER WOODS

1 Understanding through Talk

I have been concerned in my research to discover and report the experience of teachers and pupils in school. My general conceptual framework has been within the symbolic interactionist tradition of Mead, Blumer, Goffman and Becker.[1] Clearly, subject matter and methodological theory place heavy reliance on talk both as objective data and as an agency, and I want to discuss some aspects of this which seemed of particular note in my study. First, in order to have some idea of where all the talk led to, I will give a brief account of some of my conclusions, the interpretations I have made of my material, and some of the theoretical implications I have seen in them.[2]

I went into an ordinary Secondary Modern school with as open a mind as I could manage, ultimately moving freely around the school, observing lessons, sitting in the staffroom, talking to over three hundred pupils for periods ranging from twenty minutes to three hours, many of them several times over the period of the year that I was there, making field notes and recordings of as much as I could by whatever means I could. I had been impressed by the grounded theory approach of Glaser and Strauss,[3] and looked to develop my theory from the research as it unfolded. After a term in the school, I listened to all my tapes and read through my notes. There were certain regularities in the pupils' conversations with me which provided certain themes. One of their preoccupations was an aversion to being shown up by teachers.

Third-year boy: I could not stand that subject. The teacher kept being nasty and sarcastic. He called us louts and said we all had lice, that was the sort of thing, in front of all the class . . . because we had long hair, we were dirty . . . just because he had not got none.

Eric: He shows you up in front of the class.

Kay: Yeah, all the teachers embarrass you! All the boys
              look . . . horrible it is . . . horrible.

Kay: One of my friends . . . a teacher belted her ever so hard
              and she started crying and all the boys started picking
              on her . . . calling her a baby.

PW: Do you think teachers show you up on purpose?

Kay: They probably think if they show us up we won't do it
              again because we're so embarrassed.

From my material I was able to make a study of the process of showing
up, and to accumulate more details in accordance with the trends that
were revealed. These became the construction of a typology, an
examination of the internal structure of the process, a consideration
of functions and results, and of who was involved. This level of
substantive theory involved the introduction of certain basic concepts
like negative sanction, surface and deeper behaviour, the self and the
other. Formal theory, wherein we locate this within a more widely
applicable framework, requires a broader base. Tentatively, I
associated the 'showing-up syndrome' with certain pedagogic styles
which are underwritten by psychological models of teaching,
childhood and knowledge, social Darwinism and paternalist systems
of rule, all within an umbrella of alienation.[4]

Before further development along those lines, however, I returned
to my data. In talking about their school lives, many pupils spoke
frequently, intensely and at length about 'having a laugh'.

Well I think . . . 'ere we go again, another day for mucking about.

It's all right when you're at school, really, like when you can just
talk to people, have a laugh.

It's the only place we have fun, isn't it?

We aren't silly at home, not very often anyway. You act silly at
school for a laugh.

Assemblies are a waste of time. For religious people they're OK,
it's a good morning's start, but there aren't many religious people
in the school. You're all in there together, it's a great temptation to

kick somebody's legs and make them fall down just for a laugh, just temptation to trouble.

'Having a laugh' eventually gelled into another theme. What did they mean by it, how important was it to them, what kinds were there, who was involved, when did it happen, and so on? Again I structured my observations and conversations to elaborate, and to fill in the gaps. Eventually I argued that pupils have their own norms, rules and values, and that their school lives are well structured by them in ways not immediately apparent, and not always based on official criteria. In their lives, laughter has a central place, either as a natural product, or as a life-saving response to the exigencies of the institution – boredom, ritual, routine, regulations, oppressive authority. I distinguished between 'natural' and 'institutional' laughter, the latter being produced specifically by the agency of the school. Among the latter I distinguished between 'mucking about', a kind of seemingly aimless behaviour, which I saw as a reaction to boredom; and what I called 'subversive laughter', a more political reaction. Strictly authoritarian teachers can be instrumental in promoting subversive laughter, which can at times degenerate into anger and open conflict; other teachers, by aiding colonisation, avoid it.[5]

This fitted the general theoretical framework previously developed in that there were the same regularities between types of laughter and groups of pupils as between types of laughter and teachers' pedagogic orientation and control techniques. Further light on these groups of pupils came from my study of the subject choice process in the second term of my stay at the school. I concluded that pupils approach this matter in fundamentally different ways. Pupil groups develop group perspectives, and for these subject choice has different meanings, one group employing an official educational model, the other a counter-official, social model. These perspectives are connected with social class, parents showing similar interpretative frameworks as their children. Teachers mediate these filtered choices still further, motivated by a critical external influence which demands ever improving examination results, and which involves the re-channelling of misdirected choices. All of this portrays the school as a massive and relentless imprinting agency in the service of social selection.[6]

Throughout, I have favoured forms of what I call naturalistic or behavioural talk, that is talk heard and noted by me in the ordinary course of events. But how do we recognise the 'ordinary course of events'? I detected three levels of 'ordinariness' associated with three levels of access. When I first went to the school I was shown carefully pre-selected scenes and witnessed 'educationist' performances. This was the public, outer face of the school in its Sunday clothes. The second level came with the relaxation of this strict control and shop-window performance and allowed me general freedom – showing the school divested of its clothes as it were. However, it was not until more time had elapsed that I had built up enough trust and concord with the inmates for them to confide in me their innermost throughts and feelings, and thus reveal to me how the school operated in its very vitals. I was not aware of being given actually contradictory information, though it may have been limited, and hence distortional, out of context. To guard against this I employed the usual precautions – distinguishing between subjective and objective data, invoking the criteria of plausibility and reliability of informant. The main procedures were pursuing discrepancies in accounts and cross-checking them over a period of time.

I was fortunate in finding some key informants. They helped give perspective to the entire methodological front from the very beginning, for example by identifying the nature of other people's talk and behaviour. One instance of this arises from the distinction between educationist and teacher talk.[7] It is not surprising that on occasions there is a big difference between what teachers say in one context, and what they actually do in another. The gap between word and deed may well be wider if one does not progress beyond the first two levels of access, and it might be difficult to spot if there were no informants. Similarly, key informants can alert us to alternative explanations of the talk and behaviour of others that we perhaps have no other means of knowing about, so that we can recognise the various rhetorics presented to us, and how consciously and seriously they are held. It helps here to have various kinds of informants. The more they constitute a cross-section of the population in question, the better. I was lucky in being able to forge close ties not only with the reformist left-wing Art veteran and the libertarian Social Studies probationer, but with the traditional-conservative head of Games, who had academic aspirations, and the traditional-liberal Humanities teacher. On the important temporal dimension also, informants provide a sense of history, interpreting present events as part of a long, ongoing process.

My general practice was to use as many cross-validating methods and instruments as I could. For example, I would not know what to make of the content of a personal talk with the headmaster, say, on the matter of subject choice, without the benefit of other vantage points. Among these I would include his talk to the third year pupils, and to their parents, their views on it, and the views of those he has taken into his confidence – other members of staff, preferably both for and against – sought if possible in various different situations, which might include public house as well as staffroom and classroom. I never held any formal interviews. The nearest I approached it was with the headmaster, a reflection possibly of the social distance between us. But even then I made no notes on the spot, had no formal schedule, and simply tried to conduct a man-to-man discussion, leaving him to fill the scene that I set. I did as little talking as I could get away with, being intent, as Cicourel advises,[8] on elaborating his meaning. So with other members of staff. It would not be much use asking them directly what their ideologies were, because for the most part they do not consider them systematically. They are revealed by naturalistic observation, and discussion of other topics. For example, I found, on one occasion, that discussing a particular class of pupils with teachers revealed a great deal about the teachers' conceptions of knowledge, teaching and childhood. A similar result followed my production of a paper on 'pupils' views of school and teachers', which contained plenty of provocative material. Here, some of them challenged both the pupils' views and my interpretation of them. There is a neat ethical point here. It would be quite wrong, in my view, to set up conversations with teachers (or anyone else for that matter) on one subject with the intention of gaining information on another. That would involve a form of deceit. But there is nothing wrong with post-hoc analysing. Ultimately, the ethical point here rests on the use of such data, and the extent to which it impinges on the private individuals concerned.

If one of the problems in talking to teachers is identifying the various caps they wear, with pupils it is *seeing* the cap they are wearing. At least we can identify more readily with teacher culture; the road to understanding is a longer one with pupils.

Here I should say that I am using 'understanding' as Rosalie Wax does, not as some mysterious empathy, but as a phenomenon of shared meanings, when one feels part of the culture and can interpret words, gestures and so on, as they do.[9] We know some of the problems from, for example, Labov's work, where he explains that the asymmetrical interview is likely to lead in some instances to defensive, monosyllabic behaviour.[10] The problem of putting pupils at their ease cannot be met by the normal forms of proclaiming anonymity, universality and impersonality, disclaiming teacher and associate identity, and trying to get across to them in words that this was *their* platform. I felt that I had to make it their platform. This I tried to do by having conversations with them in friendship groups. I would go to a class at the beginning of a day, with the permission of the teacher concerned of course, and arrange a timetable for the day, seeing groups of about four pupils in double-period slots. Pupils were invariably split up into groups when I entered. If they were large groups, I asked them to split themselves up. Pairs of pupils I asked to invite another pair along. This technique, I believe, had several advantages. The company of like-minded fellows helped to put them at their ease. The bond between them and the way it was allowed to surface shifted the power balance in the discussion situation in their direction. As long as my interventions were not too intrusive, it might facilitate the establishment of their norms, and I might become privy to their culture, albeit in rather a rigged way. These remarks, in fact, were addressed more to the three friends present rather than to me. At other times, they prompted each other – 'Go on, tell him' – 'What about when you . . . ?' Other advantages of the group interview were that the pupils acted as checks, balances and prompts to each other. Inaccuracies were corrected, incidents and reactions recalled and analysed. Many of the conversations became, I believe, part of their experience rather than a commentary on it, and this was particularly true of the 'laughter' discussions.

This leads me to consider what these discussions actually did, in a Garfinkelian sense.[11] First, they did provide me with information, and I think the structure of the group facilitated this. Pupils volunteered information in the company of their friends, and often to them rather than to me in the context of ongoing exchanges with them, that I would not otherwise have been privy to. I doubt, for example, if I would have received this information in a one-to-one interview:

Christine: I was sitting next to Kevin, and he'd got this cartridge in his pen and he was going like that (*she indicates an obscene gesture*), and I just pushed him away, and the teacher was writing on the board and he must have eyes in the back of his head . . . and he says . . . he turns round with a fuming face and he says 'Will you two stop fiddling with each other!' I never went so bright red in all my life, and he pushed me over one side and him on the other . . . and everybody turned round, didn't they? . . . In front of all my friends! You know . . . he made such a . . . mockery . . . can't stand him! Everybody was scared stiff in that class, everyone just sits there, all quiet.

There is another side to the unstructured, naturalistic, group identification approach of course. More forthright or articulate individuals can dominate discussions and there is a danger that the outcomes can be biased in favour of the most outspoken or aggressive individuals. This may then colour the whole work, the views of one or a few pupils being presented as illustrative of a whole group.[12] If we couple with this the pupils' natural tendency in a conflict situation to regard an external interviewer as a kind of relief agency, we get an idea of the kind of bias that can creep in. I felt that, on occasions, the actual discussion made for grievance or for therapy. People can talk themselves and others into a temper, or into laughter for that matter, and sometimes I felt there was a thin divide between the two. This clearly has repercussions for their representations of past events. Such discussions should be regarded as data rather than sources of information. Thus misrepresentations, outrageous lies, melodrama, put-ons can all in fact be turned to research advantage, as long as they are identified. Perhaps the best examples again are in connection with the 'laughter' paper. Many of the discussions held with me were 'laughs' in their own right, that is to say they were generated in the discussion, and possibly the particular configuration of circumstances subscribing to it as reported by them had not led to laughter – at least so much laughter – previously. The discussion thus became part of their school life rather than a pause in it. Also of course the laughter is the important element. For added ribaldry, the facts will probably have suffered some distortion, but that is a natural concomitant of laughter-making. Consider this example:

Tracy: Dianne fell off a chair first and as she went to get up, she got 'old of me skirt, she was 'aving a muck about, and there was I in me petticoat, me skirt came down round my ankles and Mr Bridge came in (*great screams of laughter from girls*). He'd been standing outside the door.

Kate: 'E told her she'd get suspended.

Tracy: He 'ad me mum up the school, telling her what a horrible child I was.

Kate: 'Nobody will marry you,' said Miss Judge.

Tracy: Oh yeah, Miss Judge sits there, 'n, nobody will want to marry *you*, Jones,' she said. I said, 'Well you ain't married, anyway.' (*Shrieks of laughter from girls.*)

Surrendering the initiative can lead to results that are very time-absorbing, tedious and discomforting. There is a great deal of repetition. Occasionally people wander off into peripheral monologues. I remember one boy describing at great length his plans for becoming a jockey; a couple of girls their experiences with a gang of Hell's Angels in Luton; several risqué discussions with both boys and girls about sex and fornication. This last is clearly very relevant to my interest in the pupils' cultural experience with their environment. But it reminds me of another of those ethical problems. In a sense, talk is legitimation. The wise man's advice to the young lover not to declare his love until sure of the response is founded on this knowledge. Until he says it, he is free to love another. For me to talk about some things with the pupils might have the effect of legitimating them in their eyes. Even 'listening' can go half way towards this. Smoking, fornication, teacher-victimisation, all figure prominently in the pupils' school life, and thus we need to know about them. But it can be uncomfortable at times, while operating under the auspices, enjoying the hospitality of and making friendships with those who make a career of trying to eliminate these activities.

The solution of course is to take sides, and I suppose if one is going to identify successfully with a culture, it is imperative to do so. This leads me on to something else I felt these discussions did, which touches on the 'mysterious empathy' I spoke of earlier. Robert Redfield described how the form in which he came to understand the Mayan culture came to be constituted phenomenologically in his experience, and in some ways I think I went through a similar process.[13] In the early days of my study, I recorded my impressions of the cultural experiences of the pupils. I noted down what the teachers did, what the pupils did, and what they told me about it. As this was during the first stage of access it had only limited value. Later, after many discussions, when I had become what Robert Janes calls a personalised member and had developed a certain rapport with the pupils, I was keyed in to their experience via talk, and it was the talk which led to the empathy.[14] This might be already clear from the 'laughter' examples. Having listened for example to their accounts of how they occupied themselves during school assembly, it was easy to do some of the same things and share in the fun. Obviously one catches something in laughter that is not necessarily expressed in words. The same is true of other experiences, when the talk assumes an onomatopoeic quality. I am thinking here of what I discovered to be the main impact of the school on one group of pupils – boredom. As one boy expressed it:

Simon: It's not a bad school really, you know. I don't mind it, you know, but . . . coming every day, doing the same old thing one day after the other, same lessons, you know, gets a bit sickening. You can't wait until the end of the week or the end of the day, you know, when you get here.

PW: Do you find the work difficult?

Simon: No, it's not difficult, it's boring. You just sit there with a whole lot of work to do.

PW: What do you do, say in English?

Simon: Wednesday, teacher reads to you which makes you nearly fall off to sleep. I do anyway. You get so bored with it, you know.

PW: What else do you do?

Simon: It's hard to think. I remember once I got so bored I did fall off to sleep in English. Yeah, so bored with it.

The point I am making is that the way in which they expressed it cued me into the actual experience of it. One of my outstanding memories from the enormous mass of experience at the school is that of pupils talking to me about boredom. They managed to convey, largely in a very few words, years of crushing ennui that had been ingrained into their bones. Great wealth of expression was got into 'boring', 'boredom', 'it's so bo-or-oring here'. The word, I realise now, is onomatopoeic. I could never view lessons in company with that group again without experiencing that boredom myself. They would occasionally glance my way in the back corner of the room with the same pained expression on their faces, and I knew exactly what they meant. This, then, provided a platform for my understanding of the school life of one group of pupils.

The group conversations also enabled me to distinguish between groups fairly easily. There were some very large differences between discussions along several dimensions, the most general one being adaptation to the school, with conformists at one end and non-conformists at the other. Now several people have distinguished between separate groups or cultures along these lines – Hargreaves, Lacey, King, Quine – a pro-school culture and either an anti-school or a colonisers' culture.[15] But they have not used to any great extent an interpretative perspective which emphasises a pupil's own construction of events and definitions of a situation. It was possible to bunch whole groups of pupils together around two basic models. First, there was the diffident, social, counter-official chooser, who, inasmuch as he or she made a positive choice at all, employed criteria such as difficulty of work, fun, boredom, with or without friends; second, the keen, instrumental, pro-school chooser who thought in terms of future job, his own ability, the learning situation and so forth. I found a contrast between the two not only in terms of what was actually said – the informative aspect – but also between the volume of what was said, and the nature of it. Compare, for example, the following:

Dave:	I filled that form in in about twenty seconds (*laughs*).
PW:	Did you ask anybody's advice about what to do?
Dave:	I didn't 'ave time. See, I filled my paper in, I took it 'ome, see what me dad think, an' I forgot all about it, an' then, oh, [deputy head] came in and gi' me

another form an' I filled it in quick so I wouldn't lose it, because I've got a bad memory, I always forget things an' I just filled it in quick.

PW: Did you talk about it amongst yourselves?

Dave and Philip: No.

Kevin: We just said what we were doing.

Stephen: I chose chemistry instead of geography because someone advised me it would be better for the RAF than geography. I thought geography would be better, but the bloke next door thought chemistry. He knows a bloke in the Air Force, pretty important, and he was talking to Mum and Dad one night and he said chemistry was more important. I would much rather do chemistry myself than geography because you can't do geography 'O' level, but you can chemistry.

PW: Why physics?

Stephen: Well, the only other one I thought of was English literature and I'm only really interested in that, so I chose physics.

PW: The others are out, are they?

Stephen: Yeah – general science – I'm already doing chemistry. I'm not interested in biology, so I might as well do physics and specialise in something else rather than do general science.

PW: Tell me about technical drawing.

Stephen: Well, I wanted to do both that and history, I just couldn't make my mind up.

PW: What was hard about it?

Stephen: Well if I join the RAF, I want to be a draughtsman, so tech. drawing is obviously the one to do. But I'm interested in history and I enjoy it. I put history down first then thought again and changed it later.

PW: Did you talk to anybody about it?

Stephen: No. I told Mum and Dad I was thinking of changing it, and they said, 'We won't say "yes" or "no" either way.'

PW: And why woodwork in group 6?

Stephen: Well I'm not good at metalwork, I don't do needlework or housecraft, I'm no good at music, shan't mention French. I quite enjoy woodwork, but I'm not much good at it.

The first transcript displays some of the vagueness, unconcern, unawareness and lack of interest typical of the anti-official chooser; and this comes from a free-talking situation where the pupil concerned had a great deal more to say about matters that interested him, so that these qualities were all the more emphasised. The second shows the close commitment to school values, the logical and ebullient application to the task in hand, and instrumental reasoning typical of the pro-school chooser. Later, it was possible to distinguish between the parents of these two groups in a similar way as a result of interviews held with them.[16]

Finally, a brief word about my use of talk. My criteria for selecting extracts in my accounts are basically four – validity, typicality, relevance and clarity. I use extensive quotation – the subjects do a great deal of speaking for themselves. The themes are theirs, the categories are theirs. The sociologist acts first as a roving microphone, then as a book-keeper and filing clerk. By presenting a sample from his files, he can give a tidy, descriptive account organised round certain features which will have a value in its own right. These member typifications are then subjected to social and scientific analysis. They are two distinct processes, and ideally should not be confused. The 'rhetoric of interaction'[17] should not be coloured by the analysis, and should be available for alternative analyses. Some of these should be those of the subjects of study, at least those with the ability to distance themselves from the situation, and to look at the analysis impersonally and rationally. In a sense I regarded my feedback of papers to members of staff as the supreme test. One of the best commendations I received was from a teacher of different persuasion from myself who thought the subject choice analysis was 'cruel, but true'. I hope it was my quest for 'truth' (whatever that might be) that was being gratified, but that terse comment caused me to reflect that, among the oft quoted qualities required of the would-be ethnographer, such as sensitivity, understanding, power of insight and so on, a streak of sadism can, at times, be a useful attribute.

NOTES

1 MEAD, G. H., *Mind, Self and Society,* University of Chicago Press, 1934.

BLUMER, H., *Symbolic Interactionism*, Prentice-Hall, 1969.

GOFFMAN, E., *The Presentation of Self in Everyday Life*, Doubleday Anchor, 1969.

BECKER, H. S., *Sociological Work*, Aldine, 1970.

2 The full report is in WOODS, P., *The Divided School,* Routledge and Kegan Paul, 1979.

3 GLASER, B. G. & STRAUSS, A. L., *The Discovery of Grounded Theory*, Weidenfeld and Nicolson, 1968.

4 WOODS, P., 'Showing them up in secondary school' in Chanan, G. & Delamont, S. (eds) *Frontiers of Classroom Research*, National Foundation for Educational Research, 1975.

5 WOODS, P., 'Having a laugh: an antidote to schooling', in Hammersley, M. & Woods, P. (eds), *The Process of Schooling*, Routledge and Kegan Paul, 1975.

6 WOODS, P., 'The myth of subject choice', *British Journal of Sociology,* June 1976.

7 KEDDIE, N., 'Classroom knowledge', in Young, M. F. D. (ed.), *Knowledge and Control*, Collier-Macmillan, 1971.

8 CICOUREL, A. V., *Method and Measurement in Sociology*, Free Press, 1964.

9 WAX, R. H., *Doing Fieldwork*, University of Chicago Press, 1971.

10 LABOV, W., 'The Logic of non-standard English', National Council of Teachers of English/Centre for Applied Linguistics, 1969.

11 GARFINKEL, H., *Studies in Ethnomethodology*, Prentice-Hall, 1967.

12 See, for example, WILLIS, P., *Learning to Labour*, Saxon House, 1977.

13 REDFIELD, R., *Peasant Society and Culture*, University of Chicago Press, 1960.

14 JANES, R., 'A note on phases of the community role of the participant observer', *American Sociological Review*, 26, 1961.

15 HARGREAVES, D., *Social Relations in a Secondary School*, Routledge and Kegan Paul, 1967.

LACEY, C., *Hightown Grammar*, Manchester University Press, 1970.

KING, R. A., *Values and Involvement in a Grammar School*, Routledge and Kegan Paul, 1969.

QUINE, W. G., 'Polarised cultures in comprehensive schools', *Research in Education*, November 1974.

16 Other interactionist work has disputed the relevance to pupils of these broad divisions and of the notion of 'conformity'. See FURLONG, V. J., 'Interaction sets in the classroom', in Hammersley, M. and Woods, P. (eds), *The Process of Schooling*, Routledge and Kegan Paul, 1976; and HAMMERSLEY, M. and TURNER, G., 'Conformist Pupils?' in Woods, P. (ed.), *Pupil Strategies*, Croom Helm, 1980.

17 BALL, D., 'Sarcasm as association: the rhetoric of interaction', *Canadian Review of Sociology and Anthropology*, 2, iii, 1965.

HELEN SIMONS

2 Conversation Piece: the Practice of Interviewing in Case Study Research

The case for adopting a case study approach in educational inquiry has been well documented in recent years.[1] Yet little has been written about *how* to do a case study or how to interview, observe or negotiate – three processes often cited as the main tools of such research. This paper looks at the first of these; in particular at some of the problems in the practice of interviewing.[2]

Often the practice of interviewing, particularly of the unstructured kind advocated in case study research, is not discussed on the grounds that interviewing is an idiosyncratic, interpersonal process that is not susceptible to systematic analysis. Like teaching, it is seen to be a private, personal skill for which some people are suited and others are not. It takes time to develop, mostly through trial and error though the process may be helped by 'looking over the shoulder' of someone acknowledged to have the sensitivity, judgment and intellectual skills that unstructured interviewing demand. The apprenticeship analogy is often invoked to describe how people acquire such skills. But this model is expensive and inaccessible to many. If the growth of practitioners in this field is to parallel the growth of advocates I think we must begin to discuss the problems we experience in practice however self-evident, situation-specific or limited when restricted to the written word they may seem. This is not to say that personality differences are not important in interviewing – one only has to note how the same question asked by different interviewers can elicit diverse responses from the same person.[3] It is simply to suggest that there are certain points about practice we can draw to the attention of others which may speed up the learning process.

Another reason why practice is rarely described is that discussions of the interview often never get beyond attempts to conceptualise and justify its theoretical underpinning as a research tool. In this paper I hope to circumvent debate at the theoretical level by treating some of the major premises of my practice as assumptions and so proceed, more or less directly, to explicate my experience.

I start from the following assumptions:

(a) that the justification for case study research as an appropriate mode of enquiry in the study of social situations has been established;

(b) that interviewing is a useful tool in case study research;

(c) that the recording of people's subjective definitions of experience is a normal part of case study research;

(d) that whereas structured questions are appropriate when you know what you want to find out, unstructured questions are preferable when you are not sure what you want to know but are prepared to depend on your capacity to recognise significant data on appearance;

(e) that, further, it is necessary to adopt an unstructured approach (variously called open-ended or flexible) to interviewing in the study of social situations whose complexity has to be uncovered by the research;

(f) that unstructured interviewing offers more scope for involving the interviewee in the research;

(g) that because interviewing is a most penetrative way of gaining information from and about people there is a need for rules to control both the acquisition and the subsequent use of interview data.

CONTEXT

For several years now I have been interviewing in curriculum research in secondary and higher education. But what I focus upon here are some of the particular problems of interviewing in schools. Rather different problems arise with interviewing in a higher education context where both staff and students have more autonomy and more time, or in the DES or educational authorities where problems of access and protocol differ.[4] To be even more specific, what I have to say about the problems of interviewing in schools is influenced by the principles for data gathering and use adopted by the SAFARI Project.[5]

In practice, case study staff on the Project have been working to the following agreed set of rules:

- interviews should be conducted on the principle of confidentiality;
- interview data is the property of the interviewees and should only be made accessible to others with their agreement;
- how the data may be used should be negotiated with the people interviewed;
- interviewees have ultimate control over what information becomes public;
- the study is restricted to seven days in the field gathering data and twenty-one for writing and negotiating spread over a year.

At the end of the paper I will return to these rules to consider how helpful or unhelpful they are in the light of the problems I now outline.

I am going to deal chronologically with problems of access and then problems in the process of interviewing in hierarchically structured institutions. In practice, of course, the two are inevitably linked. Access to and within educational institutions is highly governed by protocol and how access is achieved has consequences for the kind of data it is possible to obtain and how it may be used.

ACCESS

With the Head there is little difficulty in gaining access. His agreement to participate in the study has to be sought. The authority of the funding agency may help to ensure access. He may have little option if he has been asked to participate by the chief education officer. But questions of entry aside, of all the people in the school the Head is the easiest person to interview. He has time (though he often denies this). He has power – nothing you say, do, or report is likely to affect his career. He is often lonely, isolated, since he alone has no peers within the institution, and is therefore usually quite willing to talk confidentially to a sympathetic outsider. He can be flattered by the interest you show in 'his' school. It is difficult to avoid interviewing him first and, in fact, it may be advantageous to do so at length to secure his confidence and involvement in the study. However, lengthy interviews with the Head may be unhelpful in terms of how they affect teachers' perception of you and your subsequent interviews with them. Already you have access to knowledge, including perhaps the Head's judgment of them, which they may not have. The Head may also have given you *carte blanche* to interview pupils, a point over which teachers might have exercised more reserve.

Teachers, on the whole, are in a more constrained position than the Head. They have less time: while a Head of Department may have a double period free, rarely is this the case with a junior member of staff. Depending upon the authority structure of the school they are less free to be open or to refuse, for instance, access to pupils. If they are innovatory they are often caught up in the struggle for resources or timetable space. Their careers may be at risk or they may think they are. In some instances, they may wish to use the interviewer to enhance their position either indirectly by eliciting your advocacy for their innovatory activities (hoping you will mention their resource difficulties etc., in the 'right places') or more directly by confirming their 'good work'.

Pupils are an important source of information but gaining access to them is the most difficult problem. Their views are often not known to the teachers or the Head. While some teachers welcome an outsider talking to pupils as an extension of the democratic principle or because they hope the interviewer will tell them 'what the pupils think', others do not. Gaining access to sixth formers or 'prize' pupils is less of a problem than getting the opportunity to talk to the 'troublemakers' or 'low-achievers'.

Socially, access is difficult for the pupils as well. They are in the least powerful position. Sixth formers may not get the reference they require if they are too critical. Fourth-year low achievers may be constrained by the low status accorded them in comparison with their successful fellows. ('It's only the clever people who have opinions.') Alternatively, of course, knowing they have no status to protect, they may talk quite freely and even adopt a bravado stance – 'I don't care what I say'.

Pupils have less time than teachers, yet more time is needed to establish trust and to understand their experience (this is particularly true of the less articulate).[6] A thirty-five minute period, often the only time available, is rarely enough to establish the kind of relationship necessary to gain accurate data.

The position is not helped by institutional 'assistance' in selecting pupils for interview. When the time is short it is frequently the teacher who selects the pupils. Not only may pupils be chosen to reflect credit on the school but the introduction by the teacher to the purpose of the discussion may be different from what the interviewer would say. It is often useful to ask pupils if the teacher indicated why he wanted them to have a talk with you so that you may confirm or correct the impression and begin to establish a relationship on your own terms. The researcher may of course ask the teacher to select specific pupils like 'the silent pupil', the 'below average' or the 'disaffected'. Or if the researcher is able to observe pupils in advance, he may select them himself. An entirely different approach is to seek a cross selection from the roll. But there is still the problem of release from classes. It is very difficult, in fact virtually impossible, to gain access to pupils without these pupils being identified by the school. This means that the possibility of anonymising pupil responses is severely restricted.

Finding an appropriate place to talk is also a problem. The Head or the Deputy Head's office won't do. Empty classrooms are rare. Sometimes one ends up in the store room where the acoustics are bad, cluttered by boxes and books. If the research issue in question is a delicate one for the member of staff you may find him or her popping in and out, disrupting the relationship you are trying so quickly to establish. Seek out the careers teacher. He is frequently willing to lend his office which is usually set apart from the main classrooms and is relatively quiet.

PRINCIPLES OF PROCEDURE

Open-ended interviewing challenges conventional expectations of the research process. Relying as it does a great deal on the personal skills and judgment of the interviewer it is also open to manipulation and distortion. Principles of procedure protect both interviewer and interviewee from misuse of the data, provided assumptions are shared. Perspectives, for instance, on the meaning of confidentiality may range from complete trust that the information will not go 'beyond the four walls of this room' to the assumption that the information may be shared with research colleagues but not other teachers in the school or to 'the secret that is passed on to only one person at a time'. Then there may be differences in status of people or information. Does confidentiality, for instance, mean the same for pupils as it does for teachers and the Head? Does confidentiality extend to data expressed in informal chat? Should the same or different rules apply to the use of the data obtained in and out of the interview situation or of data offered by one person about another? Should the same or different rules over the use of data apply to pupils as apply to teachers? What rights do, or should, pupils have?

Misunderstandings can easily arise if the rules of information use are not fully understood or respected equally by all parties. For example, if the researcher interviews pupils in confidence and does not reveal what they say, teachers may see the interviewer in a conspiratorial role with pupils. Since pupils in a hierarchical structure are often the last to be interviewed the researcher may be the only person at one point who has access to what pupils think as well as what the teachers think: staff may see the interviewer in a 'god-like role' which may strain previously established good relationships, if not governed by rules of procedure.

Staff uncertainty about whether pupils have been friendly or hostile is difficult to tolerate: direct pressure has on occasion been applied to pupils by teachers to reveal what they said in interview. But a more common response to such anxiety is to say to the interviewer, 'I know you can't tell me what they said but what did they think of . . .?' Or, if you have interviewed a pupil who is usually silent in class, 'Did she say anything?' If the interviewer fails to respond to these questions teachers may continue to try to evoke a response by giving their view of what they thought the pupils would say, expecting you to confirm or deny their statements. Comments such as 'Janet is rather slow isn't she?' or 'I expect Mark had a lot to say, he has always told me how he dislikes maths', put confidentiality at risk. To gain credibility with pupils and teachers it is essential to resist such pressure and to take care not to tell teachers anything inconsistent with what pupils are told. It also helps to avoid being seen talking to the teacher immediately after an interview with pupils, just as it helps to avoid being seen going to the Headmaster's office by the teacher or pupils you have just interviewed.

PROCESS

Judging from the questions asked of case study workers both by new practitioners and by interviewees, many assume that the interview is a one-way process, for the researcher to gain information for a particular research inquiry; where the interviewer asks the questions and the interviewee 'gives' the information. But the process is much more complex than that – more dynamic, interpersonal, intangible.

Both the interviewer and the interviewee bring preconceptions to the interview which will affect what they say, hear and report, and which may be confirmed or changed in the course of the interview. Both are making judgments of each other's attitudes and expectations as well as considering the context or implications of the questions or issue under discussion. Perceptions differ too. How the interviewee perceives the interviewer, as sympathetic, critical or threatening, for example, will influence what kind of information is offered; how the interviewer perceives the interviewee, as interested, indifferent or hostile, will affect how he or she behaves. The interview, in other words, is a complex social process in which much more than information is being sought or communicated. (It can also be an educational process as interviewees begin to reflect on their own situation and, perhaps, continue the inquiry beyond the formal interview.) The interviewer should continually be responsive to the range of social and intellectual reactions in the process of engaging the person in talk: an interview should be a conversation piece, not an inquisition.

Given this emphasis, what does the interviewing process look like in practice? The following are points I try to keep in mind. They are not meant to sound prescriptive. I am simply going to try to uncover the process of interviewing as I have experienced it – to articulate what I think are the assumptions and principles I work with, or should work with, in interviewing.

It is important at the outset to establish confidence and trust so that people will speak freely. There must be some motivation to participate other than institutional expectation. On the whole, people will treat the interview seriously if they think you can change something or if they think you accept and understand their problems. Since researchers are rarely in a position to influence events directly they have to rely on demonstrating empathy with the interviewees' concerns. What can help to secure their confidence is to indicate indirectly that you have some understanding of the problems facing them. Offering confidentiality may help if this convention has meaning for them. So might informal chat around a topic of local or personal interest to the interviewee; although informal talk is sometimes perceived to be unrelated to the formal interview.

One way to engage interviewees' involvement in the study is to encourage them to talk about what interests them much as they might in a social conversation. This also helps to break down the formality of the interview over which the interviewer is perceived to have control. Reversing expectations, however, takes time and may need prompting. Try to dispossess them of any notions that you are the expert. Shift the role to them in early interviews by asking questions which touch on their concerns and which are open-ended enough to allow them scope to reply fully. Respond acceptingly so they will feel free to talk without feeling anxious about being judged or not giving the 'right response'. Let them shift from topic to topic. Counter any question to the interviewer with one which shifts the onus back to them to demonstrate that you really are interested in their perceptions and judgments.

Information people offer on their own initiative is more true, some argue, than what they say in answering questions. Whether or not this is so, interviewees' unsolicited responses frequently alert the interviewer to consider the subject under discussion in a new light and in the context central to the person interviewed. Piaget, in criticising the questionnaire as a means of obtaining access to a person's mental processes, put this point neatly when he wrote:

> But the real problem is to know how he [the subject] frames the question to himself or if he frames it at all. The skill of the practitioner consists not in making him answer questions but in making him talk freely and thus encouraging the flow of his spontaneous tendencies instead of diverting it into the artificial

channels of set question and answer. It consists in placing every symptom in its mental context rather than abstracting it from its context.[7]

In many cases where both parties to the interview share a view of the task there is no need to ask many questions; it is more important to listen. A comparison of a tape-recording where the interviewer does not speak for half an hour with one where the interviewer asks a question every second minute may illustrate the open-ended approach better than any description. (This is not to say that the interviewer is inactive. His presence, his responses, non-verbal though they may be, and how he takes notes, contribute in quite significant ways.) Usually the issues the interviewer thought of will be raised by the interviewee if the interviewer listens carefully and refrains from asking questions too soon. Take the following example related by an interviewee:

'It is difficult for me to hold a dialogue', he said, 'someone came to interview me once and I gave a monologue for two hours . . . I liked him. He was an easy person to talk to. Then I realised the time. "You must have some questions" I said to the interviewer. "No", the interviewer replied, "you've answered them all".'

Listening by itself, of course, does not always lead to depth of understanding. Probing is necessary to get behind the expected response or to test the significance of what you are being told. Taking up cues from the interviewees, asking them to elaborate or explain why they adopted a particular view or introducing a theme for comment are all means of extending the initial response. But these can still be pursued in a non-directed way if the aim of the research is to portray the interviewees' judgments, perceptions and theories of events.

It is evident from the emphasis given to the above points that I think one of the most common errors in open-ended interviewing is failure to listen, either by asking too many questions or interrupting to confirm one's own hypotheses. A second related error is to seek closure too soon by accepting the initial response too readily, summarising erroneously or by asking questions which give the interviewee a plausible response without committing him to reveal what he really thinks or feels. (This is a special danger when interviewing pupils.) Timely summarising of course is very useful to clarify issues and shift the interview a stage further.

In summary, the kind of skill flexible interviewing calls for is what the anthropologist, Hortense Powdermaker, has called 'psychological mobility,[8] or the novelist, Sybille Bedford, 'emotional intelligence'[9]. Sybille Bedford summarises the complex skills involved when she writes:

'It takes two to tell the truth.'
'One for one side, one for the other?'
'That's not what I mean. I mean one to tell, one to hear. A speaker and a receiver. To tell the truth about any complex situation requires a certain attitude in the receiver.'
'What is required in the receiver?'
'I would say first of all a level of emotional intelligence.'
'Imagination?'
'Disciplined.'
'Sympathy? Attention?'
'And patience.'
'All of these. And a taste for the truth – an immense willingness to see.'[10]

If the study involves a series of interviews, who sets and shifts the topics may vary from interview to interview. What is appropriate at one point may not be at another, as understanding and perceptions change. At times the interviewer may want to feed in some interpretation, at other times to take up a cue from the interviewee. Towards the end of the study precisely the opposite tactic from responding to the interviewee's initiative may be appropriate, particularly if the interviewee has a habit of repeating his story over and over again. In such a case the interviewer may want to be quite assertive or exclusive about the issues he would like the interviewee to comment upon.

Interviewing encompasses more than listening, asking questions and being socially responsive. Often it is important to judge the significance of what is said by non-verbal cues such as gestures, the tone of the voice, how people dress, how they look, how and where they sit or to infer from what is not said or what is denied what the interviewee thinks or feels. At the same time acceptance of non-verbal cues may be misleading. Their significance has to be judged in relation to all the data obtained.

In what order people are interviewed affects the process and the kind of information obtained. If teachers are interviewed after the Head they may assume what he has told you and be guarded in their response. If pupils are the last to be interviewed – the usual pattern – they may feel that they are expected to confirm what the teachers said. While much of the data must remain locked in confidentiality it is difficult for the interviewer to avoid using the information gained from previous interviews to sharpen and focus subsequent ones. It may also be necessary to further understanding. But it does raise a difficult ethical question if confidentiality is assured. The interviewer may breach confidentiality quite unwittingly as he asks a question which was stimulated by information he gained from previous interviews. It is not difficult to offer a defence in such a case and thus protect previous interviewees from feeling you have betrayed their confidence. The interviewer can simply deny the inference (which may not, in fact, be true) or indicate that the issue was highlighted in a previous setting. This may seem a minor point to deliberate but it does illustrate why the interviewer needs to be continually responsive to the reactions of interviewees if he wants to retain trust and obtain reliable data.

It may also be useful to note the number and kind of interruptions accepted in the interview. Does the Head, for instance, take an interruption from the Deputy Head but dismiss one from the Careers' Officer? Does he differentiate between the telephone calls he takes and those he defers? Who comes into the room while you are there? What issues does he discuss with others while you are there and what does he reserve? Not only may these observations indicate how the interviewer or whole study is perceived, they offer useful clues for how to act subsequently.

SPECIAL PROBLEMS IN INTERVIEWING PUPILS

Many of the points already mentioned apply equally to pupils but are more difficult to put into practice. Talking too much, listening too little and suggesting answers are real traps if one is aspiring to reflect pupils' thoughts and feelings. The constraints of interviewing within the school in a short time do not make the task any easier.[11]

Pupils learn to live by rules and conventions prescribed by those responsible for the running of the school and may not *feel as free* as teachers to express their attitudes and feelings. In schools which have a fairly traditional curriculum, furthermore, pupils may not have had much opportunity to talk in class or informally to teachers outside class. A stranger coming in for a few odd days may have difficulty *beyond institutional habits*. Some pupils appear to treat the interview as a test situation, and try to give 'right' answers.

Direct questioning, while providing a check on perceptions or events described by teachers, rarely gets beyond conforming to what the teacher or institution expects and, therefore, often fails to reveal understanding of the pupil's experience. More inferences have to be drawn or a more direct indirect starting point adopted to try to free pupils from the constraints of school environment.

Where pupils have been selected by the teacher they may associate the interviewer with the authority structure and this may restrict discussion. (This differs from the authority of the research agency which, while useful to gain access, may also inhibit interaction.) You may be seen as a spy of the establishment. It may help to indicate that you were once a teacher but now are visiting schools talking to pupils about what school is like from their point of view. Or you may appeal to status 'I am from the university . . .' or to their interest in helping you with research, though this tactic appears to have low credibility. Whatever tactic is adopted it is important to try to disassociate yourself from the school establishment. At the same time to maintain credibility with staff one must avoid the opposite danger, of appearing to be on the side of the pupils.

Some pupils may be reluctant to talk out of loyalty to teachers or the institution, fear of peer group or teacher reprisal, or simply lack of interest in your enterprise or the school. But others may be quite willing to vent spleen and seek your sanction and support. 'Can you change things for us, Miss?' is a common request from the disgruntled or hapless fourth year leaver.

It is not simply a problem of getting pupils to talk but getting them to talk on relevant issues. They may well chat about school meals, assembly, uniform (which may give insight into how the school is run) but not so easily talk about teachers, subjects or school. A common response to questions about school for a fourth year leaver, for example, is to say 'It's boring'. It is important to sort out boredom or institutional responses from what they are really saying. Sometimes one of the peer group may begin to reveal the actuality. 'They say it's boring, but they don't mean that. In such-and-such a case this happened . . .' Other times the interviewer has to infer.

On page 35 I noted that seeking closure too soon was a special danger when interviewing pupils. Note the following instance where I interrrupted a pupil in an interview on the theme of participation in class discussions to summarise what I thought she might feel. The girl was a 'non-talker' in class:

'Did you feel . . . that you did have things to say?'
'Yes. But often other people said them . . .'
'And that put you off saying something another time did it?'
'Umm. If you say something you sometimes think that if you say something wrong people are going to think it is funny.'

Here the pupil dismissed my summary questions in fact to go on to say why she felt diffident about talking in class. In other cases such a question effectively closes discussion, having presented the pupil with an acceptable response. If pupils do associate the interviewer with teachers, 'wanting to please the teacher' may extend to wanting to please the interviewer.

Acceptance of non-verbal cues may be especially misleading when talking to pupils. The pupil who is having difficulty expressing himself, for instance, frequently responds to questions by saying nothing, with gestures – shifting in his seat, shrugging his shoulders – or by how he looks. Here there is often a tendency for the interviewer to rely on non-verbal cues as indicators of what the pupil thinks and feels. If you accept them too readily you may simply be creating a problem which may end up in an interviewer's monologue or a multiple choice check-out, 'Is it this, this . . . or this . . . that you think?', none of which may actually be what the pupil does think.

With pupils peer group norms may be supportive or destructive but either way quite a powerful influence. In general, if pupils know each other and have worked together in groups before, they are quite supportive in a group interview. Take the silent pupil, for instance. If she does not speak up much in a group interview other pupils will often explain what she feels or say, affectionately, 'She's all right, she's much better at writing than talking.' Or, as in the following example, she may explain herself. Carol is the pupil in question.

Interviewer:	Does the lesson help the shy ones or does it make them stand out more?
Angela:	They're so quiet and then all of a sudden one of them'll speak and you think 'What's come over them?' I suppose they've got their opinion in their head and they hear everyone else talking so they think they will.
Patricia:	Carol's quiet.
Interviewer:	You're quiet Carol?
Angela:	Not as quiet as you used to be.
Carol:	I'm better than I used to be.
Interviewer:	You didn't like speaking?
Carol:	I'd only talk when I was asked a question.
Angela:	Sort of speak when you're spoken to. I noticed that when I first met her, I thought she was quiet.
Interviewer:	But now you speak when you want to put your point of view.
Carol:	Yes. When I think someone's wrong, I'll say what I think.
Interviewer:	And how long did it take you to get to this stage?
Carol:	Well, it was more friendly, we sat in a circle and we could speak to each other. That was better and it didn't take long, only a few lessons.
Angela:	I noticed after three or four lessons Carol started speaking more.
Patricia:	I spoke the first lesson.
Angela:	So did I.
Carol:	It gets me mad when people say you're very quiet though. I enjoy other people's views as well.
Angela to Patricia:	Probably the way you shout, you probably frighten them to death.

If pupils do not know each other, peer group norms may operate in a constricting way and one may get little mileage out of group interviews with pupils. The same may be true of interviewing boys and girls together.

SOME CONTINUING PROBLEMS

However experienced in interviewing you become there will always be situations you feel you did not handle satisfactorily. Some which remain problematic for me include:

- how to get the teacher out of the room when you want to interview students;
- how to interview inarticulate pupils;
- how to respond to the person who reveals all and immediately wishes he had said nothing;
- how to evoke pupil responses which are not just responses to the interview situation;
- how to get out of the Headmaster's office deftly;
- how to get beyond the institutional response in a short time;
- how to avoid the Headmaster escorting you to coffee in the staff-room when you have arranged to interview a teacher immediately afterwards;
- how to deal with the unanticipated, like teachers not involved in the study wanting to be interviewed when you are working to a tight schedule;
- how to respond if the interviewee tries to reverse roles and assume the interviewer's position.

If some of these points sound trivial this is perhaps evidence of the extent to which we underestimate the importance and the delicacy of the social process which the case study worker is compelled to negotiate in the pursuit of data. There are no formulae, no prescriptions for resolving such problems. Resolution is a matter for personal judgment in the specific context.

A FEW SPECIFIC CASES

On the assumption that we sometimes learn from the practice of others I will indicate how I tried to resolve just three of these problems. In some cases I could not, and still cannot, think of what is the most appropriate response. I do not intend to justify how or why I responded the way I did in these instances. I don't know if my response was right or wrong. It is simply what I did.

Teachers often assume they have a right, or wish to stay in the room when you are interviewing pupils. In an institutional framework their presence usually inhibits pupils and the interviewer. On several occasions like this where I have felt impeded by the teacher's presence I have paused and said very slowly . . . looking at the pupils: 'I think . . . um . . . this may be a difficult one to answer . . . while your teacher is here, but . . .'

The teacher shifts in his seat, looks slightly uncomfortable and says: 'Shall I go?'

'No, no . . .', looking at the teacher this time, 'I don't think that's necessary . . . I'll give it a try. It's . . . (speaking quickly as though I was just about to ask the question), 'I think', says the teacher over speaking, 'that perhaps I ought to go.'

Teacher gets up quietly and leaves.

The group invariably relaxes with a sigh of relief and the interview takes a different turn. While this ploy has worked on some occasions on others it is short lived. Back comes the teacher after ten minutes just when the pupils are beginning to open up on issues which really concern them. Nevertheless, the change in their responses is worth noting. And the whole incident perhaps indicates as much about relationships in the setting as talk does. Why is such a ploy necessary, some people have asked me. Why not simply tell the teacher that you wish to speak to pupils alone? It is difficult in many settings to deal directly with this issue without engendering deep suspicion in the teacher about your purposes, or implying scepticism of the teacher's claim to enjoy a very 'open' relationship with his pupils.

How to interview inarticulate pupils is one of the problems for which I still have no adequate solution. Responding to their initiatives is clearly impossible if they don't take any. Often the interview becomes a question and answer session, with the questions getting longer and the answers shorter. Faced with a lack of response, the temptation is to try and articulate the problem for them. I have done this, but feel that all it does is to offer them an acceptable response. I have no means of knowing whether or not it is accurate.

Talking about anything other than school – football or the television, for instance – gets a conversation going, but it may not lead to discussion relevant to the study. One major exception was where the pupil in question was a Second Division football player who had a life outside school that he felt was not relevant inside school and therefore assumed nobody wanted to hear about it. On his own ground he was quite articulate and, after fifteen minutes, equally articulate about curriculum issues and the school.

On other occasions I have asked inarticulate pupils to write accounts of their experience on certain themes, but in the time available could not use these as a basis for discussion to tease out the real from the expected. It is too much like a school essay.

It seems essential to interview inarticulate pupils alone unless the peer group is particularly sympathetic. Even then I am far from confident that we can establish the trust necessary in a short time to represent their experience adequately. If part of the reason for pupils failing to talk seems to lie with the structures of the institution, one way to overcome this problem, it is often suggested, is to take them out of the school and interview them in your car or a nearby café. But this seems to me to be a solution that fails to take account of the problems of access and control. Inarticulate pupils, furthermore, are often defined as 'hostile witnesses' to the school. If you take them out of the school you may be aligning yourself with the 'hostile witnesses' and possibly lose credibility in the eyes of the staff.

How to get beyond the institutionalised response in a short time is equally problematic. I have tried presenting provocative interpretations of the school to teachers individually in the hope that they would correct the account, or a consensus interpretation to a group of teachers as a means of provoking divergent views. Both seem to work but on one occasion I ran the risk and lost the impartial and fair stance I was striving to establish. Some people, whom I feel will not misinterpret my intention and whose response I just do not believe, I have challenged directly, or I have confronted them with information that questions the position they are taking or pointed out inconsistencies in their views. Most often this leads to a modification of their first position and one which I have assumed more accurately represents where they stand.

With pupils, the problem remains acute. Starting with something immediate to their experience, like the lesson they have been drawn from, a recent event in their locality or a recent television programme, helps to get them talking and may, by comparison or direction, eventually bring them to discuss topics relevant to the study. But usually a more indirect approach is needed. I have tried to present them with the opposite of what I think may be an accurate description of the school. While they respond, sometimes quite heatedly, I suspect this simply serves to confirm the view I held. On the assumption that adolescents often have different views from their parents, I have asked pupils to tell me what their parents think of the school, the curriculum, the examination and vocational opportunities it offers, and tried to infer from their response (both spoken and observed) what they do think.

Other approaches which I have sometimes thought of trying but never had the time or the opportunity to do so include:

- asking pupils to describe 'critical incidents' in their school life;
- asking pupils to describe how they found their way around the school, who they talked to on the first day, first three weeks, who they talk to now and so on;
- following *one* pupil for two days, observing and talking intervals;
- interviewing the same pupil every time you visit the school: asking him or her to keep a diary of events and observations;
- comparing how pupils talk in class and in the playground and using this as a focus for talk in interview.

RECORDING THE INTERVIEW

Reporting information and observations is an essential part of the interview process. Whether or not to tape record interviews is often a critical issue. Arguments against using tape recorders usually centre on their intrusiveness inhibiting honest accounts or the time that it takes to process and transcribe the tapes. But in most situations I find that these disadvantages are outweighed by the advantages of tape recording.

Tape recording helps to ensure that the data is accurate. However good one's memory the distortion in reporting that can occur is considerable. It is easy to mishear. It is tempting, if the interviewer is pursuing specific themes or hypotheses, to note those verbatim quotations which fit. Accuracy can easily be checked from time to time by comparing verbatim quotations written down during the interview with what is recorded on tape. To check whether the tape recorder inhibited interaction it is useful to compare what is said when the tape recorder is off with what is said when it is on. However, it is not a *guarantee* of accuracy. Distortions and omissions in transcribing must be legion. Accents may be difficult to hear. You have been there. The secretary has not. Even intelligent guesses may need to be checked, and the omission or mistranscription of little words can distort the sense in quite significant ways like the omission of the first three words of the following sentence from a headmaster's interview: 'Some staff say I am a paternalistic dictator.'

The interviewer, relieved from the burden of having to take detailed notes, can listen, observe and respond more attentively to the interviewee. And the interviewee can feel at ease not having to worry, as John and Elizabeth Newson[12] point out, about the possible significance of what the interviewer notes down in relation to what she does not. If the researcher wishes to prepare a report that gives prominence to interviewees' perceptions and judgments and conveys the texture and meaning of what they say, it is useful to quote verbatim. It is difficult to do this accurately without a tape recording.

Even if the interviews are tape recorded, responsibility for note taking is not diminished. It is still important to take notes during the interview to remind the interviewer of issues to raise in subsequent interviews; to enable the interviewer to write a report distilling the main issues before the interview is transcribed; or to offer an editing guide to a secretary if a transcript is being prepared.

PROCESSING THE DATA OBTAINED IN INTERVIEW

I have not said much about the process of selecting and processing the data which is perhaps one of the biggest problems of all. How do you assess the worth of the data, its meaning in relation to other data obtained in the study and its accuracy? On what criteria do you select events, incidents, themes, issues to report or verbatim quotations in illustration or support? On what criteria do you structure a report?

Problems associated with processing the data are large enough to warrant another paper. But I can make a few brief points here. Criteria for selection of data change from study to study but whatever they are it is important to select themes and data against a background of what happens in the process of interviewing, when the person was interviewed (early in the morning, or at the end of a tiring day, for instance), whether the interviewee was clear about the purposes of the research and how the interview data was to be used, if the response was volunteered or elicited by questioning which took in understandings gained from previous interviews, and so on.[13]

The most skilful interviewing is often indirect, although it places a lot of responsibility on the interviewer to infer and interpret. If inferences are drawn from incidents, observations, and interviews, a full context may need to be reported so that other people have the opportunity of making different inferences.

In the context I am working in at present the difficulty of processing is eased somewhat because the intention is to reflect issues of concern to the interviewees, and the selection of which issues are to be reported is negotiated with them. This does not solve the whole problem because there are other decisions to be made. But it may help to reduce bias in the interviewer's selection.

RETURN TO THE RULES

At the beginning I said I would return to the rules. Are they helpful? Or do they, perhaps, create some of the problems I have outlined? I will comment on two which are interlinked. Giving control to participants over the use of the interview data coupled with conducting interviews on the principle of confidentiality encourages teachers to talk freely and helps to gain access to data in a short time. Both, however, have their drawbacks.

Giving blanket confidentiality creates a problem over the use of the data; it tends to defeat the aspiration to complete the study in a short time because release of data from confidentiality has to be negotiated at each stage; it sometimes means that data which could be used to break the rhetoric or push the interview forward is locked in confidence.

Giving participants control over the use of the data increases the time needed for negotiation; as teachers come to exercise control they may modify or change their minds leaving the researcher to negotiate further or incorporate their changed responses. The researcher also has to face the fact that some data may be irretrievably lost or that what is given permission at one time is retracted at another in the light of subsequent evidence.

Just as the twenty-eight day time scale poses problems for the negotiation and release of data[14] so the seven day in the field restriction is a constraint on the style of interviewing advocated in this paper. To put the principles I have outlined into practice requires more time than a thirty-five to forty minute period and a few days in a school. So many interruptions – bells ringing, room changes – and such a crowded day for teachers – collecting materials for the next lesson, supervising playground duty, attending meetings – hardly provides the private setting conducive to encouraging people to reflect on their experience. If a school is timetabled in blocks of three periods or a series of doubles the problem might be alleviated a little but teachers would still have to find free time.

Interviewing pupils in a short time remains a problem; also how to use information obtained in confidence from pupils while protecting them from any repercussions of making that information accessible. It may not be possible to convince pupils in one interview what confidentiality, let alone control, means, even if it is extended to pupils, and at this stage, with the exception of sixth-formers we have not extended negotiation of data to pupils. I can see no reason why the principle of control should not apply to them. But it adds to the problem of and may affect the degree of access granted.

One of the reasons, perhaps escape clauses, for researchers using pupil data without pupils' specific agreement (and I have done this myself), is to say that they are less easily identified. But this may not be the case if teachers selected them or released them from classes for interviews. Only reporting general issues raised by a number of pupils (if many are interviewed) may protect individuals from being identified. But this does not solve the problem of how to use the incidental comments which sometimes provide a key to understanding and which may be traceable, in the institutional context of interviewing three or four pupils.

Though difficult, the question of appropriate rules and procedures for pupil interviews in case study research ought to be explored. Such rules are likely to make research more difficult to carry out but more defensible. As case study research becomes more widely practiced and discussed, revealing its structure, methods, principles and procedures, its practitioners will be called upon to articulate a socioethical stance, which should consider all contributors to the research.

NOTES

1 See, for example, SIMONS, H., 'Innovation and the case-study of schools', *Cambridge Journal of Education*, Michaelmas Term, 1971; MACDONALD, B. & PARLETT, M., 'Rethinking evaluation: Notes from the Cambridge Conference,' *Cambridge Journal of Education*, Vol. 2, 1973; MACDONALD, B. & WALKER, R., 'Case study and the social philosophy of educational research', *Cambridge Journal of Education*, Lent Term, 1975; STAKE, R. E., 'The case study method in social enquiry', mimeo, University of East Anglia, 1975.

2 While most social science textbooks usually contain some general description of interviewing techniques, this paper addresses the particular problems of unstructured interviewing *within* a bounded institution.

3 In fact some people, like Ferdinand Zweig, argue strongly for the interviewer's personality to be an integral part of the interview.

> . . . the art of interviewing is personal in its character, as the basic tool of the interviewer is in fact his own personality . . . he has to discover his own personal truth in interviewing, how to be friendly with people without embarrassing them, how to learn from them without being too inquisitive, how to be interesting without talking too much, how to take great interest in their troubles without patronising them, how to inspire confidence without perplexing them.

He suggests further that the interviewer needs to have 'a certain understanding of himself . . .' and 'a great range and variety of personal experience . . .' in order to be able to appreciate and empathise with the ambivalent concerns of the interviewee. (Quoted by Andreski, S. 'Hiding behind methodology' in *Social Science as Sorcery*, André Deutsch, 1971.)

4 Some of these differences are discussed in a paper by SIMONS, H., 'Styles and context of interviewing', mimeo, The Nuffield Foundation, 1976.

5 SAFARI is a three year research project looking at medium term effects of four curriculum projects adopting procedures which aspire to shift control of the research data from the researcher to participants. The project attempts to involve teachers in research by giving prominence to their perceptions, by sharing and negotiating the use of interview data with them and by encouraging them to correct, modify, confirm or add to early interpretations of the researcher. In this way a shared responsibility for what eventually becomes public is developed by the participants and the researcher. One further characteristic of this study is that it attempts to abbreviate the time scale of the research so that the research process itself can be replicated by non-research workers.

6 Not all researchers take the view that trust is the most appropriate basis for interviewing in case study research. I am not concerned here to discuss different styles but rather to outline what seem to be the essential features of flexible interviewing *within* a framework of trust.

7 PIAGET, J., *The Child's Conception of the World*, trans. by Joan & Andrew Tomlinson, Routledge and Kegan Paul, 1929. Introductory chapter 'Problems and Methods', p. 4.

8 Quoted by WALKER, R., 'The conduct of educational case study: ethics theory and procedures', *SAFARI, Innovation, Evaluation, Research, and the Problem of Control*, Some Interim Papers, Centre for Applied Research in Education, University of East Anglia, 1974, p. 90.

9 Ibid., p. 91.

10 BEDFORD, S., *A Compass Error*, Collins, 1968; Fontana, 1975.

11 For those interested in interviewing pupils unconstrained by the school context and with a view to understanding their mental processes, Piaget (vide supra) is valuable reading.

12 NEWSON, J. & E., 'Parental roles and social context', in M. Shipman (ed.) *The Organisation and Impact of Social Research; Six Original Case Studies in Education and Behavioural Science*, Routledge and Kegan Paul, 1976.

13 For one example of the criteria used for editing see 'Brookland School, Brookshire County: a case study in the management of innovation', in *From Council to Classroom: an Evaluation of the Humanities Curriculum Project*, by S. Humble & H. Simons, Schools Council Research Project, Macmillan, 1978.

14 SIMONS, H., 'Building a social contract: negotiation, participation and portrayal in condensed field research'. In *SAFARI, Theory in Practice*, Papers 2, Centre for Applied Research in Education, University of East Anglia, 1977.

MARY WILLES

3 Children Becoming Pupils: a Study of Discourse in Nursery and Reception Classes

THE NATURE AND PURPOSE OF THE REPORTED STUDY

The study reported in this paper was concerned with the processes of starting school and of settling down, and with a particular aspect of it, namely, how children learn to participate as pupils in the discourse of the classroom. How do they learn the rules of the game they will play, with varying fortunes, for more than a decade, success in which will significantly affect their later lives?

Of course in asking the question, a number of assumptions are made, and, in effect, a stance is taken up. It is implied that, in important respects, lessons are games played by rules and that, in the process of taking part, participants get to know what the rules are. Children new to classrooms are obliged to learn how to interpret what teachers say, and what constitute appropriate and acceptable responses, and how and when to make individual contributions that teachers recognise as commendable. In a society like our own, where early schooling generally represents the first step taken un-accompanied from the family into a wider world, such learning constitutes (I shall assume rather than argue) a significant extension of sociolinguistic competence. In taking on his new role of pupil, the newcomer to school has to put to the test of use the language learned in interaction at home. He has to find, or to extend his resources to include, the language of a learner, one among many, in an institutionalised setting. He has to wait his turn, and recognise it when it comes, to compete, to assert his rights, and sometimes to give ground. He has, in short, to discover what the rules of classroom interaction and behaviour are, what sort of priority obtains among them, and how and when and with what consequences they can be broken. By the time children leave the Infant for the Junior school, the organisation of curriculum and routines proceeds on the assumption that they *know* how to be pupils, and understand what to expect and what is expected of them. How all this learning is accomplished is a topic interesting enough to deserve study for its own sake, with no other goal than a better understanding. I would certainly not want to overlook its possible significance for educational concerns, and my hope was, from the beginning, that I might arrive at some findings that would interest those professionally concerned with the education of young children. I would want to be very cautious, however, in making any such claim. In a context of widespread anxiety about the long term effects of early educational failure there is some risk of looking towards any such investigations for relevance to intractable problems too soon, and too optimistically.

At the outset of the study it seemed reasonable to suppose that since the regularities of classroom discourse seem, when laid out for adult scrutiny, to be quite complicated, they must be learned over an extended period of time. It is at this point that I would wish to acknowledge my indebtedness to the work of J. McH. Sinclair, R. M. Coulthard, and their associates, which has since 1975 been available in the form of a monograph *Towards an Analysis of Discourse: the English used by Teachers and Pupils*. It was anticipated by a number of informal publications before that date, and has been substantially developed since. It provided the linguistically motivated, explicit, model that this study needed, and part at least of my original intention was to put to exploratory use the tools that had been developed in the course of the work done at Birmingham, and to do so in terms which they had anticipated:

How does the five year old who speaks when he wants to become the ten year old who wants to be nominated? (*op. cit.,* p. 113).

My expectation was that nearly all these newcomers to school would make mistakes indicative of stages in the learning process. I thought I should find evidence of learning going on at different rates, and I was prepared to find teachers explaining carefully and repetitively to pupils what was required of them. Only gradually, and with a good deal of uncertainty, I surmised, would the structure of this verbal interaction in the Reception classroom come to resemble that of the

Junior and the Secondary school, and be analysable in the same terms. I started, in sum, with the supposition that children must learn how to be pupils by means of an accretion of knowledge and experience, that the process would be more rapid and steady for some than for others, and that I might be able to observe or to record some parts of it. Even with hindsight, these do not seem to me to have been unreasonable suppositions with which to begin work of this kind.

SOME UNEXPECTED RESULTS OF PARTICIPANT OBSERVATION

In one respect, and it seemed a fundamental one, the expectations with which I started were almost at once contradicted. It seemed *not* to be the case that children learned to be pupils by accumulating knowledge and experience. It became apparent that what was observable would simply not bear such interpretation.

My initial observations were made in the first three weeks of September 1974 in an Infant school that serves a large estate on the edge of a Midlands industrial town. The estate includes both private and local authority housing. The school has a well-established nursery that admits children from the age of three for half-day attendance. At the beginning of each term those who will shortly reach the age of five are transferred to the Reception class in the same building, to begin full-time compulsory attendance. They are there joined by others, some of whom may have attended pre-school groups or classes elsewhere, and some of whom have no experience of that sort at all. Much thoughtful organisation goes into the arrangements for the start of full-time schooling, and these attest the fact that the transition is, for five year olds, a significant and possibly an alarming event. Everything is done to assure the newcomer that the parting from the familiar world is no more than temporary, and that starting school full-time represents promotion, and is an experience to be enjoyed. The school has a high reputation locally for its liberal programme and progressive organisation. The opportunity to record text in the nursery, among the three to five year olds, and also in the Reception class, Class Five, was available, and I set myself to obtain as representative a collection of classroom texts as I could.

The routines of the classroom became familiar to me as they did to other newcomers, within a few days. It was evident that the contrast

between the experience of the youngest children, entering the
nursery at three, and that of the 'rising fives' entering the Reception
class, was not in the nature of the activities that made up the
school day, but in the different distribution of time among them. For
all of them, including the youngest, there were routines of
administration (registration, distribution of milk, collection of
money) where the individual found himself a unit within a group. The
ratio of adults to children made possible a good deal of small group
teaching, involving five or six children at any one time, where the
teacher judged how long, on any one occasion, the activity of the
group should continue. Larger groups, some ten or twelve strong,
were referred to as 'families'. Each child soon learned he belonged to
the 'family' of a particular teacher. There was play with all sorts of
toys, indoors or out, depending on the weather. Teachers were
generally unobtrusive in supervising play, but they talked to children,
and children to each other, in the course of it. All these activities were
part of the experience of each session, and occurred in an order which
the children quickly learned to anticipate. In the nursery, play was
valued highly, and made up a substantial part of each session, where in
the Reception class the time given to it was reduced in favour of small
and larger group teaching. My recordings of verbal interaction
during play sessions were for the most part poor in quality, subject to
interruption from noisy activity, and imperfectly representative of
what was going on. However, if the recordings represent much better
the verbal interaction of teachers with larger or smaller groups of
children, this is not wholly unfortunate or unfair. While I am sure that
decisions about the allocation of time for play were principled ones, it
was nonetheless noticeable that teachers attached to group activities,
and even to administrative procedures, an altogether different degree
of seriousness. It seemed to be the case that they perceived the
supervision of play as necessary 'minding', whereas in the presence of
a seated group they could exercise the professional skills learned in
the course of training and experience.

As for the routines deriving from the care-taking role assumed by
teachers in relation to children as young as these, they could be
elaborated in such a way as to give them some degree of educational
significance. Registration was not handled in this way, but the
distribution of milk and snacks in the nursery, and the song and story

sessions that occupied the final half-hour, and from which children were released as soon as their mothers arrived to collect them, were seen as opportunities, not to be missed, for fostering language development. To do this was, among all the teachers, a major concern. It was seen as the prerequisite of early and successful literacy, and for that and other less specific reasons, the key to eventual educational success. The pleasant welcome I received, and the readiness with which teachers complied with any request I made, stemmed in great part from their sense that any work that promised eventual better understanding of children's language use was to be encouraged.

From the beginning, from the earliest days in the nursery, where teachers were engaged with children in what they perceived as educationally significant activity, the discourse that resulted was analysable in terms of the Birmingham model. In structure, that is (though not of course in terms of its content), it was similar to the verbal interaction that typically occurs in classrooms for older children, who might reasonably be accounted experienced pupils. There were differences. I had evidence of misunderstandings and mistakes. This was not difficult to explain, given that children bring to the classroom an internalised knowledge of the most important grammatical rules of English, but have no way of knowing, until they get there, what the situational rules of the classroom are. Experienced pupils know, for example, that in classrooms a question related to an activity is to be interpreted as a directive to do it, so that 'Ashley, will you join in with us please?' is an instruction to desist from inattention, and to do so, while 'Wouldn't you like to drink yours up like Jason?' is not intended to get an expression of preference from the hearer, but to persuade him to conform. Until children have found out by experience how the things that teachers say are to be interpreted they will of course make mistakes. What is *not* easily explained is how it is that mistakes do not occur all the time. Even with the youngest and least experienced pupils, teachers assumed that questions would be correctly interpreted as instructions to do or to desist, and their expectations were often met. It may have been the case that the total setting provided enough cues to enable children often to make the expected response. It may have been that the children had already learned a very general rule of behaviour in relation to adults that might be verbalised like this: if you are noticed by an adult, stop, attend, look to see what others are doing – and do that. This second explanation implies a third: that situational rules for discourse in classrooms are not in fact so specific as that; they are rules that obtain in interactional relations characterised, on the one hand, by dependence and subordinateness, and on the other by responsibility, superordinateness and benevolence, so that the children learn, in interaction with parents and other adults, rules that the experience of school confirms and perhaps extends.

Teachers themselves, in my experience, assisted the learning of what a pupil is expected to do, but less directly than might be anticipated. They taught the children how to respond when the register was taken – and not without some difficulty. Making the required response on hearing one's name called was, for these newcomers to the educational system, easy enough. The demanding part of the task was in remaining silent before and after. In the initial weeks, these teachers did not require hands to be raised. They named the individual from whom they wanted a response, and this practice must have been useful to the teacher in imprinting each new name early and indelibly on her memory and useful to pupils, in impressing on them that everyone normally could expect to have a turn. Teachers must differ in the judgments they make about the appropriate time to insist upon bidding for the right to speak. The following excerpt was made later in the year in a summer term and sounds as if it had by that time been many times rehearsed:

Teacher: Children. What did I say?
            Children. What did I say yesterday about all shouting out together?
            Can I listen (*raising her voice*) to everybody talking at once?
Pupils (in chorus): No.
Teacher: How many people can I listen to at once?
Pupils (breaking in before she finished): One.
Teacher: One. And what happens if everybody shouts at once?
Pupils: Can't hear.
Teacher: I can't hear *anybody*.

The lesson is repeated, however, long after the Infant school is left behind. Much older pupils, excited by competition, commonly answer without waiting for nomination and it is for the teacher to decide whether and how long this may be tolerated. Bidding, even in responsive and docile classes, approximates to orderliness, and that is reckoned enough.

Explicit insistence on what pupils are expected to say and do seemed to be no more than occasional, and to relate to routines which are clearly recognisable by adults as specific to the classroom (and sometimes specific to a particular school or to a particular teacher). Teachers assumed, as a rule correctly, that even very young pupils know that a question or a statement may have a directive function (though disobedience will almost always persuade a teacher to the use of an unmistakable imperative). While children's responses were often hesitant and confused they seem rarely in doubt *when* a verbal or a non-verbal response is expected. Teachers had a great deal of discretion in the exercise of tolerance and this is the condition that permits much indirect and inexplicit teaching to be done. I found that the teacher of these newcomers to the educational system expected and tolerated from the children answers that were unexpected or inappropriate, or indeed quite inaudible, and would select from a babel of sound a response she regarded as satisfactory, or, if none was discernible, would impose upon the chorus of sound the answer that she hoped to hear, in very much the same way that the mothers in Snow's studies (1972, 1977) would interpret a sound or look or movement from their babies *as if* these constituted a turn at talking, that could properly elicit another turn in reply. Teachers behave *as if* children were already the participating pupils they will soon become. The pupil role is in any case (relative to the teacher's) an undemanding one, since to the teacher it seems natural that she should take virtually all the initiatives, should expect from the children a responding or subordinate role, and should create a framework that virtually ensures it. Children are taught to engage in the discourse of the classroom very much as they are taught a variety of other games played by rules – with minimal explanation. They are treated from the start as players, but as players whose fumbling and inaccurate moves will initially require a good deal of leniency in interpretation from those more experienced. In this respect, however, the games played in the classroom differ from those played outside it. The teacher retains the dominant role, relaxes it only intermittently, and at her own wish. The pupils' part is not only in the earliest stages, but typically, one in which real initiatives are rarely taken, and real choices rarely available. Insofar as the pupils' role is typically that of a recipient, it does not commend itself as more than a limited, and rather inflexible, medium for learning.

THE NEED FOR OTHER EVIDENCE

The experience of transcribing and analysing spontaneously recurring classroom talk produced two convictions about it. On the one hand, it seemed as if, from the very beginning, from the first days in the nursery or the Reception class, teachers and pupils produced text that was a recognisable working approximation to classroom discourse, analysable in terms of the Birmingham model. On the other, it was not the case that all the children participated in anything like the same degree. Taped and transcribed texts overlook altogether the non-participating pupils, and represent the discourse as if the class were a collective entity, making a collective response in relation to the teacher's initiatives. Such a generalised view of class behaviour is one that teachers have often to accept. They typically regard as satisfactorily responsive a class where only some of those present offer replies which they can evaluate, and the efforts they make to identify and nominate those who are reluctant to answer are necessarily intermittent. For some purposes this unevenness of response may be immaterial, but not for mine. It is certain that each child has severally to learn what is expected of him in the role of pupil and what in his turn he may expect. It was clear that the evidence of spontaneously occurring talk needed to be supplemented by evidence of another sort, having its own limitations and distortions no doubt, but avoiding this one. Some means had to be found by which I could tap the perceptions of a representative sample of children.

In working out a means of doing so, I felt able to make a number of assumptions. A child in process of learning to be a pupil can rely on his teacher to make the initiating moves. He has of course the option of doing so, but, unlike her, he has the option of *not* doing so. He must, however, be able to understand what she means, and on that basis be able to respond and to predict from moment to moment what is going to happen next. It is this – the understanding, the ability to distinguish the appropriate from the inappropriate answer – that distinguishes the capable, active and participating, even if silent, pupil from the bewildered, and silent, child who simply does not know what he should do. I needed a device that would enable me to offer children, singly and separately, opportunities to show me whether they could do these things. In addition I needed some control over the kind and the number of their responses, so that I could make comparisons among children, and between the performance of the same child at different stages of his school experience.

The materials I designed and used were a very simple way of eliciting, in something like the way that involvement in make-believe play elicits, some part of what it is that children know. They consist of an illustrated storybook, put together so as to look as much like the reading books in use in classrooms as my limited resources would allow. In two particulars, however, the book differs from the stories to be found in any book corner. It is a story about children and their teacher in school. Very few storybooks produced for this youngest age group represent this part of their experience. And it is incomplete. The illustrations are there, facing each page of text. That text however has important parts unwritten, and it was these that I invited each child to supply, drawing on his own experience of what, in such a setting, is likely to be said or done. Within the story, which the observing adult reads aloud, sitting with the child and referring to the illustrations, are recurrent opportunities to say 'And what do you think happened then?', 'What shall we make him/her say?', 'What do you suppose he/she said then?' The observer then writes into the book the completed story, and this eventually can become the property of its author, to take home, or to colour, but not before his individual contribution has been transferred onto previously prepared sheets.

The numbers in my sample were not larger than the number of children I could reasonably expect to see in the time available to me. My sample consisted of those children, not of Asian or Caribbean parentage, who started formal schooling on 1 September 1977 in seven schools, randomly selected from those in a Midlands metropolitan borough. Learning to be a pupil in a language not one's own, or in a variety of English significantly unlike that native to you, seemed so different and so important an activity as to require separate study. My observation of individual new entrants suggests that to enter an environment where the language, in addition to all else, is strange, where you can, inexplicably, neither understand nor be understood, is for some children an extremely upsetting experience. For the teacher too, the presence of a minority of newcomers whose mother-tongue is quite unknown is extremely disturbing. I have seen one teacher, herself a mother and foster mother, who had a particularly warm and affectionate relation with pupils, resort almost entirely to non-verbal interaction with a Punjabi speaking boy. I was concerned to establish a base line in respect of the learning of discourse, and I excluded these children for that reason.

In addition I worked with a small group of children, in another school, who on that day started the Junior stage of their education. In April of the following year, when the younger children were at the start of their third term of schooling, I repeated the exercise. Naturally I felt some concern that they might recall the first occasion, and simply repeat what they had said. However, their recollection of what had happened months earlier was extremely hazy. Few of them recollected even having seen me before, and I judged the possibility of some recollection less of a hazard than that involved in the task of designing a second story-task at the same level of difficulty. At the conclusion, I was in a position to compare the responses to the task given by a group of children, few of whom had reached the age of five, by the same group several months later, and by another group who, having completed two years of compulsory schooling and attained the age of seven, must be reckoned experienced pupils. I hoped to test, on a small scale certainly, two propositions that observation had suggested: that exposure to the experience of schooling, rather than chronological age, is the major determinant of ability to participate as a pupil, and that children differ in their learning rate in this respect to an extent that is not usually apparent to the observer of the behaviour of a class. As a result of what I found, I made a third visit to a selected small sample of my younger group. This was undertaken for a specific purpose, and was differently organised and recorded.

Of the initial sample of forty-two newcomers to school only four gave me clear evidence of not knowing at all what was required of them. As it happened, these included the youngest and the oldest child in the sample, but since the difference in their ages was no more than eight months, this is not especially a matter for remark. Those four whose rate of nil response was very high (thirty-five of forty-five possible responses) had already been identified at this early stage of their schooling by their teachers as silent, or very nearly so. One other boy (who in fact managed the task without difficulty) found it too long, or complained of boredom. With these exceptions, the children seemed neither surprised nor uneasy that the new experiences crowding their first days at school included a request to help another unknown adult to finish a story. They seemed to understand in general terms what was wanted, even where they could not comply with some specific parts of it. Several of them demonstrated an understanding of what it is to write in a book, remarkable in pre-literate children. Without prompting, they repeated their contributions at a considerate dictation speed. Most of them experienced (as I had hoped they would) a feeling of achievement at the completion of the task. The seven year olds found it easy, though it was not the case that the responses they produced were consistently and effortlessly well formed.

As I anticipated, I found very wide differences in the responses given by children not far apart in terms of chronological age. It seemed to be the case that at entry to school some children could readily and accurately interpret teachers' meanings and predict what was likely to happen from moment to moment in classroom settings. Others could do neither of these things with any assurance. The effect of these differences in understanding must be to produce what I had observed – a situation where a near approximation to well-formed classroom discourse is created by very inexperienced pupils in interaction with their teacher, even though some of them contribute little, and probably do not comprehend what is expected. The origin of the differences was not a matter on which I had evidence. Once in the classroom, the opportunity is available for everyone to learn from the interaction that is established from the beginning. A child who is uncertain what is meant, does not know what to say, and does not know what to expect, can exercise his option of silence until he feels confident enough to try an answer or until a question is directed at him. He can imitate somebody else's contribution which has already been positively evaluated, and expect similar success. (That expectation may of course be disappointed.) He is in a favourable learning situation and it is the fact that some newcomers are, from the start, fully participating pupils, that is in part responsible for making it so. To be a fully participating pupil is not necessarily to be an independent and well-motivated learner.

Between the first and the second set of answers, there was a very considerable difference. With a single exception, there were fewer nil responses, fewer doubtfully interpretable answers, more well-formed responses. The children's ability to predict what was going to happen seemed generally to be substantially increased, and, given that my seven year old group was very small, and the results I had from it must be cautiously interpreted, the five year olds, after two terms of schooling, seemed almost as able to make appropriate responses as were the seven year olds. Of course it would be extraordinary if a sample of newcomers to school did *not* give evidence of having learned a great deal about the discourse of the classroom in their first months of classroom experience. So far this small-scale study is wide open to the criticism that it simply confirms what is entirely apparent to anybody who gives any time or thought to considering the processes of early education. In defence of the undertaking, though, it does suggest some conclusions that are not obvious. Given that on the second occasion the younger children did only a little less well than the seven year olds, the natural explanation is that the business of learning to perform in the pupil role is an important part of the total learning accomplished in the initial months of schooling, that it starts at an accelerated rate, and continues at a slower pace through the Infant and into the Junior school stage. It was not evident at the beginning, either, how disparate the responses would be on the first occasion. Seven months later, even those who had seemed least able to accomplish the task gave evidence of considerable learning achieved. Relative to the others, though, they were still far behind. It was this observation that prompted me to plan a third visit to this small group of children for whom the process of participation as a pupil seemed to be, for whatever reasons, particularly difficult.

AN ATTEMPT TO TEACH CHILDREN TO BE PUPILS

On that third visit I hoped to adopt what on the earlier occasions I had avoided, a deliberately didactic stance. I was encouraged to make the attempt by the fact that of the four children, three, Mark, Louise and Nigel, were a source of considerable anxiety to their teachers. Robert was the only one of them concerning whom nothing had been said to me. I had not sought teachers' estimates of children's probable performance of the task I asked them to do, but it was very natural that they should talk to me about their new intake, and their expectations concerning them. I had been assured in advance of my first visit that Louise would have nothing to offer. Within a day or two of entering school she was established as exceptionally retiring and shy, and explanation was offered in terms of her family's low expectations of her possible attainment. On arrival at Mark's school, I was told that he was one of identical twins; that both boys were experiencing a good deal of difficulty in adjusting to school, not helped by some degree of visual impairment, and noticeable clumsiness of movement associated with it. The fleeting and fragmentary nature of Nigel's attention made him a perpetual focus of disturbance in his classroom. He upset and irritated other children, and his teacher coped with it all with an affectionate patience I could only marvel at, steadily opposing the suggestion that application should be made on his behalf for special education, on the grounds that the longer he could remain within the educational system, the better his eventual chances of functioning within the range of normality.

None of these children seemed at all likely to respond to anything like direct teaching from me. I planned to use as a teaching aid a Fisher Price Play School. It is an engaging toy for the age range (three to six) for which the manufacturers recommend it. Reeder (1975) made use of it in his study of the development of pragmatic competence in pre-school children. It consists of a toy schoolroom, with movable figures and furnishings. The blackboard and magnet board, and the magnetised letters and figures, are deliberately out of scale with the rest, and are of a size to be handled easily by a child. I hoped that a novel and attractive toy would help me secure the attention of each of these children in turn, and that I could show them the possibility of identifying with the figures, making them move, and providing them with things they could appropriately say. Initially, I expected to adopt the teacher role, and to show that it is the one having more attractive possibilities than any other. The teacher has a chair and a desk of distinctive size and colour, she controls the school bell, she has first claim on the board and chalk, and the letters and magnet board, to which, as if by magic, they adhere. I hoped I would soon be under pressure from the children to relinquish these privileges in their favour, and that by identifying with the teacher they would gain the beginnings of understanding what it is that teachers do, when they elicit in expectation of an answering move, direct in expectation of response, and evaluate pupils' answers and responses.

It is a commonplace that early failure in education is very hard to retrieve, that 'If at first you don't succeed, you don't succeed'. The processes of classification, which teachers cannot avoid, are often held to blame. My experience ran quite counter to any suggestion, such as is often implicit in discussion of educational difficulty and failure, that teachers discard and ignore slow, reluctant or ineffectual learners. I had some evidence that these learners experienced extreme difficulty in perceiving the discourse of the classroom as orderly, predictable, and so admitting of their participation. It could only be one of many difficulties for them, but, once identified, it seemed to be one of the more accessible to intervention. The question whether they could be helped, the process of learning to take part could be accelerated, seemed too interesting, and in human terms too important, to ignore.

The responses I got were neither expected nor uniform. Neither Nigel, nor Robert, nor Mark, on the separate occasions when I saw them, was willing to play with the materials I offered in the way that to adults, and to other children of their age, seemed obvious and natural. Their attention was caught by the items (slide, swings, roundabout and school bell) that could be easily and noisily manipulated, to the exclusion of the pupils and the teacher, the desks and the boards. When I drew their attention to these, and invited make-believe play, they disregarded my suggestions as if they had no meaning for them. Although each of the children initially found the new toy attractive, they quickly wearied of it, and looked for something else. In short, they responded just as one would expect children very much younger to do. For them the figures of teacher and pupils, desks and chairs and playground and classroom apparatus were coloured shapes to be handled, and had no representative or symbolic function.

Louise responded quite differently. When I arrived for my third visit, her teacher told me to expect a changed, and much happier, little girl. Louise had blossomed. She had, in recent weeks, since my second visit, learned to read, and with a rapidity and success that gave the lie to her family's expectation that she was the slow one. Recognition had been immediate. Louise had been rewarded by the possession of a hymn book of her own, for use daily in assembly. In one respect Louise, evidently a specialist in defeating adult expectation, defeated mine. I assumed that the Play School would have the attraction of novelty for each of the children, but Louise told me, and I believed her, that she had been given just such a toy as a Christmas present. Her play with it, which was wholly unlike that of the other children, may therefore have been rehearsed. She was no more willing than the others to accept me as a playmate, and like them she turned a deaf ear to my offer of a shared make-believe game. There, however, the resemblance ended.

Without delay, she unpacked the box, set out the pupils at their desks and the teacher at hers, and assumed the teacher role: 'You've got to write your names out proper!' she announced authoritatively. Moments later, she said, turning to me, 'The teacher's got to go to a meeting!' and as she removed the teacher to the top of a box, well out of sight of the class, '*This* little girl is going to be the teacher.' However, the delegation of authority was not a success. 'They've been very naughty!' Louise said to me with evident relish, 'All of them have been very naughty. These children are doing very naughty!' and she added, 'The teacher's talking to thin air!'

Louise's school day was interrupted by 'playtime' and 'home time', and at the end of it she carefully and quickly packed up the toys, and asked my permission to return to her classroom. Louise sustained her make-believe by telling herself a story, and she used the toy pieces to support and illustrate her narrative. She gave me a clear indication of an understanding of the roles of teacher and pupil in some respects very much more sophisticated than I had expected or had looked for. She represented the teacher as someone who organises and controls, and who has, in addition, duties that sometimes remove her altogether from the classroom. 'Being a teacher' was for Louise, after less than a year of schooling, and despite a hesitant start, a role having obligations that may be successfully or unsuccessfully discharged. Proper teachers, in Louise's experience, expect and get compliance, whereas the unlucky pupil to whom the teacher's responsibilities are delegated is likely to get disobedience. Neither the teacher nor her deputy was represented by Louise as providing information, or as checking, by means of questions, whether information had been retained. Clearly one must be cautious of inferring that these essential functions of a teacher are simply not perceived by children. In order to *represent* them, it is necessary to identify some areas of one's own experience and knowledge as potentially, but not actually, shared by others. Five year olds give little evidence of being able to do this at all readily or consistently, nor would one expect them to do so.

This experimental teaching situation I set up failed in its immediate purpose. Louise had already learned all I hoped to teach, and more. Robert and Mark and Nigel were unresponsive to what I offered. Like their respective teachers, I encountered the intractable difficulty of securing their unstable attention, and the toys I offered had not for them the meaning that I had anticipated. My experience gave no encouragement at all to the supposition that it might be possible to identify those children for whom the process of learning what to expect and what is expected in the classroom proves especially troublesome, and to teach them, in a deliberate way, what others learn without such assistance. It is not of course necessarily true that because I conspicuously failed in my efforts to assist those children who seemed slowest to learn, they could not be taught. It *is* true however that where there is a compulsory age of entry to full-time schooling, classrooms will include some children who simply have not reached a stage of development at which they can learn what is appropriate for the majority. Whether children *generally* would benefit if their teachers were, as a result of initial or in-service training, made aware of the rule governed and predictable character of the interaction that goes on in classrooms, is another question altogether. Teachers expect to insist on what is required for registration and similar processes: they expect to find a moment at which it is suitable to start teaching a class to bid for the right to answer. The principle could be extended. Given that it is to children's advantage that they should quickly find their new environment predictable and comprehensible, this seems a possibility worth pursuing.

CONCLUSION

I had at this point to review the overall results of the materials I had designed to supplement observation. The materials constitute in effect a cloze procedure for discourse. I knew from the outset that I must limit my sample to small numbers, but I hoped to demonstrate that replication with a larger sample was a practicable, and might for some purposes be a useful, undertaking. It seems to me that I had confirmation of my initial supposition, that newcomers to the discourse of the classroom do not start at a common level of ignorance and inexperience. They do a great deal of learning in the early months of schooling, but that learning occurs at very different rates, so that very dissimilar degrees of understanding of discourse persist among children who entered school at the same time. School organisation, curricula, and textbooks are organised on a contrary supposition, and the effect of all this in schools is that the realities of learning – that individuals may seem to make no headway, and then may unexpectedly lurch towards understanding – is seen as deviant rather than as commonplace. The requirement made by the materials I used, that individual pupils should predict what would happen in a fictitious situation, needs to be checked against those same individuals' classroom performance, and against other evidence – for example of their progress in reading. Both sorts of check are important, since the group of children who performed well in the story-making task is likely to include some who are, at an early stage, ready participants, and some who understand quite well what is going on, but who are, temperamentally or for other reasons, reluctant to speak. It is this second group that I dare hope might be the eventual beneficiaries of the developed work. Their number is not small, and the difficulties they experience do not automatically decrease over time. They are the children of whom their teachers regularly report 'Must take more part in class.' Naturally taciturn children are vulnerable in classrooms, not just because teachers naturally look for overt responsiveness and dislike its contrary, but because it is extremely difficult for teachers to know *what* to expect of them. A straightforward, unalarming procedure, that could be carried out by any teacher able to devote twenty minutes to an individual pupil, and that would discriminate between a silent child for whom the classroom is a place of unpredictable confusion, and another for whom it is, in essentials, intelligible and orderly, would, I believe, be worth having, and would justify the expenditure of some resources.

REFERENCES

REEDER, K. F., *Pre-School Children's Comprehension of Illocutionary Force: an Experimental Psycholinguistic Study*, unpublished Ph.D. Thesis, University of Birmingham, 1975.

SINCLAIR, J. McH. & COULTHARD, R. M., *Towards an Analysis of Discourse: the English used by Teachers and Pupils*, Oxford University Press, 1975.

SNOW, C., 'Mothers' speech to children learning language', *Child Development*, 43, 1972, pp. 549–565.

SNOW, C., 'The development of conversation between mothers and babies', *Journal of Child Language*, 4/1, 1977, pp. 1–22.

DOUGLAS BARNES AND FRANKIE TODD

4 Talk in Small Learning Groups: Analysis of Strategies

In this paper we seek to share with the reader some of the considerations which influenced us during a two-year research project.[1] We present a view of the situation in which our data was gathered, and discuss the implications of the kind of analysis which we chose to give to the data.

The questions which we set ourselves were educational and not linguistic. Was it possible to describe the talk of small groups of children in ways which would distinguish successful engagement with the learning tasks they had been set? And if that were possible, could one identify aspects of the social context and of the setting of the task which relate to successful learning? In particular, could those moves by which learners interrelate their viewpoints be identified? (Behind this last question lay Piaget's view that more adequate representations of reality are developed by the incorporation of alternative viewpoints.)[2]

Briefly, this is how we collected our data. Our subjects were fifty-six boys and girls of thirteen years of age. They came from two schools and were recorded in sixteen groups of three or four members. Approximately eleven hours of tape were transcribed in standard orthography. We worked closely with teachers of a range of school subjects. When their normal teaching approached a point where group work became appropriate, they collaborated with us in drawing up a task. Some of these tasks were tightly structured by a series of questions, while others were open according to the teacher's wishes. Those groups whom we were recording were then withdrawn from the appropriate lesson, and recorded in separate rooms.

The contexts which we thus created were therefore neither strictly experimental nor exactly like group work in lessons. We gained some control of the situation and an excellent quality of recording; we lost the right to claim that we were sampling group talk in lessons. This loss seemed less serious in that we wanted to describe talk under circumstances which in our judgment were encouraging, and particularly to understand the effect of placing more control of learning and the social context in the hands of the learners.

A central task in any study of talk must be to map out the subjects' interpretation of the situation in which they are recorded. It is not easy to construct such a map. Undoubtedly the young people saw the recording as school work and not something else: most of the talk was devoted to the given tasks and not to other purposes. Nevertheless, the problem solving strategies used were not necessarily learnt at school, since talk of this kind by pupils is not common in lessons.[3] In spite of the constraints imposed by the tasks, the pupils were free to control the cognitive strategies used and the patterns of their interaction, since no teacher exercised moment by moment control. Whatever norms they brought to the conversation were treated as less binding than those of teacher–class discussion, more open to negotiation.

So much we can confidently say about the situation apart from our own part in it as investigators. We believe that the children's interpretation of the situation differed according to the way we worked with them. We shall distinguish two phases in which our methods of collecting data were widely different: one we now call the Participatory Phase and the other the Experimental Phase. Our different methods during these two phases threw unforeseen light upon the problem of delineating the subjects' view of the situation.

During the Participatory Phase, which lasted for five months, one of us made repeated visits to a school to record four of the groups. A teacher who was sympathetic to our purposes had explained the project to the children, and we too chatted informally with them. The experimenter became familiar to the children and avoided assuming the teacherly role. During the recording the children, who were working in friendship groups, had considerable control over the tape recorder; they could switch off or play back as they wished and could decide when they should stop. They were given a promise of anonymity with respect to the school. Whether or not they indeed understood our purposes, these four groups appeared to believe that they understood, and to take our purposes as positive and non-threatening. We think they saw themselves as participating in our attempt to record good talk.

The Experimental Phase came later as an attempt to conform to a quite different research paradigm. We wished to control situational and IQ variables more sharply in order to test hypotheses. We selected children from different classes on the results of a verbal intelligence test, and grouped them arbitrarily. In order to fulfil sampling requirements it was necessary to draw children from several classes, and we therefore carried out all the recordings in one visit in order to disturb the school as little as possible. Groups were recorded rapidly one after another to conform to a tight schedule. Attempts to communicate our purposes to the children could only be brief and perfunctory; they could have gained no understanding, nor trust of our good faith. As part of the experimental design, we told some groups that they would not be tested. Inspection of the talk suggested to us that most – and perhaps all – of the children treated the exercise as a test: that is, the meaning they attributed to the situation overrode the experimental meaning which we attempted to give it. Most groups pursued 'right answers', and one group of girls were so anxious that they treated a problem-solving task as an exercise in recollection. Schools are places where assessment goes on; so powerful an interpretation is difficult to supplant.

It is not easy to estimate the effect upon the speaker of the knowledge that he or she is being tape recorded. We surmise that no groups were ever entirely unaware, though the groups recorded during the Participatory Phase sometimes seem to have forgotten briefly when they became excited. Such awareness was occasionally shown when children addressed the tape recorder: one boy said, 'We've done Two, Tape' (Question Two, that is). The difference between the Participatory and Experimental groups was not a matter of forgetting the recording but of how they perceived the audience it provided. For the Experimental groups, we never ceased to be potentially threatening outsiders; only the Participatory groups could perceive us as unthreatening. We take this to be a valuable reminder that data collected in one context should not be generalised to others without the greatest care. This applies particularly to studies in which a sample of talk is taken to represent cognitive or communicative competences possessed by the subjects.

It is now time to turn from the situation to the analysis itself. It is useful to distinguish three main levels of analysis which we will call the levels of Form, of Discourse and of Strategy. Labov[4] has distinguished between the first two as 'What is said' and 'What is done'. Similarly the level of Strategy might be characterised as 'What is to be accomplished'. (The term 'Strategy' has been chosen in order to refer to sequences of utterances which are united by a speaker's continuing purpose, whether it relates to the requirements of a learning task or to interaction with other people, or both.) These three levels of analysis can be illustrated from our materials: one of the boys said to a girl in his group, 'Do you, Diane, think he's a delinquent, Diane?' At the Level of Form this can be given phonological, morphological and syntactical analyses, that is, this level contains various sub levels. At the Level of Discourse this utterance would be identified as the speech act often called an 'elicitation'.[5] (It is important to note that a question form does not always function as an elicitation, and elicitation can be carried out by other forms as well as questions.) At the Level of Strategy, however, the utterance in question in our judgment functioned as an attempt to force the girl Diane to take a more active part in the discussion and as a judgment about her failure to do so. These levels can be represented thus:

Level	Characterisation	Description of 'Do you, Diane, think he's a delinquent, Diane?'
1. Form	What is said	Grammatical etc. description (including position of 'Diane').
2. Discourse	What is done	Illocutionary force: 'elicitation'.
3. Strategy	What is to be accomplished	Social and cognitive strategies: 'Pressure to participate'.

Our concern in this study, however, was to find ways of describing pupils' talk that threw light upon its relationship with learning, and that would be of value to teachers when they reflected upon their pupils' uses of language in lessons. This directed our endeavours towards the third level of description, that of Strategy. Nevertheless, when we set out upon the study of group talk we assumed that we would find a relationship between levels. We hoped to identify functional categories and then to be able to specify the forms that 'realised' these functions, but we found no such simple relationship between forms and functions. For example, as we were interested in identifying occasions when the children were trying to come to terms with one another's different viewpoints we tried to set up an 'index of collaborativeness', using forms such as anaphora, subordinations, repetitions, transformations and so on. However, it turned out that enumerating these forms could not serve our purposes in examining the role of collaboration in learning; indeed at times the distribution of the forms we wished to use as markers of collaboration ran counter to our intuitions about the collaborativeness being shown by the children. Links between successive utterances were left implicit in our data more often than made explicit, though the nature of the link was often clear enough even to an observer as well as to the participants. As Labov has shown[6], links between utterances are frequently carried out not at the Level of Form but via underlying propositions. Participants use their tacit knowledge to attribute meaning to what is said, but may call on different bodies of knowledge at different moments, as they seem relevant. We called these subsystems of implicit knowledge 'Frames'; they provide frames of reference within which utterances are assigned meaning and relevance. Labov cites the dialogue from a Charlie Brown cartoon.

> *Linus*: Do you want to play with me, Violet?
> *Violet*: You're younger than me. (*Shuts the door*)
> *Linus* (*puzzled*): She didn't answer my question.

Violet's utterance is only a reply to Linus if one knows that in their culture older children do not play with younger children. Violet's words 'You're younger than me' are understood by any hearer who can bring an appropriate frame of reference to bear on it; Labov calls this 'shared knowledge', though Linus clearly does not share it. In terms of our analysis (at the level of Strategy) this is part of the Content Frame which Violet is using but it is not available as part of Linus' Content Frame. The point might also be made that one cannot analyse the first two utterances at the Level of Discourse as Initiation and Response without using knowledge of the culture.[7]

We made some attempt to develop an analysis at the Level of Discourse, using categories such as 'Initiative', 'Elicitation', 'Extension', but abandoned this partly because of the more fully-developed work by Sinclair and Coulthard,[8] and partly because analysis at this level did not seem to be answering our purposes. We were not looking for those characteristics which were common to all dialogue but for those which accompanied success in carrying out cooperative learning through talk. In attempting discourse analysis, it became clear to us that such analysis cannot be carried out solely on formal grounds; throughout the analysis we were using knowledge of the subject matter and of the children and their situation in order to attribute discourse categories to utterances.

We are convinced that the cognitive and social meanings which we are concerned with require analysis at the Level of Strategy, and that analyses at the other two levels will only occasionally contribute to understanding these meanings. Labov in the paper already cited[9] suggests a hierarchy of categories of action in which higher level categories such as 'Inquiries', 'Challenges' and 'Defences' would each contain within them a group of discourse categories. We have not found a consistent relationship of inclusion between the categories of Strategy which we wished to use and those of Discourse. It is true, however, that the units of analysis we found ourselves using at the level of Strategy were often larger in scale than a single utterance, and might include more than one participant.

In describing the communication strategies which distinguish some conversations from others we have used ad hoc categories such as these:

Social Skills	*Cognitive Strategies*
Monitoring progress through the task	Constructing questions
	Setting up hypotheses
Managing conflict	Using evidence
Giving support	Interrelating viewpoints
etc.	etc.[10]

It must be stressed that these categories are not so far capable of precise operational definition, and that they do not form a system which exhausts the possibilities of meaning at this level of analysis. They are highly inferential, and may overlap, or differ in scale, so that they are not quantifiable. We justify them as a stage in the development of 'grounded theory' since they arise from lengthy work on the data, and successive attempts to find forms of analysis that were intuitively satisfying. We sought to find categories which teachers could use to understand group talk in lessons.

The incompleteness and lack of formal definition of the categories arises in part from the nature of conversation. As Garfinkel[11] and others have shown, meaning depends on the knowledge brought to the interpretation of situated utterances: it does not adhere to the utterances themselves. Since each participant in group talk brings a different frame of reference to the interpretation of an utterance, meaning must be multiple. Moreover, the meanings are also fluid and indeterminate,[12] since each new utterance implicitly reinterprets what has gone before: there is no point in the flow of a conversation at which the investigator can stop and say, 'That's what they really meant'. The frame of reference from which we interpret utterances itself changes during conversation: it is only in retrospect that participant or observer can attribute a more stable meaning to an exchange (though this attributed meaning can itself change). Thus it is useful to distinguish the 'operational meaning' which participants construct implicitly in the course of the ongoing interaction from the 'reflective meaning' which arises from later reconstruction. The meaning of talk is at once multiple and indeterminate.

We also found it necessary to distinguish what is said about the subject matter from the sending of messages about social relationships in the group. In order to assign meaning to talk, participants and observers alike must utilise Content Frames (bodies of knowledge about how the world is) and Interaction Frames (views about who the participants are and what they are doing). Content and Interaction Frames are negotiated simultaneously throughout talk, often through the same utterances.

In selecting the Social Skills and Cognitive Strategies we were uneasily aware of dealing only with the more explicit aspects of the complex events which constitute talk, 'explicit' in the sense that we could offer interpretations with some confidence that they bore some resemblance to participants' operational meanings. But these omitted the rest of the iceberg, for we were aware of similar processes going on, perhaps via intonation and gesture, or perhaps through meanings of the utterances which were unavailable to us because we had not shared the previous history of these children.

In spite of all that we have written about talk as multiple and indefinite, we must make statements about what a particular sequence of talk means if we wish to communicate our interpretations to others. In order to do so we take up the stance of an ideal disembodied observer and assume the existence of a general communicative and substantive competence, that is, assume Interaction Frames and Content Frames. But does such common knowledge exist at the level of Strategy? Although we assume this in order to discuss our understanding of our materials, we regard such competences as potentially misleading idealisations.

Conversation – even academic conversation – is characterised by ambiguity, misunderstanding, meanings that insensibly change, and by what we have called 'fuzziness', all of which arise from the nature of conversation, the diversity of participants' social experience and therefore the diversity of the frames available. We must not allow the idealised unanimity to disguise from us the reality of that diversity.

NOTES

1 'Communication and learning in small groups', funded by the Social Science Research Council.

2 PIAGET, J., *The Moral Judgement of the Child*, Free Press, 1948.

3 See BARNES, D., BRITTON, J. & ROSEN, H., *Language, the Learner and the School*, Penguin, revised edition, 1971.

4 LABOV, W., 'Rules for Ritual Insults', in Sudnow, D. (ed.), *Studies in Social Interaction*, Free Press, 1972.

5 SINCLAIR, J. McH. & COULTHARD, M., *Towards an Analysis of Discourse: the English used by Teachers and Pupils*, Oxford University Press, 1975.

6 LABOV, W., op. cit.

7 WILSON, D. & SPERBER, D., 'On Grice's Theory of Conversation', mimeographed, Department of Linguistics, University College, London, (undated), have recently argued that in attributing meaning to propositions as well as to implications (such as

Violet's) we are dependent on 'conversational maxims', i.e. presuppositions about relevance similar to those implied here in discussing Frames.

8 SINCLAIR & COULTHARD, op. cit.

9 LABOV, W., op. cit.

10 The categories are presented in full and discussed in: BARNES, D. & TODD, F., *Communication and Learning in Small Groups*, Routledge and Kegan Paul, 1977.

11 GARFINKEL, H., *Studies in Ethnomethodology*, Prentice-Hall, 1967.

12 A similar point is made by R. WALKER & C. ADELMAN, *Towards a Sociography of Classrooms*, Chelsea College of Science and Technology, Social Science Research Council, 1972.

CLEM ADELMAN

5 On First Hearing

The Ford Teaching Project made a concerted effort over nearly two years to establish and support a group of forty teachers who were attempting to self-monitor the intended and unintended effects of their actions on pupils. The central team – John Elliott and Clem Adelman – had suggested that a feedback from pupils could be got by asking them to keep diaries, by interviewing them, by recording lessons, and so on. Teachers of younger children, on attempting to put these techniques into practice, reported that 'it was no use trying to get feedback from them because they could not express themselves adequately'. Older pupils often treated the teacher's request for feedback as a cause for mirth and ridicule. Other teachers, obtaining feedback that was uncritical, took this to mean that they had no problems in communicating the intent of their actions. Only by breaking the stalemate concerning the eliciting of honest accounts could the teachers begin to monitor the extent and type of hiatus that separated their aspirations from their practices. The collaboration within a mutually agreed ethical framework deriving from practitioner's theory – action research as we understood it – could not commence until honest accounts could be obtained on the form of both teachers' and pupils' accounts. The central team was forced – indeed asked – to intervene as an intermediary between teachers and pupils, and try to elicit honest accounts from teachers and from pupils which could be fed back to each other. This intervention, then, took the form of what Cicourel calls 'triangulation'. This article reviews the practice and experience of the Ford Teaching Project when using the research strategy of triangulation. It looks at two of the triangulations that were accomplished during the course of the Ford Teaching Project. Cicourel[1] describes triangulation thus:

. . . it provides details on how various interpretations of 'what happened' are assembled from different physical, temporal, and biographically provided perspectives of a situation. Comparing the teacher's accounts of the lesson before and after it was presented, and comparing the teacher's version with those of the children produced different accounts of the 'same' scene. It was sometimes difficult to recognise that the children and the teacher witnessed the same event. The children's responses during the lesson provided different conceptions of correct and incorrect answers which contrasted with the teacher's expectations stated prior to and subsequent to the lesson. The children seemed to receive and organise the lesson in terms of their own orientation at the time of the event, and these conceptions do not always match the teacher's account of the lesson's purpose and conduct.

When the first Ford Teaching Project triangulation (the 'tin' study included below) was commenced in March 1973, this book by Cicourel had not been published. I had to draw on incomplete accounts, for instance in other work of Cicourel[2] and of Garfinkel.[3] Guidelines for interview were adapted from Frake[4] and Black and Metzger.[5] Harré and Secord[6] suggest asking the actors for their accounts, but their suggestion was hypothetical, rather than arising out of practical problems of such an enterprise.

Now, at least, with some practice and experience as a basis, it seems to me that triangulation involves getting people to give accounts of what their actions were. These accounts are, however, not elicited through questions constructed from the interviewer's own interpretations of the actions, but through the interviewer's reporting or replaying some sort of representation of the actions. A film, tape-slide, video-tape, tape recording, or notes, are made available to the interviewees. Our practice of triangulation involves an attempt to relate the way people give accounts of what they do, to their accounts of the representation of what they do. Then, we subsequently elicit their interpretation of an account of what other people say they do. Any evaluation of self or other focuses on the actions of the actor in a role, rather than an evaluation of the person.[7] The underlying idea here is that no action is self-contained; people can have intended actions which are constrained by context. No actions are untrammeled, all actions in the social world are interactions. Interaction necessarily involves a reciprocation and thus a reciprocal viewpoint. Triangulation, then, does not treat the speech act as self-contained action. A speech act is seen as incomplete, needing reciprocal interpretations to complete its meaning in a social context. These practices are supported by the ideas of illocutionary force and uptake[8] and central to 'taking the role of the other' as propounded by George Mead.[9]

The practice of collecting discrete accounts from witnesses of an event has been well established by law enforcement agencies and disseminated to a wider public over time by authors such as Wilkie Collins, Arthur Conan Doyle, Georges Simenon. The attribution of blame during rule enforcement in schools usually involves the collection of accounts from witnesses and the pursuance of discrepancies. (One significant exception to this custom of schools was the practice of A. S. Neill, who depended on pupils giving accounts of their own actions.) Although the eliciting of accounts is central to ethnographic studies, accounts are never reported back by the ethnographer to other members of the primitive culture. (Is this because ethnographers are afraid to taint one member of another culture, so blurring the boundaries?) So Frake,[10] for instance, vividly illustrates that participants' accounts of the same event were not at all similar, but dependent on status relationships and so on.

Students on teaching practice are observed by one or more college staff often on separate occasions. There is, then, an established judgmental ethos of which the action of giving accounts is emblematic, although contexts may vary. In ordinary social life people do not give frank, honest accounts about people's actions: politeness and courtesy, respect for others' feelings, are involved. We precede the 'crunch' utterance with such words as 'to be frank', and then the unashamed utterance.

The transformations a hearer has to make of another's utterance in any context, to understand the intended meaning of the utterance, are based on cultural knowledge of person, role and context. The eliciting of honest accounts depends on certain contextual conditions and, even when these things are established, the elicited utterance is not necessarily self-evident in meaning. But at least constraints of politeness, status differential, retribution, courtesy, etc. are reduced in effect. Accounts that appear judgmental do show these qualities.

Accounts that are honest and reflexive showed reduced phatic features.[11]

But to get back to the substantive problem, how to accomplish triangulation. When the central team realised that they would have to intervene in the teacher's own research to attempt to provide the teachers with honest pupil accounts, triangulation seemed to be the appropriate research strategy. As the effects of triangulation on teachers and pupils were unknown the procedural guidelines were exploratory, yet the attempt seemed crucial to initiate the project. We selected two teachers whom we considered from early observations to have certain problematic aspects in their classrooms, yet were reflective enough to take part as collaborative partners in the triangulation. We hoped that they would not subsequently reject further involvement in the project. We were taking a risk. We envisaged that if the triangulations from these two teachers could be circulated (with the permission and editing of the participants) amongst the other teachers, then the breakdown of the stalemate in obtaining honest accounts would begin. Other teachers might, if we could get substantial feedback from pupils, begin to take seriously (as valid rather than reliable) pupils' accounts of teacher actions.

THE PROCEDURES IN TRIANGULATION

The accounts of participants in a classroom event are elicited by an observer, who was witness to that event. The observer attempts to maintain an unbiased relationship to what goes on but this non-evaluative stance is only possible through a certain amount of awareness of one's own beliefs and values that one brings to the classroom. The observer has to hold in reflexive suspension his own beliefs and values about an activity.

Stage One

The observer has already recorded the lesson. The form of recording might be notes, tape-slide, tape recording, and so on. The observer has to decide what the sequence of interviews would be – if the pupils first, then the observer, acting now as interviewer, would be asking the pupils to give their account of the lesson. Eventually the onus would be on the pupils to account for discrepancies in their first account as compared with the teacher's first account. If the teacher is interviewed first, then the onus would be on the teacher to give an account of the discrepancies between his account and the pupils' account. As the project was concerned with the problems of teachers researching their own teaching, the onus had to be on the teacher.

Stage Two

Pupils' accounts are elicited. Pupils are selected in several ways. Where the teacher mentions a particular event, the pupils in that event are asked for their accounts. Where the teacher subsequently talks generally, the central team member would talk to pupils who had worked alone, pupils who had worked in a group, and especially to pupils who seemed to the observer to be involved in some misunderstanding or miscommunication with the teacher. The particular sections of the lesson that the teacher self-selected from a recording, or the observer questioned the teacher about and then repeated to the pupils, were important. The observer's questions are based on the teacher's first account; thus not only does the observer collect the pupils' interpretation of events selected as 'significant' by the teacher, but the interviewer may introduce through his own questions the teacher's first account for the pupils to comment on without mentioning the source as being the teacher.

Stage Three

The pupils' accounts are played back to the teacher with the questions asked by the interviewer. The teacher then gives his understanding and explanation of the pupils' account. That is, this is the point when the onus is on the teacher to account for discrepancies between his first account of his intentions and the pupils' account of their interpretation of his action. This is the time when the teacher – if he does at all – makes most explicit his beliefs and values, his tacit assumptions about his actions and their effects. This is also the time when the self-esteem of the teacher is likely to be threatened by being presented with discrepant accounts from the pupils. The interviewer has to encourage the teacher to give his account, at the same time drawing on the accumulative store of trusting and non-judgmental relationship with the interviewer/observer. The fact that the interviewer has also witnessed the original event is invaluable in helping to ground the proceedings and realities that can be referred to by the teacher. He has the knowledge and confidence that the observer is capable of giving yet another account, one which is fair, unbiased, and full of genuine doubts about the observer's own interpretation. The implication of the necessity for the observer to be a witness to the actual event is highlighted if, say, a video recorded event is the information source of the triangulation. In this case the observer maybe watched the lesson on an outside monitor screen. Although the triangulation can give a lot of information about video recordings, it does not give much information about the actual event.

When the teacher has successfully begun to self-monitor and through self-monitoring become self-aware, the interviewer can make the intent of his questions explicit – he can study his own interpretations – for through his monitoring the teacher collects and can cite information to refute or confirm the observer's interpretation. The observer's interpretations in the early stages of the project were sometimes interpreted as confrontation, but later they were seen as genuine enquiries.

Stage Four

The lesson and the accounts are transcribed. The transcripts are carefully reviewed to collect together the separate accounts that focus on the same and on similar topics. These are juxtaposed. The interviewer's accounts of the teacher's first account, the pupils' first account, the teacher's second account, are placed alongside each other topic by topic. In the Ford Project we used triangulation as a source of evidence to formulate hypotheses about the effects of certain actions on pupils for the teachers to test subsequently in their own classrooms. However, our acts of intervention through triangulation were only carried out during the initial to middle stages of the project. Once the honest account stalemate was broken, the teachers found they could begin to get feedback on their own initiative from pupils and begin to formulate and test their own hypotheses. Especially in the initial stages of the project, the feeding back of the triangulations we hoped would encourage teachers to start research into their own teaching. We hoped that the triangulations would be clear evidence that there were often gaps between the stated intention and the actual effects of actions.

I will now provide some extracts from two triangulation studies, collected during the Ford Teaching Project, to illustrate Stages One, Two and Three.

In Stage One, the teacher is asked to be concerned with his account of the lesson. This account tends to be descriptive and the extent to which the teacher introduces explanations tends to depend on the amount of threat he feels and the extent to which he feels the interviewer is evaluating his teaching. As with the later stages, two and three, the honest, frank account is likely to be forthcoming if all parties' actions are predicated by a mutually agreed ethical framework which specifies rights and duties of participants in the project, especially regarding control of data. Trust between the observer/central team researcher and teachers and pupils develops within this agreed way of working.[12]

When I was envisaging this article, I had strong retrospective impressions that the initial interviews with the teacher were those where the teacher's descriptions and to a lesser extent his explanations of the events within the lesson, would be prominent. The same qualities would be perceivable in the pupils' first account. Only on the second order account, when the teacher heard the pupils' account, would the beliefs and values, especially the values of the teacher, be made explicit by him. However, when I look at the two triangulation studies I do not find clear cut distinctions between description and values. I account for this in the following ways.

The published triangulations were accomplished during the early stages of the project, before we had much experience of the research strategy itself. Specifically they lack experience in asking non-leading questions and in encouraging, by our questions, the teacher to stay at a descriptive level. After a teacher's first order account, after seeing a tape-slide recording of his lesson, he has requested that the recording be paused at a particular place; the interviewer has talked with him about an issue that he has raised and then brings him back to the point at which the recording was paused:

Interviewer: Did you want to say something about the talk with the boys about the tins? Have they got any comment to make about their problem as they saw it? Do you want to hear it?

Teacher: No, I can recall it. The tin and the rusting. The tin as a metal or the tin as a tin. Well, they were confused, weren't they? I think the problem I had there was to get over the concept of tin as a metal and a tin as a container. That was their problem. Tin to them was a container, wasn't it? I don't suppose they would come into contact with tin in any other way.

Interviewer: As a metal?

Teacher: Not as a metal, because it's not used a lot, is it, except for plating. I was just trying to think.

Interviewer: What you were trying to get from them was whether tin rusts.

Teacher: Yes, but they didn't know because they had no *concept of tin*, had they?

Interviewer: No.

There are several things to be said about this sequence. The interviewer's initial question raises the talk with the boys about the tins only on the initiative of the teacher who has specified the point at which the recording should be paused, this point being the incident with the tins; thus, the interviewer is talking in order to recover the topic that the teacher himself raised. The teacher's description picks out the topics of tin and rusting, the tin as a metal or the tin as a tin (can). He then gives his understanding: 'Well, they were confused, weren't they? I think the problem I had there was to get over the concept of tin as a metal and a tin as a container.' The interviewer prompts the teacher's memory with 'What you were trying to get from them was whether tin rusts.' This is not, then, a leading question in that it is descriptive of the content of the event that the teacher has raised. Teacher agrees, 'Yes, but they didn't know because they had no *concept of tin*, had they?' This is the teacher's belief being raised. The interviewer says at this point 'No', *not* because he himself has understood the interaction to indicate that the pupils had no concept of tin (he himself believes that the pupils have a strong concept of tin), but mainly that the teacher has not disambiguated tin (metal) from tin (can). However, he says 'No' at this point because if he said otherwise he would have prevented and inhibited the teacher from giving his own particular interpretation. It is important, it would appear, that the truth value of a teacher's account is not made the first criterion for effective eliciting. The problem of eliciting overrides the interviewer's judgment about truth.

In Stage Two, the interviews with pupils, the sequence is:

Interviewer: Go on, say what you want to say. (*The recorded section having been played back yet again.*)

Pupil 1: I don't think chrome is a metal is it?

Pupil 2: The magnet wouldn't pick it up, would it?

Pupil 1: No.

Interviewer: It wouldn't pick up chrome?

Pupil 1: No. It picked up copper.

Pupil 2: When we said the copper would rust, we were right. We've got some in the pond now and it is rusting.

Pupil 1: Yes, but I think Mr J said it was more corrosion than rust.

Interviewer: Yes, that's right – it doesn't rust, chrome doesn't, and it isn't a metal – that's what you are saying. Still can't get to the point. . . . What are you trying to tell Mr J about the tin?

Pupil 1: We are trying to tell him that they rust.

Interviewer: And what's he saying to you?

Pupil 1: I think he is trying to get into us that he doesn't think tin rusts.

Interviewer: He's trying to get you to say that tin doesn't rust?

Pupil 1: He's saying that them tins weren't tins.

Pupil 2: Yeah, and how we knew it was tin.

Interviewer: Ah, now that's good. So at that point . . . ? Yes, go on.

Pupil: At that point we did think they were tin.

Interviewer: So what sort of sense were you making of what Mr J was saying?

Pupil 1: . . . Well, he kept saying that tin didn't rust and we kept trying to say to him that tin would rust.

Pupil 2: Then he said look it up.

Interviewer: Did you manage to make Mr J understand what you meant by tin?

Pupil 1: Not really, did we?

Pupil 2: I think we understood that we thought it was tin because it was called tin, I think he understood that. I suppose that

was why we said tin would rust. I think he knew that we
call that tin and that was tin, thought that was tin.

This is a complex section where the interviewer is trying to represent
as accurately as possible the teacher's account by posing statements of
the teacher as questions to the pupils to get them to give their
accounts. The encouragement of the pupils to give their account
overrides in priority a concern for eliciting 'right' answers about the
original event. 'Go on, say what you want to say' is said after the third
replay of the section which the teacher has originally selected. The
boys reconstruct what they have been doing, describing the
experiments that they were involved in. Also, trying to recall, as in
'But I think Mr J said it was more corrosion than rust', the teacher's
replies and interventions in their experiments. Just as with the point
where the interviewer agrees 'no' that the pupils don't have a concept
of tin rather than contradicting the teacher, in this account where the
interviewer says 'Yes, that's right – it doesn't rust, chrome doesn't, and
it isn't a metal' he is contradicting his own scientific knowledge to
recount 'that's what you are saying'. The interviewer at this point
is trying to get the pupils to make the reciprocal account to the first
order account of the teacher, that is to test out the teacher's account
with the pupils. At least he gets a response through asking a leading
question 'What are you trying to tell Mr J about the tin?' However, it
is only leading in the sense that it leads back to the teacher's first
account and to the topic originally raised by the teacher and the
interviewer is still acting as a go-between trying to retain the original
force of the teacher's first account.

Later, at the point where the interviewer says 'Ah, now that's good
. . .' the interviewer's own enthusiasm comes out because he feels he is
beginning to make sense of what went on initially; this has overriden
his sense of the principle that one should act as a non-evaluative go-
between. Eventually, at the end of this sequence, the point where the
interviewer asks whether the pupils manage to make the teacher
understand what they meant by tin, the second pupil makes it clear
that the problem was one of terminology – that of 'tin' and 'tins'.
Having clarified that the pupils did have this distinction, the interviewer could take this knowledge back with him when he made the
second order interview with the teacher.

In Stage Three, the pupils' accounts are played back to the teacher
and the teacher says:

Teacher: I think they are a bit confused personally.
Interviewer: Yes, yes. What's their confusion?
Teacher: Well, I think it is partly due to the fact that they haven't
                got the concept of the tin, the coating of tin is almost
                infinitesimal, so thin. They are probably thinking it is
                quite thick. I would want to get round to scratching it,
                this is what I would lead up to. They don't seem all that
                clear. I think the problem is putting it in a form which
                they understand. You felt that did you? (*Addressed to the
                interviewer*).

The teacher, within the second order, is expressing his beliefs and
values about the pupils' account, rather than describing the original
lesson incident. The crucial point, then, is that ideally the fullest
eliciting of beliefs and values should be encouraged at the second
order accounts. It seems to me that it should be possible by carefully
framing questions to the teacher to reduce the expression of values in
first order accounts to allow there to be symmetry between teacher's
descriptions and pupils' descriptions.

However, I wonder, even on inspection of much later triangulation,
whether this is in fact possible during interview. The values are
embedded in the descriptions.

Even with further experience and hindsight, this second, much
later, triangulation does not have the ideal separation of values from
description.

One incident within this lesson is chosen by the teacher as being
significant and problematic. The teacher with a group of pupils is
looking at specimens of pond water in polythene bags.

Teacher: I arrived three years ago. If you went down there three
                years ago, it was different from what it is now; the
                difference is quite obvious. In fact you notice the difference.
                Yesterday, even though you'd never been there before, you
                saw something new, you know what it was? (*Pause*) What
                are they doing all the way round?

Children: Making . . . Putting down grass in some places but people have been treading it too much.

Teacher: But there's something happening perhaps a little way away from the pond, which might be having an effect on it.

Child: Those houses, big houses.

Teacher: Very big houses – estate, you remember the big housing estate. Now, you've got a nice . . . I don't know, what do you think?

Child: . . .

Teacher: Yeah.

Child: It's got a fence round the back of it.

Teacher: But I think, the – supposing I was the, the builders and I said right I'm – I'm building right down through that field. What's your reaction to that?

Children (*Several overlapping replies, the last to the effect that it's coming more into the village, and will spoil it with the fence.*)

Teacher: Yeah, but supposing I was a town person, I'd say I like village life, so why can't I come and live in your village?

Children: (*Overlapping replies*).

Teacher: Yeah, I will because I'll be living in a modern house, because I want my modern houses coming all the way down, but why can't . . . But the old village would still be the old village.

Child: Yes but unless you made the new estate, you know, new shops and things, it would be old one side and new the other side.

Teacher: Well is there anything wrong in that?

Child: It would look strange.

Teacher: Does that matter?

Child: People in the village might want it to remain a village.

Teacher: Well, should we take any notice of what they say? I mean after all there are only a few villagers, should we ...

Child: They should vote on it.

Teacher: But supposing, you see I mean supposing I'm living in London and I think, well, I want a nice place in the country, why can't I come out and move in to that estate to get out of the big city into the village and then I could, I could go to the

village pub for a drink in the evening you know . . . sit
round the pond on a Saturday afternoon, why not, why
can't I?

On the first interview with the teacher he says:

Interviewer: I find that interesting.
Teacher: Well we went down to the pond actually when was it – on
Wednesday, and as they say they all expected it to be
lyrical and beautiful with the trees and with ducks on the
pond. We'd go down and there will be reeds and ducks on
the pond. Now I knew it would be a bit tatty down there
and what I wanted was their reaction as soon as they got
there. Now you got the reaction there, you know, their
first thought was pollution and all the rest of it, so
obviously it was guided, and it was their reaction.
At the same time it was a reaction I was expecting and wanting. And in fact you notice I think
when you look at that particular section, a couple of times
there were, it's guided quite strongly, at one stage it
changes away from the pond, it goes on to the village.
Interviewer: Yes right.
Teacher: And in fact there's one little bit there where Alison I
think, obviously thinks I'm still on about the pond, and she
says, the effect is going to be that rubbish is going to be
thrown in the pond and so on.
If they wanted to continue that, fine, it would have
continued but the others picked up very quickly that it
was going to have an effect on the village itself. Now
whether there was too much leading and feeding there.
What do you think from . . .
Interviewer: Well you shifted from sort of observing the specimens,
making notes about that, to . . .
Teacher: Yeah we had.
Interviewer: To actually moving onto a sort of ethical problem. That
change of tack seems to have thrown the big girl.
Teacher: Big change wasn't it?
Interviewer: Yes a big shift and different sort of talk . . . much more of

a discussion of course, then, than before where you . . . information about particular live creatures and plants.

Teacher: But do you think the, looking at it from outside, that the change was too abrupt?

Interviewer: Well it didn't seem to be for most, for well for four of the girls . . . but we only in fact heard, how many speak, two or three?

Teacher: Well the whole thing changed as you say from looking at the water to looking at the pond and the problems of looking at the village, and the problems of encroachment on the village.

Interviewer: Yes. I would have thought it's always fairly difficult to make such big, sort of topic changes; you . . . you know even though they are connected up. I mean the bags, and jars with these specimens in, still there . . . (*both talk*) the whole sort of context is one of observation and note making about specimens.

Teacher: I think this is the danger when you, the big danger when you've got an idea in your head: you see pollution was the obvious thing we were looking at. But there is the danger that you rush on too quickly and I think perhaps there's got to be a lot more time spent on those specimens, I would hope to be able to come back to them, spend a lot of time on those specimens. But at the same time, you know, I think we want to be looking at the wider thing as well.

Interviewer: I think you did bring that topic forward yourself quite strongly, I mean it wasn't their own independent reasoning . . . that led them on, I mean, most, how many of them, three of them at least know what you were getting at. But they didn't actually shift the talk from the specimens to wider problems of pollution and so on.

This is much later in the Ford project, towards the very end; the accumulated trust shows in that the interviewer himself expresses his own ideas quite freely to the teacher as if he feels that they are elicited to get the teacher's responses to these ideas. The interviewer/observer no longer – as he did at the beginning of the project – feels that the teacher will be threatened by his honest accounts. The teacher now gives forthright replies and even raises issues for response from the observer/interviewer. I feel that this sort of relationship is one outcome of the project; the relationship between the central team researchers and the teachers. That is after the teachers had done sufficient research on their own teaching and to an extent had become self-evaluating, their accounts no longer have to be delicately prised out by the interviewer. The teachers are self-critical and do not become defensive about the topics that the interviewers raise. The teacher, pupil, and observer's accounts become more congruent as the teacher becomes more self-aware through self-monitoring.

When the section that the teacher has selected is played back to the pupils, the recording goes:

Teacher: But I think, the – supposing I was the, the builders and I said right I'm – I'm building right down through that field. What's your reaction to that?

The girl indicates she wants to say something and says:

Girl: I wasn't talking about that point, he started talking about something behind it, the houses have taken me right off the subject and then suddenly he changes right back.

Interviewer: Does that make you feel sort of uncomfortable . . . or what?

Note the hesitancy and lack of clarity here. As the interviewer I would account for this by saying I was trying not to make what was obviously a leading question but trying to raise a question that was based upon the issue raised by the previous speaker, that is what I took to be the changing subject. The lack of clarity in this formulation leads to misunderstanding so that the next speaker, the girl, says 'Well it does spoil the village life', which is not the topic that the interviewer hopes to elicit further comment on. The interviewer says 'No what he has just done, taking you off the subject'. He has to specify explicitly at this point what the topic is that he perceives the first girl to have mentioned.

Girl: You don't really know what you are meant to be doing.

Interviewer: Yes.
Girl: . . . at the time.
Interviewer: Sorry? Say that again?

The interviewer asks her to say it again because he was not sure whether he heard it.

Girl: You don't know what you're meant to be doing at the
                  time, if you're meant to be talking about the pool . . .

The second girl continues the sense of this:

Girl 2:   . . . pond or the village life or what.
Interviewer: Oh, you don't quite know how to respond sometimes to
                  his questions. Did you feel that that time then?
Girl: Oh yes.
Girl 2:   Yes.
Interviewer: Why are you . . . you know, how much . . . how much do
                  you think you have a chance to direct the way in which
                  the conversation goes in this bit you've just seen?
                  (*Slide on the screen*)
Interviewer: How much can you say about the things you want to say?
Girl: I more or less said all I wanted to say.
Girl 2:   If you want to say something you just say it, you know.
Interviewer: What? You mean you can just sort of chip in and . . . ?
Girls: Yes.
Interviewer: So there's no . . . you don't feel as if Mr E is sort of
                  directing you a bit too much?
Both girls: No.
Interviewer: Now you always get – always get a chance to say it?
Girls: Yes.
Interviewer: What about this little bit we've got to now where he
                  changes to start to talk about the buildings and that. Did
                  you want to talk about that?
Girl: Well, no, not really. Well we just wanted to talk about
                  the samples more.
Girl 2:   Hmm. He went to William P to get the samples. We

weren't going to go around the outside, looking what's on the outside. We go to the pond, we're meant to look at it.

Girl: Yes.

The girls here, then, are contradicting themselves. They are protecting the teacher from the intrusiveness of the interviewer's questions about whether they can say what they like, to which they answer 'yes' and yet they answer that they did not actually want to talk about the effects of house building and this emerges from the section where they say the teacher should change the subject. On playing back some of the pupils' account to the teacher some of the comments were as follows:

Interviewer: Well, yes, well then another thing they raised was you know that part where you were talking about the specimens, and then you talked about the pond that they visited, then you went on to talk about the housing, the Wates development in. . . . They said there was . . . that when you changed to start talking about Wates housing that they got confused, they didn't know at that point whether you were supposed to . . . whether they were supposed to be concentrating on what they'd been doing about the pond with samples and so on or about the ethical problem that you raised about housing in . . . in the locality. And – and you know what's . . . it seemed to me, I mean the way I interpreted it was something like this: that – that things were going quite well, that you'd gone through the discussion of the samples, it then got to their experience when they were around the pond, and I felt maybe that you went a little bit beyond the information that they had, and started discussing something at a slightly higher level than they were capable of.

Teacher: You know, I think the point that . . . the part that I noticed most of all is that – the pollution thing I think was important, that we got to the stage – the pond was polluted, I think we could . . . it was within their experience to say that this might have something to do with the housing which is developing around the pond.

But then I think it's as I was saying before, this question of stepping in with both feet and going on beyond, and I think there is a tendency to get carried away. You think yourself of the ethical problem, and think well there's a good source of discussion there, and move it along, the discussion then starts . . . it started to sort of flounder a bit at one stage because as you say, I think it was Alison, I think, didn't really realise what we were talking about, or what I was talking about and she was still referring to the pond, while I was developing another way.

Interviewer: Yes.

Teacher: Hmm. Yes I think this is a – a pretty common error that I make actually, it happened with another group – the same sort of thing – developing along ethical lines. Hmm. I don't think I intend to when it starts out, but something comes up like that and it seems the discussion could develop quite well. What I've got to learn to do is stop at their level. I think it's a very valid criticism, if that's one they made . . .

I think that the second order of account, the teacher's account of the pupils' account, tends to focus more on the teacher's values than a description of the original event. In other words the teacher focusing on his values becomes reflective about the effects of his actions as accounted for by the interpretations of the pupils. I would feel in the triangulation that it had not been effectively accomplished if the second order accounts by the teachers continued to concentrate on the original event rather than the pupils' accounts. However, in the teacher's first order accounts, as has already been mentioned, although values get more than a mention, they mainly concentrate on the description of the original event. This movement away from the descriptive to the reflective is a gradual way of getting reflectiveness in the teacher's account.* The interviewer has to check the participants' reconstruction of the original event before he can act as

---

*The pupils' first order accounts are reflexive. The pupils are necessarily observers and interpreters of the teacher's actions, whereas the non-self-monitoring teacher does not begin to test his assumptions or habitual interpretations of the pupils' responses. The non-self-monitoring teacher's accounts are not reflexive. In the example of the second triangulation, however, the teacher is reflexive.

a go-between to ask questions which are based upon the first participants' account of that event. At this point, when the participant is asked to reconstruct the original event, tape-slide recordings are of great value. To go back to the teacher with a tape-recording of the pupils' accounts within hours of the lesson taking place doesn't allow the teacher to have time to absorb the event into his own experience – his personal history. The interviewer would have to fill in some of the goings-on to make sense of the talk with the teacher. We found within the project that a replay of tape recordings so soon after the event was interpreted by the teacher, especially in the initial stages of the project, as a case of pupils' accounts against the teacher's. They took it as a confrontation. Because the images of a tape-slide presentation are intermittent the person watching the replay has to concentrate on the talk in order to make sense and fill in the information between the images. The freedom to stop the recording at 'points of interest' commits the teacher to giving an account of why that point is significant to him or her. At these points the teacher often makes tacit knowledge explicit. The account given by the teacher or any other viewer is based upon the work he has done in filling in the information and this in itself is based upon his beliefs and values about the situation. When a number of these accounts are collected, very interesting and frank group discussions ensue. However, with video-tape recordings of the events, the viewers tend to concentrate on non-verbal communication signs, on idiosyncratic features of the person's activities, not so much on the talk; the continuous images of video are self-evident. They are not questioned, they seem to fill in all the details of the event themselves and can be taken as the 'real event'. They tend to threaten the self-image and self-esteem of teachers far more than the less rich information from a tape-slide recording.

The collecting of accounts by witnesses to an event followed by the feeding back of at least one of the accounts to other participants for comment, both on the other's account and to compare with their own account – triangulation – has been found to be a useful research strategy within the Ford Teaching Project. The symbolic interactionist, Austin/Searle, idea of the speech act which derives much of its meaning from context, illocutionary force and uptake and response to response, underlies the attempts to accomplish a triangulation.

NOTES

1 CICOUREL, A. V. & JENNINGS, K. H. *Language Use and School Performance*, Academic Press, 1974.

2 CICOUREL, A. V., *Cognitive Sociology*, Penguin, 1972, p. 128.

3 GARFINKEL, H., *Studies in Ethnomethodology*, Prentice-Hall, 1967.

4 TYLER, S. (ed.), 'Notes on queries in ethnography' in *Cognitive Anthropology*, Holt, Rinehart and Winston, 1969.

5 In Tyler, op. cit.

6 HARRÉ, R. & SECORD, P., *The Explanation of Social Behaviour*, Blackwell, 1972.

7 ELLIOTT, J. & ADELMAN, C., 'Reflecting where the action is', *Education for Teaching*, November 1973.

8 AUSTIN, J. L., *How to do Things with Words*, Oxford University Press, 1962.

9 MEAD, G. H., *Writings*, ed. A. Strauss, Chicago University Press, 1962.

10 FRAKE, C., 'Struck by speech', in J. Gumperz & D. Hymes (eds) *Directions in Sociolinguistics*, Holt, Rinehart and Winston, 1972. See also Margaret Mead in *Growing Up in New Guinea* and the chapter on child and adult knowledge of houses in the village.

11 ELLIOTT, J. & ADELMAN, C., 'Teachers' accounts and the objectivity of classroom research', *London Educational Review*, Vol. 4, Autumn 1975.

12 ELLIOTT, J. & ADELMAN, C., 'Stranger in the classroom', *Ford T Project*, Centre for Applied Research in Education, University of East Anglia, (p. 11), 1974.

NOTE: The term 'triangulation' is used by Webb *et al.*, and Denzin to refer to the cross-checking of quantitative and qualitative data. In this article 'triangulation' refers to the eliciting of accounts of interpretations of events, to assist the observers' understanding of the event (E. J. Webb, D. Campbell, R. G. Schwartz & L. S. Sechrest, *Unobtrusive Measures: Non-Reactive Research in the Social Sciences*, Rand McNally, 1966; N. Denzin, *The Research Act*, Aldine, 1970.)

PAUL ATKINSON

6 Inspecting Classroom Talk

The purpose of this paper is not to attempt any novel analysis of
classroom life or teaching talk. No new 'findings' are offered. Rather,
I shall outline some of the analytic issues raised by the examination of
classroom talk from the perspective of 'conversational analysis'. This
approach, as I shall indicate below, pays close attention to the fine
grain of the social organisation of talk in naturally occurring settings.
It provides a set of general perspectives for the analysis of transcripts
of recorded talk, and as such is therefore a valuable resource for
anyone who wishes to engage in the systematic analysis of the
language used in educational settings, such as school classrooms,
university seminars and so on.

Anyone who has attempted to make an analysis of a transcript of a
classroom lesson will probably have found it a difficult sort of task. In
the first place, faithful and detailed transcripts of naturally occurring
talk (of any sort) are – or should be – extremely complicated,
fragmented and 'messy'. It is well known, of course, that people do
not normally speak in grammatically well-formed sentences. But until
one has examined a transcript – and, better still, actually transcribed a
tape – then one will not really be aware of just how true that is. False
starts, interruptions, hesitations, 'ums' and 'ers', incomplete words,
inaudible stretches and so on are perfectly normal features of such
material.

If one is not careful, one can easily 'tidy up' the talk when
transcribing it. We do not normally hear conversation as disordered:
on the contrary, we normally hear it as orderly, smooth and coherent.
We do not hear the false starts and so forth. It is all too easy to let our
everyday assumptions about language colour the way we produce
transcripts as data, and implicitly impose a spurious order on them. It
is actually very hard to distance oneself sufficiently from the language
to produce even a moderately sensitive and detailed representation

which includes all the troublesome features which we normally pass over in our everyday talk – what we hear but don't hear, or what is heard but unnoticed.

To some extent, then, the discipline of making a transcript is a very valuable one. We are thus forced to engage in a 'slow reading' of the language, in a way which forces attention on the complexity of the discourse, rather than allowing us to do the everyday 'skimming' of a stretch of talk or text. We are therefore forced to see the language in a fresh light.

The problem of 'familiarity' is an issue which contributes to the difficulty of work like the analysis of classroom talk. Usually when we listen to tapes of, say, school lessons, we are forcibly struck by the very familiarity of the social scene captured by the tape recorder. Usually even the most casual scanning of transcripts would leave the reader in little or no doubt as to the nature of the occasion. It is usually the case, for instance, that educational encounters are almost immediately recognisable for what they are.

Consider the following transcript of a Maths lesson, for example:

T: This is the heading for today.
P1: Sir, I wasn't here.
P2: Sir, are we starting a new subject sir?
T: No, it's a continuation.
P3: Sir . . .
T: No, I've started now Tony, you've spent all your time nattering, you'll just have to sit there. If you can't get yourself organised with a book before now you'll have to wait. Now of course because we are now metric we are used to working in groups of ten. All our work so far has been in groups of ten. Now I gave you a suggestion as to how that came about. A very simple suggestion. That was what? Can anybody remember why we started working in ten? Groups of ten?

Now I don't think that any member of our culture would have any difficulty in recognising that sequence as the introduction to a classroom lesson (or something remarkably like it). Quite apart from particularities of subject-matter, there is something massively familiar and 'typical' about talk of this sort. Irrespective of whether the teaching is regarded as 'effective' or 'ineffective', good or bad, or the pupils as 'bright' or 'dull', the language is instantly recognisable.

This sense of familiarity is one which confronts all social scientists, or potentially does so at any rate. It is a particular problem when working with interactional materials from natural occasions. The very familiarity of mundane, ordinary social activity can be a great barrier to analysis. Too easily one thinks, 'Yes, I see what's going on here . . .', without really getting to grips with the data. One has to work rather hard to make the effort of will and imagination to render what is familiar *strange*. One has to approach the data as if one were an anthropologist, confronted with a new, alien and exotic culture, and hence forced to suspend one's own commonsense, culturally given assumptions. This is what ethnomethodologists mean by the task of making everyday life 'anthropologically strange'.

This does not mean, of course, that we can escape totally from such culturally given knowledge and meanings. Clearly one has to draw on such background assumptions in order to make some preliminary sense of the data: but such readings must then be set aside and constituted afresh as part of the topic of inquiry. Turner (1971) summarises this process for us:

A. *The sociologist inevitably trades on his member's knowledge* in recognising the activities that participants to interaction are engaged in; for example, it is by virtue of my status as a competent member that I can recurrently locate in my transcripts instances of 'the same' activity. This is not to claim that members are infallible or that there is perfect agreement in recognising any and every instance; it is only to claim that no resolution of problematic cases can be effected by resorting to procedures that are supposedly uncontaminated by members' knowledge . . .

B. The sociologist, having made his first-level decision on the basis of members' knowledge, must then *pose as problematic* how utterances come off as recognisable unit activities. This requires the sociologist to *explicate the resources* he shares with participants in making sense of utterances in a sketch of talk. At every step of the way, inevitably, the sociologist will continue to employ his socialised competence, while continuing to make explicit *what* these resources are and *how* he employs them. I see no alternative to these procedures, except to pay no explicit attention to one's socialised knowledge while continuing to use them as an indispensable aid. (*italics as in original*)

Clearly, school classrooms are very familiar social settings. Quite apart from problems of linguistic analysis, it is all too easy for an observer to sit and watch hours of classroom life without being able to generate any lines of inquiry or working hypotheses, other than a paraphrase of 'what happened', or a commonsense evaluation of the teacher and pupils. After all, 'everyone knows' what classrooms are like, and even experienced researchers can find it difficult to transform such overwhelmingly 'obvious' material into fruitful data.

The availability of a permanent recording will not in itself guarantee the necessary degree of 'estrangement'. Recording and transcribing does not substitute for the necessary intellectual discipline which is the prerequisite to analysis. Nevertheless, as I have indicated already, the 'slow reading' which is necessitated does encourage the right approach. Furthermore, it permits repeated re-reading: one can go on inspecting transcripts until, perhaps, they *cease* to 'make sense' in a commonsense fashion, and one is forced to look at them afresh.

Inexperienced observers who are engaging in work of this sort can easily experience profound disappointment. They often expect, if only at a sub-conscious level, to 'find' educational, sociological or psychological concepts staring them in the face or leaping out at them from the data. It is a common enough misconception to expect to stumble across 'authoritarianism', 'social control', or whatever, and to be disappointed – even to feel betrayed – when such things are not given to direct observation.

Yet it is certainly the case that one cannot just 'read off' such analytic concepts from transcripts. It is, perhaps, part of the frustration felt by some novices that records of actual interaction look awfully 'ordinary', and lacking in 'news'.

Rather than being disappointed, however, one should treat those apparently 'obvious' – even 'boring' – features which so massively characterise talk. Furthermore, rather than attempting to 'see through' the talk, to identify things like authoritarianism, one should pay due attention to the social organisation of the talk itself. This is an eminently reasonable perspective, in that educational work is overwhelmingly conducted by and through language – it *is* talk (or writing).

The first point to note about school classrooms, as revealed through recordings and transcripts, is that they are very *busy* places. In terms of spoken activities (let alone unspoken activity) there is a very great deal going on in a forty-minute school lesson. By this I am not referring to whether or not teachers and pupils are working 'hard' and working 'effectively', in conventional educational terms. Rather, my point is that in approaching data it is a good maxim that 'nothing never happens'. In other words, whatever it may look like, social interaction is always being *done*, being accomplished by the participants. They are actively engaged in communicative social action, however 'ordinary' it may appear. As Payne (1976), for instance, notes in this context:

> In a school, lessons do not 'just happen'. They, like all other social occasions, have to be achieved by the participants whose methodic procedures constitute any social event for what it is.

In other words, *all* social settings are 'busy' in the sense I mean, although I think that there are good grounds for suggesting that classrooms are particularly busy places. The sheer *amount* and *pace* of the interaction is a striking feature of most classrooms. Teachers and pupils alike are engaged in 'rapid-fire' collaborative work in constructing a school lesson. In saying that teachers and pupils collaborate in making a lesson happen (in Payne's phrase), this is not to imply that classrooms are to be thought of entirely in terms of 'harmony', 'cooperation', 'compliance' and so forth. It is not to say that teachers and pupils always say and do what they want of each other, that pupils always pay perfect attention and so on.

What this does mean is that a great deal of the discourse to be found in classroom transcripts is very *orderly*. It is orderly in terms of its sequential organisation, for instance, and its topical coherence. More will be said about these things later. For the moment we will simply note that there are long strings of talk in which each utterance, by either teacher or pupil, displays some sort of relevance to the preceding utterance: the talk is not made up of random utterances, and the participants do not just pursue their own line of talk with no reference to that of any other participant. This order is the outcome of the busyness I referred to, and shows how the teachers and pupils are 'working' at it all the time.

Now the construction of an orderly social event like a school lesson is something which the participants do as they go along. Of course, neither teachers nor pupils embark on a forty-minute period with totally blank minds and with no relevant expectations. They know roughly how long the lesson should take; there will normally be a subject specified for the lesson (French, Chemistry, Humanities and so on); the teacher will normally have a theme or topic in mind for the lesson; pupils too may have an idea of what will be talked about and done. But these plans, projections, expectations and assumptions do not provide a *script* for the participants to work through in a routine fashion. In order to get through the lesson in a relatively coherent fashion the teacher and pupils have to be engaged in a continuous process of mutual interpretation, and the joint production of orderly discourse.

Taken individually, then, teachers' or pupils' utterances may appear to be incomplete or ill considered. But when classroom discourse is looked at as a whole, it is normally the case that a high degree of order is detectable. Lessons unfold utterance by utterance. From the teacher's point of view, for instance, if he or she has a theme or *agenda* in mind for a lesson, it will still be necessary to improvise a way through the period, in order to attempt to 'cover' the relevant points and arrive at the desired outcome. From the pupil's point of view, although there is plenty of scope for *not* paying attention, he or she is expected to monitor closely the talk of teacher and fellow pupils, and may be called upon at any time to make a relevant contribution.

These facts of orderly classroom talk have now been remarked on by other authors (e.g. Payne, McHoul, Mehan). They are, however, precisely the sort of features which are readily overlooked, particularly by researchers who are searching for more apparently 'exciting' topics, who wish to expose otherwise arcane phenomena, or construct prescriptive views of classroom practice. Now I am not suggesting that the organisation of classroom talk is the *only* sort of research topic which is worthwhile, nor that it has to be thought of as *prior* to any other sorts of concerns. Rather I am trying to point out that the social organisation of classroom talk provides (indeed, has provided already) a very rich field for research.

In thinking about these fundamental issues of social organisation, I want to follow Sacks, Schegloff and Jefferson (1974). They comment:

> Turn-taking is used for the ordering of moves in games, for allocating political office, for regulating traffic at intersections, for serving customers at business establishments, and for talking in interviews, meetings, debates, ceremonies, conversations etc. – these last being members of the set which we shall refer to as 'speech exchange systems'. It is obviously a prominent type of social organisation, one whose instances are implicated in a wide range of other activities. For socially organised activities, the presence of 'turns' suggests an economy, with turns for something being valued – and with means for allocating them, which affect their relative distribution, as in economies. An investigator interested in the sociology of a turn-organised activity will want to determine, at least, the shape of the turn-taking device, and how it affects the distribution of turns for the activities on which it operates.

This passage, in what is now a classic paper, summarises one of the main preoccupations of 'conversational analysis': that is, its sequential organisation into socially distributed 'turns'. As I have suggested above, the *fact* that talk is organised in a turn-and-turn-about manner is not in itself startling. A moment's reflection shows that it is so. What is not so obviously apparent – and what constitutes the field for investigation – is *how* such orderly, sequential activity is done.

It is not my purpose to review all aspects of sequential analysis as a preliminary to talking about some issues relevant to classroom talk. Rather, I shall move straight on to note some general features of classroom talk which are very obvious to any reader of transcripts. Following the economic analogy presented in the extract from Sacks *et al.* quoted above, we can set about inquiring about the valued *goods* or *rights* which might be differentially distributed in classroom systems.

Two points are very clear from any preliminary investigation. First one party – the teacher – has many more turns than any other single party (pupil). Secondly, the teacher often has *noticeably* longer turns than do pupils. They are not necessarily longer, but it is rather a matter that teachers tend to have 'long turns'. For the moment I shall not attempt to specify what 'long' means in any definitive sense. The following extract from a classroom transcript of a science lesson illustrates these points moderately well:

P: What's happening? Miss, is there air left in it?

T: Well there might be a little bit. There's still bubbles coming out when Paul was heating it. There might be a little bit of air left. Now I'll tell you what's happening there. At the moment you've still got a little bit of air in there.

P: Shall I heat it?

T: No, listen, the flask is still, what is it cold or hot the flask?

P: Hot.

T: So there's a bit of a battle going on there 'cos the air was still trying to expand, whatever air there was in there trying to push the water down and the water was trying to rush in and fill up some of the space.

P: Now what?

T: Now what, what are you going to do? You leave that now and write it up.

We have, then, one of the basic features of the 'economy' of classroom talk as a speech-exchange system. That is, turns are unequally distributed, and the overall amount of talk is also differentially distributed.

Two further features are noticeable about many transcripts of classroom talk. When there is 'public' talk in the class, pupils do not normally speak to pupils unless specifically directed to do so by the teacher. Secondly (and closely related), the selection of the next speaker (by a present speaker) is not an 'open' issue in the classroom. This contrasts with 'ordinary' conversation. Sacks *et al* (1974) have formulated a set of rules which generate the distribution of turns in conversation. For simplicity's sake I shall cite Atkinson and Drew's simplified version of their rules (1979):

Firstly, a current speaker may, if he chooses, construct his utterance so as to select the next speaker, by using certain speaker allocation techniques. . . . The person thus selected, and importantly, *only* that person, then has rights and obligations to take the next turn to speak. However, if a current speaker has not allocated the next turn to some party, the second rule operates, which is that at a first point in the current speaker's turn at which the *completion* of that turn might be detected, another party may select themselves as next speaker by starting to speak first. . . . Finally, if a current speaker has not selected a next speaker, and if no one else self-selects at an initial transition-relevance point, then the third rule applies, which is that the current speaker may (but does not have to) continue until one of the first two rules operates, and transfer to a next speaker is effected.

Such a set of rules provides for the characteristic organisation of conversation, such that (apart from minor perturbations) only one party speaks at once and speaker change recurs. This is managed locally, and is done in an unfolding stepwise manner.

'Informal conversation' is one polar type of speech-exchange system. At the other pole is the highly formal, ritualised exchange in which the allocation of turns is predetermined. Sacks *et al.* suggest the existence of a continuum of 'kinds of talk' along this dimension:

The linear array is one in which one polar type (exemplified by conversation) involves 'one–turn–at–a–time' allocation, i.e. the use of local allocational means; the other pole (exemplified by debate) involves pre-allocation of all turns; and medial types (exemplified by meetings) involve various mixes of pre-allocational and local-allocational means.

Most classroom situations fall at some intermediate point on this 'array'. Turn-taking has certain sorts of restrictions, but is not totally predetermined.

In terms of the turn-taking system outlined above, it is clear that teachers and pupils have very different options available to them in terms of 'current speaker selects next'. In the overwhelming majority of cases, the pupil can 'select' the next speaker only from a class of one

– the teacher. This is so whether this is a pupil-initiation ('Please, Miss . . .'), or is the outcome of a reply to a teacher's initiation. The teacher, on the other hand, can select the next speaker from among a much larger class (literally, the whole class of pupils, however many they may be).

What this means, in terms of the comparative analysis of speech-exchange systems, is that most classroom interaction can be described as 'orchestrated encounters' (cf. Dingwall 1977). That is, whereas in 'mundane', 'ordinary' conversation the allocation of turns is an 'open' matter, 'it is the essence of an orchestrated encounter that one party has the ultimate right to determine when the other party or parties may speak and receive attention and what they may speak about'.

Within lessons, of course, there may be segments of talk which approximate to mundane conversation. For instance, when pupils work in pairs or in small groups (as in practical work in science), without the teacher's intervention, then talk reverts to the laissez-faire 'informal' type. When the teacher is dealing with the entire class, or a large sub-set of it, then the situation becomes a 'focused encounter' (cf. Goffman 1972). On occasion, of course, there may also be 'conversation' between pupils within the lesson which is not sanctioned by the teacher, and constitutes 'trouble' for the teacher – particularly in terms of securing attention on himself or herself as the focus of the classroom encounter.

The turn-taking machinery of the classroom has been summarised along these lines by McHoul (1978), who proposes a series of context-specific modifications to the Sacks *et al.* 'simplest systematics' referred to above. Simplified a little, McHoul's rules propose the following. If the teacher's turn is so constructed as to select the next speaker, then the right and obligation to speak is given to a single student: no other student may speak. If the teacher's turn does not use the 'current speaker selects next' technique, then the teacher must continue. For a student's turn, if the 'current selects next' rule operates, then the teacher is selected, and no other may speak; if not, the teacher may self-select at a transition-relevant place; otherwise the student may continue, until the teacher self-selects. McHoul summarises this sort of system in the same terms as Dingwall: *'Only teachers can direct speakership in any creative way'* (italic as in original).

It is largely a reflection of such considerations that teachers can and

do have much longer turns than pupils – that they can 'hold the floor'
almost as long as they choose to. Put more formally, teachers' turns
are often continued past many possible turn-completion points, when
no pupils self-select as next speaker. As McHoul points out, this
means that it is possible for teachers' turns to be punctuated by quite
lengthy pauses. If such pauses intersperse mundane conversation, then
parties may self-select to take the next turn: since the teacher has
control over speaker-selection he or she can readily continue to hold
forth.

Without attempting to go deeply into the technicalities of how
speakers, including teachers, manage to hold the floor (and it is not a
pure and simple matter), we can note the following. One of the very
characteristic features of teacher-talk is the use of particular
linguistic items, such as 'right' and 'okay'. These items have many
different functions in classroom discourse, and it would be quite
erroneous to look for *the* use (let alone *the* meaning) of them. Often
they appear to be used to attract and check pupils' attention. Often
too they are used to mark openings and transitions in the teacher's
talk. They can indicate 'we have dealt with that topic, now we are
going to go on and deal with the next one'. It is in this vein that items
like 'right' and 'okay' are often used in the course of 'long' turns, to
indicate a teacher's continuation of a turn beyond a possible
completion point (other such terms include 'now', 'so', 'well'.)

The following are examples, from Science and Maths lessons
respectively, of long teacher turns which are constructed in the way I
have just suggested:

Yes and underline any of your sideheadings would be nice as well.
It makes your work look a lot clearer, a lot easier for you to read it
when you're revising for a test. Right, so if you turn to page sixty-
one, is it sixty-one? Just a minute, no its fifty-nine I want you to
turn to, sorry. Right, if you have a look there's a heading four
hundred and nineteen, solids, liquids and gases. Again, everybody
find that on page fifty-eight. Right there's a heading on page fifty-
eight. . . .

Good nine. So nine dots altogether because we've got one group of
five and four parts of another group of five. So if you add the two

together you've got five plus four giving you nine. So we're working the other way round with question two. So now you've got an answer to question one to refer to, you've also got an answer Q-two to refer to. That should mean you can do five in question one on your own and four in question two on your own. Right let's do that then please. Do question one first and question two second.

Here then we have the elements of the speech-exchange system of the classroom, and some relevant characteristics we might use to compare classroom events with other social activities (university seminars, committee meetings, courtroom proceedings etc.)

One further topic can be dealt with briefly. As indicated already, classrooms are busy places in which a great deal of talk gets done. Now it is clear that the collaborative work teachers and pupils do means that they must monitor each other's utterances, in order to produce appropriate talk. It is a normal feature of classroom discourse that teachers ask a great many questions, and consequently that pupils do a great deal of answering.

This accounts for the very characteristic pattern which is to be found over and over again in classroom transcripts. That is, a teacher question, a pupil response and a follow-up of some sort from the teacher. Mehan (1978), for instance, reports that such three-part sequences accounted for fifty-three per cent of the total interaction in the nine lessons analysed by himself and his associates. This is the sort of sequence identified by Sinclair and Coulthard (1975) as comprising Initiation – Response – Evaluation. An instantly recognisable example of this sort of thing in practice (together with an equally characteristic 'long turn' from the teacher) is available in the following transcript:

T: . . . Right, what's this flask containing out of interest?

P: Air.

T: Yes, air, the flask containing air. People might have said nothing – then we'd have had problems. Okay. Obviously it's got air, its got a mixture of different airs and it's got carbon dioxide like those little sweets that Akis has brought in. Okay. It's got a certain amount of carbon dioxide, what other kinds of gas has it got in it? Janet.

P: Oxygen.
T: Oxygen. Any other gas?
P: Nitrogen.
T: Nitrogen. It's got a mixture of N O and CO_2 in there. Michael, are you still with me?
P: Yes.
T: Yes, good. Right . . . etc.

Exchanges of this sort illustrate very well how the orderliness of discourse is accomplished by the 'tying' of utterances to the immediately preceding one. The most elementary form of this is the minimal 'adjacency pair' (Sacks *et al.*), such as a greeting and a reply. Mehan has suggested that the three-part teaching sequence can be thought of formally as comprised of two coupled adjacency pairs:

> The initiation-reply is the first adjacency pair. When completed, this pair itself becomes the first part of a second adjacency pair. The second part of the second pair is the evaluation act, which comments on the completion of the initiation-reply pair.

Diagrammatically, Mehan expresses it like this:

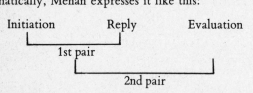

It is obviously not the case that any old response on the part of a pupil selected to speak by a teacher will pass muster, and produce a favourable evaluation from the teacher. Normally speaking, pupils need to display the relevance of their replies to teachers' questions, and produce, if not *the* right answer, at least the right sort of answer.

Teachers' questions are *indexical*: that is, they cannot specify in so many words precisely how they are to be interpreted and answered. (A moment's reflection will show that a question which did satisfy that condition would prove to be a very odd 'question' indeed.) In providing responses to teachers' questions, then, pupils must work on the question in order to attempt a reply which will 'count' as an acceptable one. As Hammersley (1977) remarks:

Being able to produce 'the answer' to the teacher's question
requires knowledge of the conventions governing a particular kind
of teaching and the ability to 'read the signs' in the teacher's
structuring of the lesson. Together these are both a necessary and a
sufficient condition of answering the question.

In answering a question, then, pupils have to recognise the possible
relevances which underlie them. Hammersley again says:

> . . . the pupils can, and must, assume that they only have to search
> their world-within-reach for an adequate method of answering
> the question. They can assume, at least as a working hypothesis,
> that everything they need to know to answer the question has been
> provided. The pupil must search his surroundings and his
> knowledge for possible methods of answering the question.

This is not to imply that pupils are always in a state of agonising over
teachers' questions and their replies to them. Often they find
appropriate answers with apparent ease, and the discourse is quite
'routine' and uneventful. This does not mean, however, that no such
judgmental or inferential work needs to be done. Even if a question is
treated as 'straightforward', and the reply equally so, the pupil still
needs to decide that that is the case. Hence we return to the theme of
'busy-ness' in classrooms, since a school lesson will normally involve a
great many exchanges which depend upon such inferential work. By
the same token teachers must work on the pupils' responses, and
inspect them for their relevance to the teacher's own frame of
reference. Even where the teacher judges the answer to be 'wrong',
he or she may still need to evaluate it from the point of view of
'building' on it, perhaps in providing clues for the same or other
pupils, to help them grope towards more acceptable responses. For a
development of this facet of classroom discourse, see also French and
MacLure (1979) and MacLure and French (1980).

The teacher's control of the speech-exchange economy, and the
normal requirement of mutual monitoring, provides the teacher with
a resource in checking pupils' attention and participation in the work
of the lesson. By exercising his or her right to select the next speaker,
the teacher may distribute turns in such a way as to ensure that

selected pupils are required to 'pay attention' and 'join in', or alternatively that their lack of attention is manifest. This point is made by Hammersley:

> On such occasions the teacher is attempting to maximise the attention of the class by demonstrating the potential built into directly selective questions for the embarrassment of pupils who have not been 'following' the lesson.

The following extract from a Maths lesson provides a fairly commonplace example of this sort of thing:

T: Can we now switch to question two. Milton? And question two says show these base five numbers as groups of dots. Okay? Now we'll go to two-a.

P: Sir, do we leave a gap?

T: Yeah and don't write it down yet. I'll leave it on the board. Two-a is written as one, four base five. One, four base five. Martin, how many dots?

Ps: Sir, sir.

P: Four, two er er . . .

Ps: Sir, sir, sir, sir!

T: You think you know it all but you sit there chatting!

This issue has been elaborated by Payne and Hustler (1980) in their analysis of how a teacher manages the class as a 'cohort', where they argue that this is accomplished not only by addressing the class as a class, but also through the manipulation of the situational turn-taking system.

In these various ways, then, the basic turn-taking devices of classroom discourse furnish fundamental ways in which teaching and the practical management of the class get done. As I indicated at the outset of this paper, no attempt has been made to indicate novel methods or findings. Rather, I have attempted to indicate how one sets about looking at transcribed classroom interaction in a sociological fashion: how one can set about inspecting the organisation of classroom talk as a speech-exchange system and identify its particular local characteristics. I have also attempted to indicate briefly how attention to such formal features of classroom discourse can also offer analytic purchase on matters of more 'general' educational interest, as it were. The social organisation of classroom talk provides teachers, pupils and observers alike with methods for the display of 'attention' and 'participation', 'decision-making' and 'control', 'knowledge' and 'ability'.

REFERENCES

ATKINSON, J. M. & DREW, P. (1979), *Order in Court*, Macmillan.

DINGWALL, R. (1977), 'Orchestrated encounters: an essay in the comparative analysis of speech-exchange systems', unpublished paper, Centre for Socio-Legal Studies, Wolfson College, Oxford.

FRENCH, P. & MACLURE, M. (1979), 'Getting the right answer and getting the answer right', *Research in Education*, 22, pp. 1–23.

GOFFMAN, E., *Interaction Ritual: Essays on Face-to-Face Behaviour*, Penguin, 1972.

HAMMERSLEY, M. (1977), 'School learning: the cultural resources required to answer a teacher's question', In P. Woods and M. Hammersley (eds.), *School Experience*, Croom Helm.

MCHOUL, A. (1978), 'The organisation of turns at formal talk in the classroom', *Language in Society*, 7, pp. 183–213.

MACLURE, M. & FRENCH, P. (1980), 'Routes to right answers: on pupils' strategies for answering teachers' questions', in P. Woods (ed.), *Pupil strategies*, Croom Helm.

MEHAN, H. (1978), 'Structuring school structure', *Harvard Educational Review*, 48, 1, pp. 32–64.

PAYNE, G. (1976), 'Making a lesson happen: an ethnomethodological analysis', in M. Hammersley & P. Woods (eds), *The Process of Schooling*, Routledge and Kegan Paul.

PAYNE, G. & HUSTLER, D. (1980), 'Teaching the class: the practical management of a cohort', *British Journal of Sociology of Education*, 1, 1, pp. 49–66.

SACKS, H., SCHEGLOFF, E. & JEFFERSON, G. (1974), 'A simplest systematics for the organisation of turn-taking for conversation', *Language*, 50, pp. 696–735.

SINCLAIR, J. MCH. & COULTHARD, R. M. (1975), *Towards an Analysis of Discourse*, Oxford University Press.

TURNER, R. (1971), 'Some formal properties of therapy talk', in D. Sudnow (ed.), *Studies in Social Interaction*, Free Press.

MICHAEL STUBBS

7 Scratching the Surface: Linguistic Data in Educational Research

Since the early 1970s, an increasing amount of educational research has been concerned with language in education, and in particular with language in the classroom. This article discusses some problems which arise when such studies attempt to use language as *evidence for educational statements*. It does not discuss any practical problems of collecting or analysing linguistic data; but considers problems involved in relating linguistic data to educational statements in a principled way. It suggests that many studies which do select aspects of language as data for educational statements have no principled basis for this selection, since they ignore the depth of organisation of the language itself. They often merely scratch the surface of the available linguistic data, restricting their attention to superficial characteristics of language in use.

We are, then, concerned with the question: How can language be used as data in educational research, in ways (to use J. R. Firth's phrase) that will avoid 'loose linguistic sociology without formal accuracy'? The argument in this article will be based on examples from educational research, but the argument could be made more general by substituting 'sociology' for 'education' throughout.

Although this paper will be entirely at a theoretical level, its argument has developed from empirical analysis of sound recordings of classroom language (Stubbs, 1975, 1976a) and other types of discourse (Stubbs, in preparation). In this data-based work, I often commit the sins of which I here accuse other researchers.

LANGUAGE AS EVIDENCE

Language as a 'marker' of educational processes
There is now a large volume of work which uses linguistic data as 'markers', 'indices', 'indicators' or 'evidence' for social-psychological

statements which are of interest to educational theory and practice. Much of this work is concerned with studying classroom language: with recording, observing and analysing teacher-pupil interaction and using the language as evidence about teaching and learning processes and outcomes.

Between the fieldwork and the published report some sequence of decisions such as the following inevitably takes place. The researcher returns from the field with his video recordings, audio recordings, notebooks or other data. From these recordings or notes, he *selects* for quotation and discussion short *extracts* of, say, teacher-pupil dialogue. From these extracts, and probably more generally also within his corpus of data, he further *selects* particular *features* of language which he regards as *evidence* for educational statements. However, precisely how such extracts do illustrate claims about the educational process is often not discussed. It is often simply assumed that particular details of what teachers and pupils say can be quoted, and can serve unproblematically as demonstrations of some educational process. Readers are expected to be able to recognise a particular teacher-pupil interchange or sequence of utterances as, for example, an instance of a 'closed teaching style', a 'democratic teacher' or a 'divergent pupil'. The fact that extracts of talk are quoted does, of course, mean that readers are free, to some extent, to form alternative interpretations. However, I want to question whether quoted utterances or surface features of language do provide evidence of anything non-linguistic.

Work of the type I have in mind includes many excellent individual studies which provide close, perceptive analyses of the ways in which language is used in schools and classrooms; and some generalisations have emerged about the relationships between 'language' and 'education'. But it is difficult to see in what way such studies are cumulative or even comparable. Certainly, they do not constitute a paradigm (Kuhn, 1962) tackling a well-articulated set of problems in well-defined ways, with agreed standards of solution and explanation, and drawing on a consensus of theory. As a whole, the studies lack coherence.

I am referring to studies of classroom language by researchers such as Adelman, Barnes, Cazden, Delamont, Flanders, Hammersley, Hawkins, Keddie, Mishler, Rosen, Sinclair, Stubbs, Torode, Walker and many others. I am not, of course, implying that these researchers think that they have much in common. But it is perhaps disappointing that such studies have very little in common beyond a loose notion that somehow 'language' is important in 'education'. I emphasise that individual researchers usually have well-defined notions, but overall there is nothing more than this loose consensus. The fact, for example, of studying language *in the classroom* provides no principled basis for relating such research. The fact that different pieces of research are carried out in similar physical settings can provide no rationale for them (Atkinson, 1975: 180, argues this point very clearly).

Unprincipled selection of data

The very tenuous and unprincipled relationship between the kinds of studies I have cited is evident from two things.

First, different studies claim to relate features of language to a very mixed collection of social-psychological concepts, including: the educability and cognitive orientation of pupils (Bernstein, 1971a); teaching strategies, for example 'open' versus 'closed' (Mishler, 1972); the teacher's role, for example democratic versus authoritarian (Flanders, 1970); methods of social control in the classroom (Hammersley, 1974; Torode, 1976); different types of classroom organisation (Walker and Adelman, 1976); pupils' and teachers' differing concepts of classroom knowledge (Keddie, 1971; Furlong, 1976). These are a few examples of rather different types of educational process for which language is used as evidence: the list could, of course, be extended.

Second, different studies select a wide range of not obviously related linguistic units, both formal and functional, as 'indicators' of these social-psychological and educational processes. These include: different teachers' use of pronouns (Mishler, 1972, Torode, 1976); the complexity of nominal group structure in children's language (Hawkins, 1969, 1977); the functions of teachers' questions and different types of question-answer exchanges (e.g. Barnes, 1971; Mishler, 1972); functional categories of speech acts (Stubbs, 1976a); intonational and paralinguistic features (Gumperz and Herasimchuk, 1972); the overall structure of teaching 'cycles' (Bellack *et al.*, 1966). This list could also be extended.

It is not unfair to say that many researchers seem to feel justified in picking out, as evidence, any feature of language which appears intuitively to be interesting. Mishler (1972:297) is one of the few researchers to admit that he has been 'relatively eclectic in the types of linguistic units used in drawing inferences'. Less misleading terms than 'eclectic' might be *ad hoc* or *unprincipled*. Given how little we know about the communicative functions of different aspects of language, it would clearly be a mistake to *restrict* enquiry to any one particular type of linguistic feature, and I am certainly not proposing that. Walker and Adelman (1976) have demonstrated very clearly that utterances with educational significance may be found in unexpected places. However, this is only to admit that research is still proceeding along heuristic and therefore unprincipled lines, still searching for the socially significant features of language. This does not mean, however, that one is condemned to pick and choose linguistic items at random, unrelated to the organisation of the linguistic data as a whole. This would, in any case, merely lead to the unending task of looking for more and more particular features of language, unless these particulars are related to a coherent framework. I am, then, using the term 'unprincipled' to refer to studies in which surface features of language are picked out at random and not related to underlying linguistic statements and descriptions.

Two things might immediately strike the linguist about such research. First: linguistic items are selected, usually with no explicit justification, from several different levels of language – including lexis (i.e. individual words), syntax (i.e. grammatical structure), semantics (i.e. meaning), language function, and discourse (i.e. overall conversational structure). Second: these items, either as unique items or according to their linguistic class membership, are then often related directly to social-psychological categories, rather than being first *related to the linguistic and sociolinguistic systems and structures in which they are terms.*

For example, the fact that a teacher uses pronouns in a certain way has been said to be evidence of his style of social control (Torode, 1976) or of his pedagogical message (Mishler, 1972). And the fact that children use pronouns in a certain way has been said to be evidence of their intellectual orientation (Hawkins, 1969). It is not obvious, firstly, that the use of pronouns can be considered apart from other characteristics of the speaker's language. Nor, secondly, is it obvious that the use of pronouns relates *directly* to social and psychological processes.

These two related points amount to the criticism that such studies characteristically attempt to relate isolated linguistic variables to social-psychological categories, *as though the language had no organisation of its own*. This point is well made in an article by Coulthard and Ashby (1976). They argue, with reference to sociological studies of language, that 'sociological categories should not be used to classify stretches of speech as though [the speech] had no other organisation'. This means that these studies often attempt to relate concepts at quite incompatible levels of abstraction and generality. Isolated, surface features of language are taken as indicators of deep, general and highly abstract social-psychological categories.

One body of work which does explicitly discuss how to relate linguistic and sociological categories at an equal depth of generality is Bernstein's. His work is an attempt to state causal relationships between a theory of educational transmissions and pupils' social class, family type, cognitive orientation and use of language. He accuses other researchers of not having recognised the depth of abstraction of the problem (Bernstein, 1975:25). Unfortunately, the deep, underlying principles and categories which Bernstein proposes are entirely unrelated to any naturalistic linguistic data. Bernstein has never made any statement which formulates precisely either how sociolinguistic codes or the concepts concerned with educational transmission (e.g. 'framing') are realised in language.

REDUCTIONIST DESCRIPTIONS

Most important twentieth century work in linguistics has been concerned with the complexity of surface and underlying systems and structures in language, and has consequently ignored the relations between language and its social contexts of use. (This is true at least of mainstream American linguistics in the Bloomfield to Chomsky tradition, but less true of British work from Firth to Halliday). However, recently much attention has been paid to the importance of relating language to its social contexts of use. Within linguistics, Hymes (1964) and Labov (1970) in particular have led the attack on the Chomskyan concept of a grammar which is independent of social context and on the concept of context-free grammatical competence. In addition, within sociology, much attention has been paid to the importance of studying social interaction in social contexts. The arguments here are well known: that a failure to study contexts reifies the object of study, by neglecting the interpretative procedures by which situated meanings are constructed, and by failing to treat as problematic the ways in which social order is successfully accomplished by members. The arguments usually amount to the criticism that context-free studies of language are reductionist: they reduce praxis to process; they reduce the study of meaningful behaviour to the study of ideal-typical structures, taking for granted how such structures are interpreted and used in context; and they refuse to study the essential meaningfulness of human behaviour, and how people make sense of social interaction.

I have also discussed elsewhere (Stubbs, 1975) how studies of classroom language are often decontextualised by being treated in strange isolation from other types of social interaction, such as casual conversation, doctor-patient consultations or committee meetings, which are organised by comparable sociolinguistic rules; and also in isolation from sociolinguistic findings about radically different kinds of classroom organisation in other cultures. Again, just the fact of collecting data in the physical setting of classrooms does not mean that the study will be an adequate account of language in context. Studies of classroom language will remain theoretically *ad hoc* unless they are related to general sociolinguistic principles of language behaviour and draw on observations of everyday life in other settings.

It is therefore no solution to reductionism to make loose references to context and to interpretative procedures *if this ignores the inherent structural and systemic complexity of language*. To proceed directly from isolated features of language to social-psychological categories is itself severely reductionist, for it ignores the partly autonomous, complex organisation of the language itself. Many levels of organisation are simply bypassed.

I use *systemic* in this paper in its technical linguistic sense, as the adjective corresponding to a linguistic *system*. A *system* is a closed set of choices or options in a language which are mutually defining. Thus, English has a number *system* comprising two *terms*, singular and plural. Old English had a three-term system, comprising singular, dual and plural. Clearly, plural means something different in two-term and three-term systems. Most linguistic systems are, of course, much more complex than this. Languages are then regarded as systems of systems. Systems may be identified at different *levels* of description.

Linguistics traditionally uses the term *level* to refer to phonology, morphology, syntax and semantics, but usage here is variable.

Two examples

To make these points clearer, I will discuss briefly two extreme and well-known examples of studies which pass directly from isolated, surface features of language, to social-psychological statements, whilst entirely ignoring the inherent linguistic organisation of the data.

Flanders' (1970) work on teacher-pupil interaction in classrooms is well-known and has been very influential. The basic research procedure involves coding teachers' and pupils' utterances, every three seconds, into a series of discrete categories in a pre-prepared category system. There are now a large number of articles which criticise Flanders, and similar research, for bypassing all the interpretative problems involved in 'coding' language data. A linguistic version of this criticism is that such a coding scheme necessarily ignores any inherent linguistic organisation which the talk itself has. Flanders' interaction analysis categories (FIAC) require utterances to be coded directly as pedagogical acts (e.g. lectures, praises). The codings of these acts are then taken as immediate evidence of 'indirect' or 'direct' teaching: the teacher's 'I/D ratio' being computed directly from the simple addition and division of utterances coded into different categories (Flanders 1970:102). This I/D ratio is then further taken, by implication, and with no further intervening argument, as evidence of a teacher's social role, e.g. 'democratic' or 'authoritarian'. This procedure thus takes us directly from utterances (the language data) to social role (a very high level social-psychological concept), with no intervening discussion of *how the language itself is organised*.

Specifically, the sequential organisation of the classroom dialogue is ignored. Flanders (1970:2) claims to study the 'chain of small events' in the classroom. But FIAC cannot be used to study the structure of classroom talk, because 'events' are defined arbitrarily as 'the shortest possible act that a trained observer can identify and record'. That is, the 'chain of events' has nothing to do with the autonomous organisation of the talk itself. This organisation is taken for granted in the observation. Briefly, we have to know where an event occurs in structure before we can know what kind of event it is.

A second study which passes directly from surface linguistic features to deep social-psychological categories is the well-known experiment by Bernstein's colleague Hawkins on how young middle class (MC) and working class (WC) children talked to a researcher about a series of cartoon pictures showing some boys kicking a ball through a window. Hawkins found that the WC children used more pronouns, whilst the MC children used more nouns and complex nominal groups in their narratives. Hawkins takes this finding about the complexity of the nominal group as direct evidence of different cognitive orientation in the two groups. His argument is that the MC children have more possibilities of elaborating and differentiating what they are talking about (since one cannot modify a pronoun with an adjective: one can say *good boys*, but not *good they*).

An alternative interpretation is, of course, possible: the pronouns used by the WC children take account of the conversational context in which the language is used. The hearer can see the pictures and does not need to be told explicitly who *they* are and where they kick the ball. That is, the pronouns do not necessarily have any cognitive function: they might have a discourse function, that is, a *linguistic* function. The data could be explained with reference to factors in the conversational context: that is, they could be given a *sociolinguistic* explanation. They do not have to be accounted for in psychological terms. When Bernstein himself discusses the experiment (1971a:219) he relates the different language use to context, and not directly to intellectual potential.

More recently, Hawkins (1977) has written a book in which he himself provides a very considerable reworking and reinterpretation of the data in his 1969 article. In his book, Hawkins takes, like Bernstein, a much more cautious line, and admits that in his earlier work he has crucially ignored the social context and the functions of the language. But he may have weakened his claims so much that there remains nothing left to argue with. He has, for example, entirely dropped all references to cognitive ability, claiming now simply that WC and MC children talk differently in the interview situation (which, it is pointed out, is broadly similar to test situations in school). It is further claimed (pp. 200 ff.) that the children talk differently because of speech differences in their home backgrounds. This would be interesting if it could be documented, but the only evidence presented (pp. 64, 202) is hypothetical interview data:

mothers were asked how they *would* talk to their children in different situations.

There are, however, major points to be gained from the book. First, it emphasises the widely divergent interpretations which can be placed on data about social class variation in language-use. Second, it demonstrates that everything is vastly more complex than popularised accounts of an elaborated/restricted dichotomy suggest. Hawkins' analysis is careful and painstaking: what we are dealing with is differences in relative frequency of items which all the children use, and therefore with performance not competence (pp. 108, 186–7). The care which has gone into the linguistic analysis of the nominal group is considerable, and if readers get nothing else from the book, they ought at least to see the sophistication required of such analyses, and therefore the total inadequacy of impressionistic comments on WC and MC language. Finally, however, as a result of this detail, Hawkins' analysis could be interpreted as data against the codes-theory altogether, on the grounds that if no absolute and clear-cut differences exist between children's language, and if it is all a matter of relative frequencies in usage, and is all highly context-dependent, then there does not seem to be much support for the notion of two discrete underlying codes. At most we have (that characteristically Bernsteinian term) 'orientations' (pp. 183, 203 and elsewhere). (See also Stubbs, 1978.)

SOCIOLINGUISTIC WORK ON LANGUAGE AND SOCIAL CONTEXT

The question arises, then, of what kinds of relationship linguists have found between language and its social contexts of use. I will take some examples from Labov's work to illustrate the depth and complexity of these relationships.

In his original work on the social stratification of English in New York, Labov (1966) found strong correlations between speakers' social class and their use of phonological variables. (Labov, 1966, is now out of print, but most of the material has been revised and included in Labov, 1972.) For example, simplification of word-final consonant clusters (e.g. *tol'* for *told*) correlates more strongly with working class than middle class membership. Such linguistic variables therefore have predictive power: they are socially significant and can be interpreted as an index of social structure. Note two complications however.

First: Labov found a great range of absolute values of such phonological indices, but agreement in the pattern of variation. When he looked only at the speech of individual speakers he found oscillations, contradictions and alternations which were inexplicable. On the other hand, the language turned out to be highly determined when charted against the overall social variation between speakers. In other words, the language of a speech community turns out to be more regular and predictable than the speech of an individual. Thus the absolute use of an isolated linguistic variable tells us nothing: correlations are found only by looking at the relative frequency of use of linguistic variables across a speech community. What one finds is that, if speakers are rank-ordered both in terms of their use of selected linguistic variables and in terms of their social class, these rank-orders coincide (apart from various 'cross-over phenomena' connected mainly with particular linguistic sensitivity in the lower middle class to features of language in the course of change).

Second: some linguistic variables are entirely ambiguous as indices either of the social class of speakers or of the formality of the conversational context. That is, some linguistic items serve both as demographic and as stylistic markers. One can therefore draw no inferences from a speaker's language about his social class, unless one also knows whether the social, conversational context was formal or informal. In Labov's words, one cannot tell a casual salesman from a careful pipefitter.

Labov distinguishes, in fact, between different types of linguistic item. An *indicator* correlates with some demographic characteristic of the speaker, say, social class; but does not vary in the speech of the individual. A *marker* is evidence of, say, social class, but also varies stylistically according to the formality of the situation. Empirically, both types of item are found.

In more recent work, Labov (1973) has studied the language of pre-adolescent Black gangs in New York. He has found the boys' language to be a sensitive *index* of how closely the boys are involved in the street culture. The language of core members of the gangs (discovered independently by sociometric techniques) turns out to be different in describable ways from the language of peripheral members ('lames'). But the important point is that the language is not different on the surface, for example, in the use of particular words or isolated items. There is, in fact, no absolute difference between the language of the groups. That is, for any feature of Black English Vernacular which core members use, lames will also be found to use it. What is different is the whole system. Labov's finding is that the core members' language is more consistent in its use of the rules of Black English Vernacular. Thus, they might delete the copula in 100 per cent of cases (in sentences like: *He my brother*) where lames will follow the rules only some of the time. The *index* of membership of street culture is therefore provided only by the *overall consistency of the whole grammatical system*.

> . . . the consistency of certain grammatical rules is a fine-grained index of membership in the street culture.
> . . . It must be remembered that all of these boys appear to speak BE [Black English] vernacular at first hearing.
> . . . All groups use the same linguistic variables and the differences in the system are internal variations in the organisation of similar rules: differential weightings of variable constraints.
> (Labov, 1973:81, 88).

Labov also points out the severe practical and theoretical problem that the core members of the sub-culture, whose language is most consistent, are precisely those who are most inaccessible to researchers. It is the lames, whose knowledge of the sub-culture is inadequate, who are most likely to be informants for educational researchers.

The main warning from such work is that, if language is to be used as evidence of social structure and processes, then the language must be examined *as a system*, not as isolated items. Relationships are found between linguistic *systems* and sociological categories. Therefore, the language data must be studied for its own linguistic, systemic organisation. In general, then, the relation between language and educational statements is much less direct and more abstract than many educational studies assume.

Sociolinguistic studies of the relationship between language and context also recognise the importance of speakers' attitudes and perceptions of language, as an intervening link in the chain between language forms and social processes. Much recent sociolinguistic work has concentrated not only on features of how language is used in context, but on the social values which speakers attach to language. (For American studies of language in education which emphasise this, see especially Cazden *et al.*, 1972.) Labov (1969) has suggested that a speech community is defined by speakers who hold the same linguistic attitudes and stereotypes. The phonological variables which are indices of a speaker's social class are often raised to the status of stereotyped and stigmatised features for speakers themselves. But there is a complex relation between speakers' perceptions of other speakers' speech and actual behaviour. Labov's general finding is that people perceive in categorical terms what is, in fact, variable speech behaviour. Thus, a speaker who simplifies word-final consonant clusters in some linguistic environments some of the time may be perceived as doing it all the time, if the frequency of consonant cluster simplification rises above a critical perceptual threshold.

There has been little work on the institutionalised attitudes to language transmitted by Colleges of Education and schools. But what little there has been suggests that schools and colleges often take highly prescriptive attitudes to pupils' language. (See Milroy and Milroy, 1974, for data on Belfast, and Macaulay, 1977, for data on Glasgow).

I now move on to discussing one particular level of linguistic organisation whose study cannot really be avoided by educational researchers.

CLASSROOM LANGUAGE AS A DISCOURSE SYSTEM

Much classroom research is actually concerned with studying classroom dialogue: in terms of teachers' questioning strategies, pupils' responses to teachers' questions, the kinds of exploratory discussion amongst groups of pupils working on tasks, and so on; if not immediately concerned with studying the dialogue itself, much work nevertheless draws its data from such sources. And much other work admits that it ought to be concerned with teacher-pupil interaction, or that study of teacher-pupil interaction would be required to provide empirical substance to theoretical points (see Keddie, 1971:156, and many other examples).

The organisation of classroom discourse

Most studies of the classroom are, then, inevitably concerned with how teachers and pupils interact; that is, with aspects of teacher-pupil dialogue, discussion, conversation or discourse. There are now many studies which demonstrate in detail that discourse (multi-party conversation) is a complex linguistic system: a highly patterned, rule-governed activity describable in terms of several interrelated ranks of description. That is, *discourse has its own organisation*. Major studies of how spoken interactive discourse 'works' are by Sacks (e.g. 1972) and his colleagues in the USA; and by Sinclair and his colleagues in Britain (Sinclair and Coulthard, 1975). This latter work is on teacher-pupil discourse amongst other discourse types. Many quite specific proposals have now been made concerning how spoken discourse can be analysed structurally and systemically, in terms of the linguistic 'mechanisms' which make it 'work'. Much work has been done for example on minimal interactive units, at the rank of question-answer pairs. (Cf. Sinclair and Coulthard, 1975, on exchanges; Sacks, 1972, on adjacency pairs; Goffman, 1971, on interchanges.) Often classroom researchers (e.g. Barnes, 1969) have worked with an intuitive notion of such discourse units. Larger discourse units are also discoverable. Schegloff and Sacks (1973) suggest ways in which whole conversations are structured. The most specific suggestions have come from work in Birmingham (Sinclair and Coulthard, 1975) which proposes several hierarchically ordered ranks of structural units into which discourse can be analysed on formal grounds. The details of such analyses are not important here. What is important is that any attempt to relate isolated linguistic units to non-linguistic categories completely bypasses these levels of conversational organisation.

The general point is as follows. Language is a relatively autonomous system, or more accurately a system of systems. Within language, discourse or conversation constitutes a relatively autonomous level of linguistic organisation. That is, it is possible to formulate discourse structures (including two-place structures such as question-answer) and systems of choices (if A says x, then B will say $y1$ or $y2$, and will not say z). In other words, it is possible to begin to specify how conversation works. It is also possible to specify how different discourse types work, for example, how teacher-pupil dialogue typically differs from a doctor-patient consultation. Treating teacher-pupil interaction as a linguistic discourse system means studying the formally recognisable linguistic 'mechanisms' by which the talk is organised and made coherent. That is, studying, amongst other things, how topics are introduced, sustained and closed, or how one speaker's talk is related to another's. Many formally identifiable markers of discourse cohesion have now been identified, including lexical repetition, parallelism of syntax and intonation, anaphora, ellipsis, and sentence continuations. (Halliday and Hasan, 1976, is a very detailed discussion of these topics.)

If language data are selected from observations or recordings of classroom language, these data are necessarily abstracted from their context in discourse structure. Any principled study of such data must therefore take account of their own organisation.

The transmission of educational knowledge

There is another powerful reason why educational researchers should be interested in such linguistic organisation. In ignoring it they are in fact ignoring a vast resource, much deeper and richer than surface linguistic items. Studying teacher-pupil interaction as a linguistic discourse system can provide educationally interesting insights which are not available to studies which bypass this organisation. One example is as follows.

Much recent educational research has been concerned with the sociology of knowledge: with how educational knowledge is socially defined, selected and made available to pupils. Much of this work raises 'predominantly conceptual issues' (Young 1971:2) and provides no detailed specification of how knowledge is actually transmitted from teachers to pupils. There is much theorising, but few case studies. (Case studies based discursively on classroom interaction include Keddie, 1971, Furlong, 1976.) Studies in this area can usefully be done at different levels: one can study, for example, how the curriculum defines knowledge (e.g. Hamilton, 1976). However, description of how teacher-pupil discourse is sequentially organised could also provide much information for the educationalist interested in how teachers control the knowledge which is presented to pupils.

By studying discourse sequencing, one can study in empirical detail: how teachers select bits of knowledge to present to pupils; how they break up topics and order their presentation; how these discrete items of knowledge are linked; how distinct topics are introduced and terminated; how pupils' responses to questions are evaluated; how pupils are made to reformulate their contributions; how bits of knowledge are paced and allowed to emerge when the teacher considers it appropriate. I cannot see how such topics could be studied, other than in an *ad hoc* way, by looking at isolated utterances or features of language. But by studying the overall structure of the teacher-pupil interaction as a discourse system, these topics are inevitably studied.

Studying teacher-pupil talk as a discourse system would, for example, provide one way of studying how classroom knowledge is 'framed' (Bernstein, 1971b). Only by studying how teachers control the classroom discourse itself can one then study how this also controls the transmission of educational knowledge. Only preliminary studies have so far been done on how the concept of framing may be grounded in sound recordings of classroom language (Walker and Adelman, 1972, 1976; Stubbs 1976b, chapter 7).

Such topics of study are simply not available to researchers who treat language at the level of isolated surface features, ignoring its abstract, underlying, sequential and hierarchical organisation.

POTS AND KETTLES

It often happens that educationalists, and sociologists in general, accuse linguists of ignoring the contexts in which language is used. 'Contexts' here generally mean social and cultural contexts. Such accusations are often true. (The fact that they are also no news to linguists, who are quite aware of the idealisations they make, and have strong reasons for making them, is often ignored by critics, but this is another matter which does not concern us here.) But in this paper, I am accusing educationalists, in their turn, of ignoring contexts. By 'contexts', *I* mean levels of linguistic organisation in the data: one such level is discourse sequence.

I am not claiming that, by taking account of linguistic organisation, everything can be explained. This would clearly be factually wrong.

Reference to the social context is often necessary in order to account for how language is used.

Nor am I arguing that the social functions of language ought to be related explicitly to the linguistic forms that realise them: the problem of the relationship between language forms and functions is a quite separate issue, which I have only mentioned in passing in this article. It is well known, in academic debate as in everyday life, that we often think people are saying what we expect them to say. When linguists talk about language, they are often heard as insisting that educational and social researchers pay more attention to language forms. But this is only one concern of linguists, and it has not been my concern in this article.

What I am arguing is that it is often tempting to proceed directly from language to social context, bypassing levels of organisation in the middle. As a principle, and even if it does not always work, one ought to try and account for linguistic data on its own terms before turning to sociolinguistic, sociological or psychological explanations. The argument is not that one ought to study language as a system *instead of* studying the social context; but that one ought to study language as a system *before* trying to relate it to the social context. Linguists and educationalists both accuse each other of being reductionist.

CONCLUSION

I have discussed some theoretical problems in relating linguistic data to social-psychological statements in a principled way. There are various ways of thinking about these problems.

First, it is the problem of how the researcher can place some control on his intuitions. What is to stop the researcher picking out isolated linguistic items or classes of items and taking these as 'evidence' of democratic social control, closed learning sequences, or whatever? Second, it is the problem of idealisation. Descriptions of phenomena have to simplify and idealise: otherwise they would merely reproduce the features of the original under study, rather than make hypotheses about what it is significant to describe. Third, therefore, it is the problem of how to avoid reductionist statements. Clearly, descriptions of language which ignore its social context of use and social meanings are severely reductionist and unlikely to be of any interest to the educationalist. But in concentrating on the use of language in context, one must not ignore the complexity of the language system itself, by reducing the linguistic data to a string of isolated features.

As a whole, studies of language in education have attempted to relate a mixed collection of surface linguistic features to a mixed collection of deep social-psychological categories. This is a prima facie indication that such studies are unprincipled in that they treat the linguistic data as a mere resource, as though it had no organisation of its own. I suggest finally that classroom researchers are inevitably concerned with using teacher-pupil dialogue as a source of data, and that they should therefore be concerned with how the dialogue works: that is, with teacher-pupil discourse as a linguistic system in its own right. To ignore teacher-pupil talk as a discourse system is, in any case, to throw out the baby with the bathwater, and to ignore a much richer source of data than isolated and surface linguistic items.

I find it difficult to see what direct relationship there could possibly be between isolated, surface features of language and learning and teaching strategies. For example, the cognitive complexity of an argument will never be computed merely by calculating the number of subordinate clauses it contains, the mean length of its sentences, the complexity of its noun groups, or the rarity of its adjectives. Nor can a teaching style ever be defined merely in terms of the number of closed questions the teacher asks or the number of pupil initiations. The relationship between language and educational processes is much less direct than this, and seems to depend crucially on a notion of the organisation of the language as a *system* of communication. This is a much deeper, more powerful and more interesting concept of language. At present, many educational studies are only scratching the surface of the language data which they use.

REFERENCES

ATKINSON, P. (1975), 'In cold blood: bedside teaching in a medical school', in G. Chanan & S. Delamont (eds), *Frontiers of Classroom Research*, National Foundation for Educational Research.

BARNES, D., BRITTON, J. & ROSEN, H. (1971), *Language, the Learner and the School*, Penguin, revised edition.

BARNES, D. & TODD, F. (1977), *Communication and Learning in Small Groups*, Routledge and Kegan Paul.

BELLACK, A. *et al.* (1966), *The Language of the Classroom*, New York, Teachers College Press.

BERNSTEIN, B. (1971a, 1975), *Class, Codes and Control*, vols 1 and 3, Routledge and Kegan Paul.

BERNSTEIN, B. (1971b), 'On the classification and framing of educational knowledge', in Young (ed.), 1971, and in Bernstein, 1971a and 1975.

CAZDEN, C., JOHN, V. & HYMES, D. (eds) (1972), *Functions of Language in the Classroom*, New York, Teachers College Press.

COULTHARD, R. M. & ASHBY, M. C. (1976), 'A linguistic analysis of doctor-patient interviews', in M. Wadsworth & D. Robinson (eds), *Studies in Everyday Medical Life*, Martin Robertson.

DAVIES, A. (ed.) (1977), *Language and Learning in Early Childhood*, Heinemann.

FLANDERS, N. (1970), *Analysing Teaching Behaviour*, Addison-Wesley.

FURLONG, V. (1976), 'Interaction sets in the classroom', in Stubbs & Delamont (eds), 1976.

GOFFMAN, E. (1971), *Relations in Public*, Allen Lane.

GUMPERZ, J. J. & HERASIMCHUK, E. (1972), 'The conversational analysis of social meaning', in R. Shuy (ed.), *Sociolinguistics: Current Trends and Prospects*, Georgetown Monographs on Language and Linguistics.

HALLIDAY, M. A. K. (1961), 'Categories of the theory of grammar', *Word*, 17, 3.

HALLIDAY, M. A. K. & HASAN, R. (1976), *Cohesion in English*, Longman.

HAMILTON, D. (1976), 'The advent of curriculum integration: paradigm lost or paradigm regained', in Stubbs & Delamont (eds), 1976.

HAMMERSLEY, M. (1974), 'The organisation of pupil participation', *Sociological Review*, August 1974.

HAWKINS, P. (1969), 'Social class, the nominal group and reference', *Language and Speech*, 12,2.

HAWKINS, P. (1977), *Social Class, the Nominal Group and Verbal Strategies*, Routledge and Kegan Paul.

HYMES, D. (1964), 'Directions in (ethno) linguistic theory', *American Anthropologist*, 66,3,2.

KEDDIE, N. (1971), 'Classroom knowledge', in Young (ed.), 1971.

KUHN, T. S. (1962), *The Structure of Scientific Revolutions*, University of Chicago Press.

LABOV, W. (1966), *The Social Stratification of English in New York City*, Washington.

LABOV, W. (1969), 'The logic of non-standard English' in N. Keddie (ed.), *Tinker, Tailor*, Penguin, 1974.

LABOV, W. (1970), 'The study of language in its social context', *Studium Generale*, 23,1; revised version in Labov, 1972.

LABOV, W. (1972), *Sociolinguistic Patterns*, University of Pennsylvania Press.

LABOV, W. (1973), 'The linguistic consequences of being a lame', *Language in Society*, 2,1.

MACAULAY, R. K. S. (1977), *Social Class and Education*, Edinburgh University Press.

MILROY, J. & L. (1974), 'A sociolinguistic project in Belfast', Mimeo.

MISHLER, E. (1972), 'Implications of teacher-strategies for language and cognition', in Cazden *et al.* (eds), 1972.

SACKS, H. (1972), 'On the analysability of stories by children', in J. J. Gumperz & D. Hymes (eds), *Directions in Sociolinguistics*, Holt, Rinehart and Winston.

SCHEGLOFF, E. & SACKS, H. (1973), 'Opening up closings', *Semiotica* 8,4.

SINCLAIR, J. McH.& COULTHARD, R. M. (1975), *Towards an Analysis of Discourse*, Oxford University Press.

STUBBS, M. (1975), 'Teaching and talking: a sociolinguistic approach to classroom interaction', in G. Chanan & S. Delamont (eds), *Frontiers of Classroom Research*, National Foundation for Education Research.

STUBBS, M. (1976a), 'Keeping in touch: some functions of teacher-talk', in Stubbs & Delamont (eds), 1976.

STUBBS, M. (1976b), *Language, Schools and Classrooms*, Methuen.

STUBBS, M. (1978), 'Review of Hawkins' *Social Class, the Nominal Group and Verbal Strategies'*, *British Journal of Educational Studies*, 26,2.

STUBBS, M. (in preparation), *Discourse Analysis*, Basil Blackwell.

STUBBS, M. & DELAMONT, S. (eds) (1976), *Explorations in Classroom Observation*, Wiley.

TORODE, B. (1976), 'Teachers' talk and classroom discipline' in Stubbs & Delamont (eds), 1976.

WALKER, R. & ADELMAN, C. (1972), *Towards a Sociography of the Classroom*, Report to SSRC, Mimeo, HR/1442/1.

WALKER, R. & ADELMAN, C. (1975), *A Guide to Classroom Observation*, Methuen.

WALKER, R. & ADELMAN, C. (1976), 'Strawberries' in Stubbs & Delamont (eds), 1976.

YOUNG, M. F. D. (ed.) (1971), *Knowledge and Control*, Collier-Macmillan.

GORDON WELLS

8 Describing Children's Linguistic Development at Home and at School

The aim of the first phase of the Bristol Longitudinal Language Development Research Programme is deceptively simple: to describe how children learn to talk. We have set ourselves two general questions to answer: first, to what extent do all children develop language in the same way? And second, what environmental factors affect the rate and success of this development? In order to provide a corpus of data to answer these questions, over the first three years (1973–76), we systematically collected regular samples of spontaneous speech from a representative sample of children. The 128 children being studied, half of whom were aged 15 months and half 39 months at the beginning of the study, were selected to give equal representation to both sexes, four classes of family background and all four seasons of birth. Each child was observed at three-monthly intervals over a 2¼ year period, and on each occasion, in addition to the recording in the home, tests of various aspects of linguistic ability were administered under more standardised conditions in the Research Unit. The recordings themselves were made by means of a radio-microphone, worn by the child, which transmits to a receiver linked to a tape recorder that is pre-programmed to record 24 90-second samples at approximately 20 minute intervals throughout the day between 9 a.m. and 6 p.m. This technique obviated the need for a research worker, whose presence would have contaminated the naturalness of the speech to be recorded; the lack of on-the-spot contextual information was compensated for by playing back the tape to the mother in the evening and asking her to recall, in as much detail as possible, the participants and activity for each of the recorded samples of speech. When transcribed and checked, these recordings, of which we have made approximately 1,280, provided the raw data for our study.

The nature of linguistic interaction

Before one can analyse the data to provide answers to questions about language development, one first has to decide what one means by language. Although to the layman the answer may seem straight-forward, linguists are by no means agreed on the form the answer should take. Consequently, what it is that a child acquiring language is said to be acquiring will depend to a considerable extent on what theory of language is espoused by the person conducting the research. Ten years ago, the dominance of Chomsky's transformational-generative grammar was so great that Halliday, a linguist, was taken to task by two psychologists for suggesting that different linguistic theories should 'be regarded as appropriate to different aims rather than as competing contenders for the same goal' (Marshall and Wales, 1966, p. 185). And indeed, the papers collected in Smith and Miller (1966) did seem to suggest that there was general agreement that research on language acquisition should be concerned to study the acquisition of the rules of a generative grammar. This was the heyday of syntax; but the unanimity was shortlived, and within a few years the same group of psychologists was criticising the narrowness of Chomsky's goals, 'from which by far the most important linguistic ability has been omitted – the ability to produce or understand utterances which are not so much grammatical but, more important, appropriate to the context in which they are made' (Campbell and Wales, 1970, p. 247). With the concern with appropriateness in context came a renewed interest in semantics, and semantically based theories of language (e.g. Fillmore, 1968; Chafe, 1970). Still more recently it has been the pragmatics of language that has been the focus of attention and various attempts have been made to incorporate the speech acts that utterances perform within the scope of linguistic theory (e.g. Searle, 1969), and also to include the structure of discourse at levels higher than the sentence (e.g. Sinclair and Coulthard, 1975).

How then, should one describe what it is that a child has to acquire when he is learning to talk? Our decision, when in 1972 we devised the coding scheme for the analysis of our data, was that all these aspects of language – syntactic, semantic and pragmatic – should be taken into account, and that language acquisition should be seen as the acquisition of the ability to communicate through language in

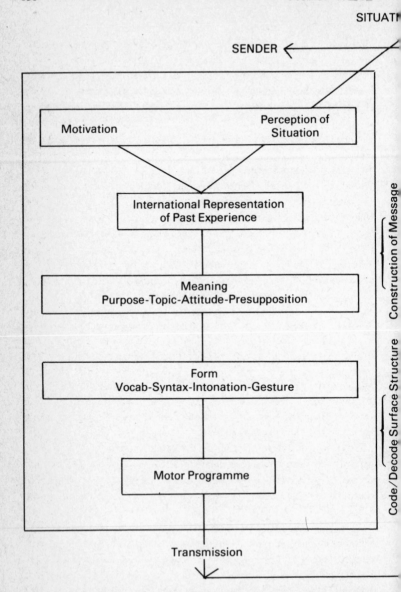

Figure 1: A Diagram of the Communication Situation (from Wells, 1976)

JATION

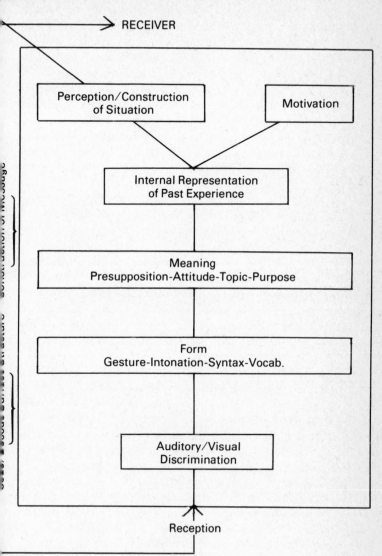

RECEIVER

situationally contextualised conversation. Linguistic communication, we argued (Wells and Ferrier, 1976), is but one form of purposeful interpersonal behaviour, and individual utterances are typically constituent parts of larger sequences of interaction, and are constructed to take account of the context, both linguistic and non-linguistic, in which they occur. In describing any particular utterance, therefore, an account needs to be given of its context and of the speaker's intended purpose, topic and expressed attitudes, as well as of the surface form in which these intentions are realised.

The way in which we see these components being related in the production and reception of a single utterance is illustrated, in a simplified and schematic form, in Figure 1. From the point of view of production, it is suggested that an utterance originates in the current state of motivation of the sender – the plan that he is currently pursuing – which requires him to interact with another person in order to achieve the purpose he has in mind. This purpose is, of course, related to the situation as he perceives it, and both purpose and perception of the situation are dependent on the internalised representation of the world that the sender has gradually built up on the basis of his past experiences. Drawing upon what is relevant in this past experience, the sender formulates a 'meaning intention' which he wishes to be understood by the receiver. This meaning intention has three major components: a purpose that he wishes his communication to achieve in relation to the receiver; a topic to which his communication refers; and his attitudes both to the receiver and to the topic. The sender also makes judgments about knowledge and attitudes in his receiver which he can take for granted, both as a result of what he knows about him and in the light of the preceding conversation, if any. As a result, the message that he constructs is formulated to provide just that information which he judges will most help the receiver to arrive at his meaning intention at this particular point in time. If the message is to be communicated linguistically, it is then coded by the sender selecting, from the linguistic resources available to him, those lexical items, syntactic structures and intonation patterns that best realise his intended message. The resulting plan for the utterance is finally transmitted by the appropriate motor acts of speaking.

Comprehending an utterance is typically quite similar to

production, for the aim of the receiver is also to construct a message – the message he judges the sender intends. In doing this he draws upon a number of sources of information. First, his own past experience and current purpose lead him to perceive the situation in a certain way, thus predisposing him to expect messages with certain purposes and topics rather than others. Second, non-verbal information from the situation, and shared information, built up during the preceding conversation, may also be available, providing further expectations about the message to be received. Finally, the utterance itself has its own internal structure which allows quite precise semantic, syntactic and phonological expectations to be set up and verified in terms of the sequence of linguistic elements of which the received signal is made up. These various sources of information then have to be compared until a match is achieved and understanding is reached.

The interactive context of language development

Considered within this theoretical framework, then, language development entails learning how to produce and receive utterances in situational contexts. In very general terms, we see this developing out of the pre-linguistic communication established in the first year of life (Trevarthen, 1975; Bruner, 1975), through which the child learns to make sense of the world in which he finds himself. Through his observations of the constantly recurring patterns in his environment and through information derived in relation to his actions, both physical and interpersonal, upon the people and objects in that environment, the child gradually builds up an internalised model of the relationship between people, objects and events and their characteristic attributes, and this model allows him to form expectations in terms of which to comprehend new experiences. Linguistic communication forms part of this environment from the beginning, as adults comment on the activities in which child and adult are jointly engaged; at first the child is only able to share in communication exchanges at a pre-verbal level and his messages are exclusively social in meaning. But this social experience of reciprocal vocalisation and turn-taking provides a framework of inter-subjectivity, which is an essential basis for the development of linguistic communication about the shared environment. This is obviously a cumulative process with certain features of utterances coming to function as cues to the sender's meaning intentions, whilst others are still ignored. Gross intonational distinctions seem to be the earliest to achieve this status, as signallers of the interpersonal functions of utterances; then specific words and simple grammatical patterns come to serve as cues to the topics of communication during the course of the second year, whilst most of the remaining grammatical distinctions are acquired during the third and fourth years of life. Put very simply, the child's task in learning to comprehend the speech of others is to make the match between the messages that he can expect in well-understood contexts, and the linguistic forms of utterances that are addressed to him in such contexts.

Learning to produce utterances, on the other hand, must involve somewhat different processes. Whereas the child can use expectations derived from previous experience to help him guess the meaning of speech addressed to him, and is not dependent on a morpheme-by-morpheme analysis of the input, the essential requirement for producing an utterance is that the meaning to be communicated should be converted into a temporal sequence of speech sounds, organised through grammatical structure. Taking for granted the ability to articulate particular sound sequences, the problem then becomes one of using those linguistic cue systems that are already functioning in comprehension to organise these articulations. In a sense, therefore, acquiring productive control of the formal linguistic systems can be thought of as developing strategies for realising atemporal representations of meanings through temporal sequences of sounds that have socially significant patterning. There are three factors that aid the child in this task. First, the recipient of his message, typically the mother, is already predisposed to attribute meaning to his attempts to communicate, and with the support of intimate knowledge of his habits and interests and of the situational context, she will probably 'guess' correctly on a high enough proportion of occasions to provide encouragement. Second, and closely related to this, mothers and other adults provide various types of feedback, both verbal and non-verbal, that are contingent upon the child's communications. Third, there is another strategy open to the child, and that is that he may use segments of the utterances addressed to him as ready-made chunks in the construction of his own utterances, only later discovering the internal structure of such segments.

Clearly this general sketch of language development relies heavily on the belief that language develops on the basis of cognitive representations of experience, through the matching of linguistic forms to expectations derived from this experience. Rapid development of language could be expected to be dependent, therefore, on availability of model forms, on the concordance between utterances addressed to the child and the expectations that he has already derived from his understanding of the situation, on the actual simplicity of the linguistic distinctions to be learned, and on feedback of appropriate quality and quantity.

Here then are a number of hypotheses to be tested on our data. In devising our coding scheme, however, we decided not to gear it to specific hypotheses, but rather to code all the syntactic, semantic and pragmatic categories that we thought would be relevant to testing these and many other hypotheses. Under the pragmatic heading, each child utterance is coded for the context in which it occurs, the purpose of the conversation of which it is a part and the function that it specifically performs in that conversation. In addition, the functions of preceding and following utterances by other speakers are coded, as are the appropriateness of fit between child utterance and the utterances by other speakers that immediately precede and follow it. The semantic coding describes the state or event that is the topic of the utterance and the temporal, aspectual, modality and manner modifications of that state or event. The way in which the utterance is modified to fit its textual context is described in terms of voice, thematic organisation and cohesion. Finally, the actual surface form of the utterance is described as a linear sequence of constituents at different levels. A typical utterance requires somewhere between 50 and 100 separate codings. (The full coding scheme can be found in the *Coding Manual* (Wells, 1973).)

At the time of writing, all the recordings have been transcribed and coded, and the codings checked and transferred to computer store. We are now embarking on the phase of data analysis. This is taking two forms. First, a description of the speech samples collected at specific age-points in terms of the frequency of occurrence of specific categories and sub-categories. So, for example, we can say what proportion of children's utterances at a particular age have the function of question, or refusal of a command; what proportion contain multi-clausal structures; what proportion refer to past and future as opposed to present events, and so on. We can also describe the relationship between these proportional frequencies and demographic variables such as class of family background, position in family, etc. Second, and rather more interestingly perhaps, we can use the same data, viewed longitudinally, to test the sort of hypotheses that can be derived from the general theory of language development outlined above. These are of two kinds: first, hypotheses about the order in which certain linguistic distinctions will be acquired, for example, that children will learn to ask grammatically well-formed Yes/No questions before questions with 'who', 'what', etc.; and, second, hypotheses about environmental factors, particularly about characteristics of the conversations in which the children participate, that influence the rate of development.

To date our results suggest that there will turn out to be a considerable degree of similarity between children in the sequence of their acquisition of the major semantic and syntactic distinctions, but that for particular sets of distinctions there may be different routes to the same goal. As far as environmental factors are concerned, it appears that demographic variables, such as class of family background and position in family, are not strongly associated with rate of development, but that, as predicted, there is a much stronger association between rate of development and qualitative aspects of the child's linguistic experience (Wells, 1974, 1975). However, such results must be treated with caution, as the bulk of the analysis still has to be carried out.

Language and educational success

Our interest in language development is not restricted to the pre-school years, however, for we believe that the study we are engaged in has, potentially, some light to throw on the vexed question of the causes of differential educational achievement, insofar as these are related to language, and to the success with which children are able to meet the linguistic demands and expectations of schooling.

Starting school involves a change from one social setting to another that differs from it in a number of ways: in size, in organisational patterns and routines, in the possibilities for one-to-one interaction, in the goals that are set and the means that children are expected to use in achieving them, and in the values that are put on different skills and competences. From all these points of view, what is central to the transition is a change in patterns of social interaction, and since this interaction is quite largely mediated through language, particularly in the school setting, the ease with which the transition is made will depend to a large extent on the child's ability to communicate effectively through language. It is not surprising, therefore, that 'linguistic disadvantage' has often been considered the major cause of lack of success at school. However, whether this is in fact the case, and if so, precisely what this disadvantage consists of, still remains open to question. What makes the issue more difficult to resolve is the fact that it is the child from a low socio-economic background who is statistically most likely to fail at school, and his environmental disadvantages are likely to include relative poverty, poor accommodation, overcrowding, low aspirations, etc., in addition to the putative linguistic disadvantage that is associated with membership of this low-status group (Tizard, 1974).

Those who believe that language is the key factor fall roughly into two groups. On the one hand there are those who argue that such children simply have a deficit – a lack of vocabulary and syntax necessary for coherent, logical communication. Bereiter *et al.*'s (1966) statement that 'the language of culturally deprived children is not merely an underdeveloped version of standard English, but is a basically non-logical mode of expressive behaviour' is probably the most extreme version of this position, but meetings with teachers working in the poorer districts of our cities confirm that this is a quite prevalent view. Of course, there *is* a very small proportion of children with very severely retarded language development, and within the large majority of normal children there is considerable variation in the rate of development, but whether the relative retardation of those children who fall below the mean is associated with later educational failure has still to be established.

Opposing the 'deficit' view, on the other hand, are those who claim that the language of the children who fail is not deficient or inferior, but simply different from that which is the norm in schools (Labov, 1970). Although such differences between home and school have not been clearly established, they might occur at one or more of several levels: the topics and purposes about which people communicate; the syntactic forms in which meanings are realised; or the accent and paralinguistic features associated with speech. All such differences are seen as being related to cultural or sub-cultural differences, and it is argued that no one set of language norms is superior to any other. However, although the case for recognising the value and effectiveness of distinctive speech styles within the communities that use them has been conclusively made (Labov, *op. cit.*), it may still be true that differences in speech style between home and school can, in practice, put a child at a disadvantage because they impede effective communication.

There are two ways in which we are attempting to contribute evidence relevant to this debate. First, by following some of the children through the first two years of schooling, recording samples of their typical linguistic interaction in school, we hope to find out the extent to which this differs from their pre-school experience of linguistic interaction at home, and whether such differences, if they occur, are related to the children's success in school. Second, we intend to carry out retrospective comparisons between the children in the sample who are found to be markedly different in school success and effectiveness of linguistic communication in school, in an attempt to identify characteristics of pre-school linguistic experience associated with differential success in school.

Children's experience of linguistic interaction

In this latter context, we are particularly interested in investigating the specifically interactive dimensions of the children's pre-school linguistic experience. In our present coding procedure, each child utterance, with its context of preceding and following utterances, is coded relatively independently. Although this is quite adequate for the types of analyses already described, it fails to capture the full interactive nature of conversation – the way in which a second or subsequent utterance in a conversation, as well as having its own specific purpose and topic, picks up and, in various ways, develops that stated and implied meaning of the previous utterance (Turner, 1975). One of the ways in which this is achieved is by means of various cohesive devices, and occurrences of these are already accounted for in our coding scheme. But equally important, as a means of relating one utterance to what went before, is the system of differential information focus, signalled by the placement of tonic stress, which allows a second speaker to indicate how his contribution, for example, accepts or contrasts with the preceding utterance. Intonational characteristics of utterances, such as choice of tone and unusually large changes in pitch, also play an important part in what Barnes and Todd (1975) have identified as the management of the interpersonal relationship in conversation. Management of the joint construction of the topic, on the other hand, is more centrally carried out by the selection of options from the mood system, for example, interrogative as opposed to declarative, and by various types of modification.

An example will help to illustrate what features of the interaction are being focused on. It is taken from one of the 90-second samples recorded when the child in question was 2¼ years old. (The full text and the conventions of transcription are given in Appendix I.) Jacqueline (J) is in the kitchen with her Mother (M), who is at the sink, washing the dishes. J is playing with the clothes that have been tipped out of the laundry bag in preparation for washing.

4	" ↑Put all. 24 ʼthing in"	[J is putting washing
5	↓I'm putting 35 ʼthings <u>in</u>	in the bag]
6		M: 24 ʼ<u>No</u>/53 ʼdarling (v)
7		M: No ↑no↑↑no 15 ʼno (accel.)
8	❘I want to ↑↑❘ put those	12 ʼthings (accel.)
9		M: 33 ʼYes
10		M: 2 ʼWhen they're 243 ʼwashed you can
11		M: 2 ʼNot 243 beʼfore

In 4, J is commenting on the activity she is engaged in and, in 5, she repeats her utterance, addressing it to M. Her intention is two-fold, to describe her activity and to invite M to share her interest. In 6 and 7, M, who has turned to pay attention to J and seen what she is doing, utters a series of prohibitions, being more concerned with her own

purpose than with taking an interest in J's. The increase in the pitch
and pace of her second utterance acts as a vocal substitute for
physically curtailing J's activity. After a short pause, J reaffirms her
own intention, and uses the same intonation features of rising pitch
and increasing pace to ward off M's interference. In 10, M recognises
the validity of J's intention and grants deferred permission, coupling
this, in 11 and 12, with a statement of the conditions under which the
activity will be permitted. In doing this she also provides a linguistic
formulation of the temporal sequence of events within which J's
intended activity will be appropriate at one stage rather than another.

Later, within the same 90-second sample, there is another
negotiated interchange, in which M attempts to understand J's
meaning and to help her to clarify her understanding of the situation.
Jacqueline has seen a pair of her socks in the pile of washing and recalls
that they had been given to her by Auntie Linda. She tries to share this
interesting information with M (20–33), but has difficulty in
organising the form of her utterance to encode her meaning intention.

20 Wash 243 'Linda's—   [Auntie Linda had given J some socks
                                   which she refers to as Linda's socks]

21 3 'There's *24 'socks

22   M: * * *

23 14 'Linda/3 'bought you
     34 'socks/54 mum (v) (you = me)

24   M: 34 'Yes/there's 24 'your socks

25 Lin—

26   M: Mummy's 24⁻¹ washing them

27   M: I've got to 243 'do all that now

28 24 'Linda/3 'brought you
     45 'socks/54 'Mum(v)

29   M: 34 'Yes

30   M: Linda bought you 45 'socks (softly)
                                      . . 5 . .

31   M: They're 24 'dirty

32   M: They've 3 'got to be 24 'washed

33 Did . Linda bought <you> –
    me got . washed (false starts)
    (=? have the socks that Linda
    bought me got to be washed?)

34   M: 31 'Pardon?

35 24 'Linda wa—/324
    'wash them

36   M: 23 'No

37   M: 23 'Mummy's going to/35 'wash them

38 15 'Linda wash them

39   M: 24 'No/Linda's 34 'not going to/
                                  45 wash them

40 24 'Linda not going to/
    54 'wash them

41   M: 35 'No

42   M: 35 'Mummy wash them
                                 . . .

In 33, J tries to express all the information in one confirmation-seeking utterance, but has difficulty in coordinating the parts. M asks for a repetition (34) and J, assuming that 'socks' as topic is jointly understood, tries in 35 to express her observation in a simpler form, but, as the hiatus suggests, still has difficulty. The arrangement of the components 'Linda' 'wash' and 'them' (= socks) in the utterance she produces encodes a simple Agent-Act-on-Object clause, in which 'Linda' is the Agent. But this does not correspond with the situation, nor, as far as one can judge, with J's intention. The problem seems to result from a conflict between two intentions: the first is to ask for confirmation of the proposition that the socks are to be washed; the second is to focus attention on the fact that it was Linda who gave her the socks. But having reduced the topic, 'socks', to the status of the anaphoric pronoun 'them', she can no longer qualify it by means of a relative clause in which 'Linda' as Agent could be given information focus. In 36 and 37 M rejects J's statement as inaccurate and, using marked tonic placement, offers a contrasting true statement, which matches the surface form of J's utterance. J seems unable to accept this way of putting it and in 38 reaffirms her original formulation, using contrasting marked tonic placement. M again rejects J's statement, and this time explicitly negates it (39). In 40, J, using marked tonic placement, restates her understanding of the fact that it is not *Linda* who is going to wash the socks, and signals her wish for confirmation of this statement. M confirms the correctness of J's negative statement and (41–42), picking up the contrastive implication of the tonic placement in J's utterance, restates the situation positively with 'Mummy' as agent. J's silence is to be taken as agreement with this jointly constructed description of the situation. It will be noticed, however, that the meaning that has been negotiated represents a compromise between what seem to have been the separate intentions of the two participants.

These episodes have been commented on in some detail, because they bring out rather clearly the way in which the mother's speech is relevant, not only to the external situation but also to her understanding of the child's intentions. The second episode, in particular, suggests one way in which, through participation in dialogue in which meaning is negotiated, the child learns to control some of the formal systems that allow speech to be made relevant to the situational and interpersonal context.

It is this characteristic of 'mutual relevance' in a child's experience of conversation that we think may be important for his success on entry to school. Discussion of linguistic disadvantage has usually distinguished between children in terms of size of vocabulary, range and complexity of sentence types used, and so on; however, it is clearly not the ability to produce linguistic forms, as such, that is the mark of the linguistically successful child, but rather the ability to use these resources of vocabulary, syntax and intonation to communicate effectively in a range of situations, where effectiveness is quite largely a matter of making what is said relevant to the needs of the listener as well as to the intentions of the speaker.

To achieve this communicative competence the child needs appropriate experience of such use of language in his pre-school home environment. Research to date (e.g. Snow, 1972; Cross, 1977) has shown that parents, particularly mothers, modify their speech style when speaking to young children by restricting the length, complexity and range of vocabulary of their utterances, and by producing frequent repetitions of well-formed, contextually appropriate models. But how far do all parents provide the essential experience of jointly constructed meaning-making, from which the child can learn how to match what is said to the total requirements of the communication situation?

By way of contrast with Jacqueline, consider Jane, whose typical experience is well illustrated by the two samples presented in Appendix 2. The physical situation is not dissimilar to Jacqueline's, and Jane, who is by no means a 'non-verbal' child, chatters away while her mother is engaged in the domestic task of preparing the dinner. However, all that Jane can be assumed to be learning from this experience is that speech is a means of expressing individual concerns and attitudes; there is nothing of the cooperative endeavour to achieve mutual understanding that characterised Jacqueline's experience. When Jane's interests and intentions conflict with her mother's, her mother makes no attempt to negotiate a mutually agreed resolution; what Jane is learning is not to expect responses that are relevant to her intentions and ultimately, one might expect, not to listen nor to adjust the expression of her own meanings to take account of the needs of others. Jacqueline's mother in a similar situation attempts to treat Jacqueline as an individual with interests and intentions of equal validity to her own. She listens to what Jacqueline has to say and continues the dialogue until discrepancies are resolved. What Jacqueline is learning, we can assume, is that, in communicating with someone else, it does matter how one's meaning is expressed and that where there is disagreement, it can be resolved by verbal negotiation. When she fails to make her meaning understood, she has the support of an adult who attempts to understand her intention and helps her to find the form that matches that intention.

Lest this marked difference between the two mother-child pairs be attributed to the effects of social class, it is worth noting that both Jacqueline and Jane come from the same class of family background: both fathers are construction workers and none of the parents has had more than minimal education. Nor is there a simple contrast in terms of code. As in most adult/pre-schooler conversation, interchanges in both homes are restricted in form and closely tied to context. The important difference is that, unlike Jane, Jacqueline is learning that in order to communicate successfully one has to modify one's message to take account both of the situation and of the knowledge and purposes of one's listener, and that, on occasion, this requires one to make one's meaning explicit.

Jacqueline and Jane are now nearing the end of their first year of formal schooling, during which time they have been observed as part of our study of *Children Learning to Read* (Wells and Raban, 1978). It is not surprising to learn that Jacqueline is rated by her teacher as a high achiever, whereas Jane is rated as well below average; since entering school, Jacqueline has learned to read quite fluently, whereas Jane's teacher is having difficulty in getting her to engage in any form of school activity.

If the ability to take part in dialogue by adapting one's speech to the requirements of the communication situation is as important as has been suggested, the linguistic disadvantage experienced by some children on entry to school may not be so much due to a lack of formal linguistic resources, nor to differences of dialect and accent (although teacher expectations based on stereotype responses to such features of children's speech are probably important (Giles, 1970; Shafer and Shafer, 1975)), but rather to what their pre-school experience has taught them – or perhaps not taught them – about what people do with language. In the classroom environment, where intentions have to be explained and actions justified, and where each child is expected to share his news with teacher and fellow pupils, it is a disadvantage indeed not to have learnt to play one's part in dialogue, but to be restricted instead to the unilateral expression of one's own individual point of view.

To stress the importance of being able to take the point of view of the person with whom one is interacting is not new, of course. It has been a pervasive theme of Piaget's writings on cognitive development, and, in a pedagogical context, it has been one of the main aims of most of the 'functionally' oriented language intervention programmes such as those of CUES (1976), Blank (1973) and Tough (1973). Where we hope to make a new contribution is in the exploration of the ways in which this ability is acquired and of the types of linguistic experience that provide opportunities for its acquisition. The examples discussed above illustrate what it is we plan to investigate: our task now is to find some systematic way of exploring the means whereby mutual relevance is achieved.

Postscript

In the time that has elapsed since this paper was first written (for the SSRC Conference in 1976), considerable progress has been made in the analysis of the pre-school data, and the predictions that were made then are beginning to be confirmed. As was to be expected, very considerable variation has been found in rate of development, as is shown in Figure 2, in which one particular global index of development, Mean Length of Structured Utterance, is plotted against Age at three-monthly intervals from 1½ to 5 years. The broken lines represent two standard deviations above and below the mean for the sample as a whole at each age. Variation on a similar scale has also been found in more detailed investigations, such as that of the

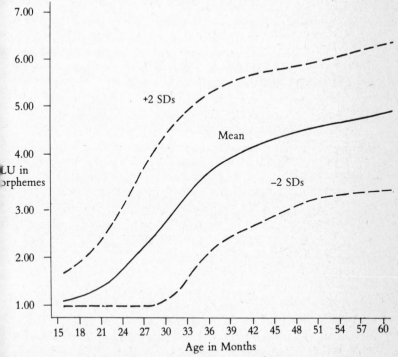

Figure 2: Mean Length of Structured Utterance × Age.

development of the auxiliary verb system (Wells, 1979): the age at which the children reached the criterion chosen as indicating control of this system ranged from 21 to more than 42 months, with a mean of 31:7 months. However, on none of the dimensions so far investigated has there been significant sex-related variation (Woll, 1978), nor is there any straightforward association with class of family background (Wells, 1977, 1979).

On the other hand, the one measure of the qualitative aspects of children's linguistic experience that we have so far devised, namely the extent to which parents accept and develop children's verbal initiations, is proving to be a more powerful predictor of level of linguistic development on entry to school and, to an even greater extent, of reading attainment after two years in school (Wells and Raban, 1978).

As the research programme has followed the children into school, we have become more and more convinced that one of the most important dimensions of variation, both at home and at school, is the quality of adult-child interaction that the child experiences. Certainly there is considerable variation between homes in this respect, leading to differences between children in the ease and speed with which they tune in to the expectations embodied in teachers' questions and instructions. But there is also variation between teachers, both in the extent to which they make their intentions and criteria of assessment explicit, and in their ability or willingness to accept and develop the children's contributions (Wells, 1978). And because interaction is a reciprocal activity, in which the quality of one party's contribution is related to the quality of the other's, adults are likely to communicate most effectively with those children who are themselves the most effective communicators. Success in linguistic communication has to be thought of, therefore, as a shared achievement, whether at home or at school. The same is equally true for lack of success.

Our current pre-occupation, therefore, is to achieve a more coherent description of linguistic interaction, with the ultimate aim of giving substance to such elusive terms as 'quality', and 'effectiveness', so that hypotheses that employ them can be tested and a better understanding developed of the role that language plays in differential educational achievement.

Note: A fuller account of the programme, papers reporting results to date, and selected sets of transcripts are available from the Secretary, 'Language at Home and at School', University of Bristol School of Education, 19 Berkeley Square, Bristol BS8 1HF. The research is supported by grants from the SSRC, the Nuffield Foundation and the Boots Charitable Trust.

REFERENCES

BARNES, D. & TODD, F., *Communication and Learning in Small Groups*, Final Report to SSRC, 1975.

BEREITER, C. *et al.*, 'An academically oriented preschool for culturally deprived children', in Hechinger, F. M. (ed.), *Pre-School Education Today*, Doubleday, 1966.

BLANK, M., *Teaching Learning in the Preschool: A Dialogue Approach*, Charles E. Merrill, 1973.

BRUNER, J. S., 'The ontogenesis of speech acts', *Journal of Child Language*, 2.1: 1–20, 1975.

CAMPBELL, R. & WALES, R., 'On the study of language acquisition', in Lyons, J. (ed.), *New Horizons in Linguistics*, Penguin, 1970.

CENTRE FOR URBAN EDUCATIONAL STUDIES, *Language for Learning*, Heinemann, 1976.

CHAFE, W. L., *Meaning and the Structure of Language*, University of Chicago Press, 1970.

CROSS, T., 'Mothers' speech adjustments: the contribution of selected child listener variables', in Snow, C. & Ferguson, C. (eds), *Talking to Children*, Cambridge University Press, 1977.

FILLMORE, C. J., 'The case for case', in Bach, E. & Harms, R. T. (eds), *Universals in Linguistic Theory*, Holt, Rinehart and Winston, 1968.

GILES, H., 'Evaluative reactions to accents', *Educational Review* 22, 211–227, 1970.

HALLIDAY, M. A. K., *Intonation and Grammar in British English*, Mouton, 1967.

LABOV, W., 'The logic of non-standard English', in Williams, F. (ed.), *Language and Poverty*, Markham, 1970.

MARSHALL, J. C. & WALES, R., 'Which syntax: a consumer's guide', *Journal of Linguistics*, 2, 2: 181–188, 1966.

RABAN, B., *Self and Self-Concept*, unpublished M.Ed. thesis, University of Bristol, 1975.

SEARLE, J. R., *Speech Acts – An Essay in the Philosophy of Language*, Cambridge University Press, 1969.

SHAFER, R. E. & SHAFER, S. M., 'Teacher attitudes towards children's language in West Germany and England', in Moyle, D. (ed.), *Reading: What of the Future?*, Ward Lock Educational, 1975.

SINCLAIR, J. McH. & COULTHARD, R. M., *Towards an Analysis of Discourse: The English used by Teachers and Pupils*, Oxford University Press, 1975.

SMITH, F. & MILLER, G. A., *The Genesis of Language: A Psycholinguistic Approach*, Massachusetts Institute of Technology Press, 1966.

SNOW, C. E., 'Mother's speech to children learning language', *Child Development*, 43, 549–565, 1972.

TIZARD, B., *Pre-School Education in Great Britain*, SSRC, 1974.

TOUGH, J., 'The language of young children: the implications for the education of the young disadvantaged child', in Chazan, M. (ed.), *Education in the Early Years*, University of Swansea, Faculty of Education, 1973.

TREVARTHEN, C., HUBLEY, P. & SHEERAN, L., 'Les activités innées du nourrissant' (Psychological actions in early infancy), *La Recherche*, 6, 56: 447–458, 1975.

TURNER, R., 'Speech act theory and natural language use', *Pragmatics Microfiche* 1, 1. A3, 1975.

WELLS, C. G., *Coding Manual for the Description of Child Speech*, University of Bristol, School of Education, 1973.

WELLS, C. G., 'Learning to code experience through language', *Child Language*, 1, 2: 243–269, 1974.

WELLS, C. G., 'The contexts of children's early language experience', *Educational Review*, 27. 2: 114–125, 1975.

WELLS, C. G., 'Comprehension: what it means to understand', *English in Education*, 10.2: 24–36, 1976.

WELLS, C. G., 'Language use and educational success: an empirical response to Joan Tough's "The Development of Meaning" (1977)', *Research in Education*, 18: 9–34, 1977.

WELLS, C. G., 'Talking with children: the complementary roles of parents and teachers', *English in Education*, 12. 2: 15–38, 1978

WELLS, C. G., 'Learning and using the auxiliary verb', in Lee, V. (ed.), *Language Development*, Croom Helm, 1979a.

WELLS, C. G., 'Variation in child language', In Fletcher, P. & Garman, M. (eds), *Language Acquisition*, Cambridge University Press, 1979b.

WELLS, C. G. & FERRIER, L., 'A framework for the semantic description of child speech in its conversational context', in Von Raffler-Engel, W. & Lebrun, Y. (eds), *Baby Talk and Infant Speech*, Swets and Zeitlinger, 1976.

WELLS, C. G. & RABAN, E. B., *Children Learning to Read*, Final Report to SSRC, 1978.

WOLL, B., *Sex as a Variable in Sociolinguistic Research*, Paper given at Child Language Seminar, York, April 1978.

Appendix 1

LANGUAGE DEVELOPMENT PROJECT

Conventions and layout for transcription

The speech of the child being studied is set out in the left hand column. The speech of all other participants is set out in the centre column, with identifying initials where necessary. Each new utterance starts on a new line.

Contextual information is enclosed in square brackets [ ] and set out in the right hand column.

Interpretations of utterances and descriptions of tone of voice, where applicable, are enclosed in round brackets ( ) and included immediately after the utterance to which they apply.

Utterances, or parts of utterances, about which there is doubt are enclosed in angular brackets < >; where two interpretations are possible they are both given, separated by an oblique stroke.

Symbols of the International Phonetic Alphabet are used for utterances, or parts of utterances, which cannot be interpreted with certainty. Phonetic symbols are always enclosed by oblique strokes. Except where there is doubt about the speaker's intended meaning, the speech is transcribed in Standard English Orthography.

The following is a list of additional symbols used, with an explanation of their significance. (Stops and commas are not used as in normal punctuation.)

?   used at end of any utterance where an interrogative meaning is considered to have been intended

!   used at the end of an utterance considered to have exclamatory intention

'   apostrophe: used as normal for contractions and elision of syllables

*   used to indicate unintelligibility, for whatever reason. The number of asterisks corresponds as nearly as possible to the number of words judged to have been uttered

. . . stops are used to indicate pauses. One stop is used for a very short pause. Thereafter, the number of stops used corresponds to the estimated length of the pause in seconds. Pauses over 5 seconds in length are shown with the figure for the length of the pause, e.g. . . 8 . .

— underlining. Where utterances overlap because both speakers speak at once, the overlapping portions are underlined

" " inverted commas are used to enclose utterances considered to be 'speech for self'

+ plus mark indicates unbroken intonation contour where a pause or clause boundary might otherwise indicate the end of an utterance

- hyphen indicates a hiatus, either because the utterance is incomplete or because the speaker makes a fresh start at the word or utterance

(v) used to indicate that the preceding word was used as a vocative, to call or hold the attention of the addressee

Intonation

Some of the transcripts include a representation of intonation, in which case the following additional conventions apply:

/ Tone unit boundary. Where an utterance consists of only one tone unit, no boundaries are marked

ˈ This symbol immediately precedes both prominent and tonic syllables

Prominent syllables [1] take a single digit before the symbol to indicate their relative pitch height

Tonic syllables [2] take two or more digits before the symbol to indicate the onset level, range and direction of significant pitch movement (see 'Pitch Height' below)

↑↓ Shift of pitch range relatively higher or lower than that normal for the speaker

↑↑ ↓↓ Shift to extra high or extra low pitch

: Lengthened syllable. The symbol follows the syllable to which it applies

Pitch Height. The height, direction and range of significant pitch movement is represented by a set of digits corresponding to points on a scale. The pitch range of a speaker is divided into five notional bands, numbered 1–5 from high to low, thus:

1
2
3
4
5

The following information is retrievable from this coding:

Direction of Movement	Halliday (1967) Tones
Falling: (e.g. 13, 25)	Tone 1
Rising: (e.g. 31,43)	Tone 2
Level: (e.g. 33)	Tone 3
Fall-Rise: (e.g. 343) or (e.g. 342)	Tone 4 or Tone 2 [3]
Rise-Fall: (e.g. 324)	Tone 5

Notes

1. Prominent syllables are salient with respect to combinations of pitch, duration and intensity.

2. Tonic syllables carry at least the onset of significant pitch movement. Significant pitch movement in its entirety may, of course, occur on a single syllable or be spread over a number of syllables.

3. Fall-Rise movements may be of two types, corresponding to Halliday's Tone 2 and Tone 4. They are conventionally denoted in the transcripts as follows: Tone 2 is represented with a higher terminal pitch than its onset (e.g. 342), whereas Tone 4 is represented as having a terminal pitch no higher than its onset (e.g. 232, 354).

Name: Jacqueline   *Record Number*: 5
Date of Birth: 26.8.1970   *Date of Recording*: 1.12.1972

Sample Number: 1   *Participants*: Jacqueline, Mother, Jane (13 mths)
                                              Time: 9.15 a.m.
                                              Location: Kitchen
                                              Activity: Jacqueline playing with laundry, Mother washing up

1 "24 Laundry bag" (sing-song)   [J picks up laundry bag]

2 "35 'Laundry bag"

3 "In 14 there"

4 "↑Put all . 24 thing in"   [J is putting washing

5 ↓I'm putting 35 things <u>in</u>   in the bag]

6   M: 24 'No / 53 'darling(v)

7   M: No ↑no ↑↑no 15 'no (accel.)
                                   . . . .

8 ↑I want to↑↑I 'put those 'things (accel.)

9   M: 33 'Yes

10   M: 2 'When they're 243 washed you can

11   M: 2 Not 243 be fore
                                   . . .

12 What's 24 'that / 54 'Mum(v)?

                                   . . . .

13 3 You: dirty 45 cat (to Jane)

14   M: 34 Oh: / she's 24 not: (softly)

   (laughs)

15   M: She's 3 not a dirty 43 cat

16   M: 24 Are you / 43 darling(v)? (to Jane)
                                   . . . .

17   M: 323 No (command to Jacq.)

18   M: 2 Leave Mummy's washing 343 a'lone /
                                      43 please

19   M: Mummy's got to 354 'wash all that (firmly

20 Wash 243 Linda's –

21 3'There's * 24 'socks

22   M: <u>* * *</u>

23 14 'Linda / 3 'bought you
   34 'socks / 54 'Mum(v) (you = me)

24   M: <u>34 'Yes / there's</u> 24 'your socks

25 <u>Lin</u>

26   M: <u>Mummy's</u> 24 'washing them

27   M: I've got to 243 'do all that now

28 24 Linda / 3 bought you
   45 socks / 54 Mum(v)

29   M: 34 Yes

30   M: Linda bought you 45 socks (softly)
                                   . . 5 . .

31   M: They're 24 dirty

32   M: They've 3 got to be washed 24 washed

33 Did . Linda bought <you> —
   me got . <u>washed</u> (false starts)
   (=? have the socks that Linda
   bought me got to be washed?)

34   M: 31 Pardon?

35 24 Linda wa —/ 324 wash them

36   M: 23 No

37   M: 23 Mummy's going to / 35 wash them

38 15 Linda wash them

39   M: 24 'No / Linda's 34 'not going to /
                                               45 'wash them

40 24 Linda not going to /
      54 wash them

41   M: 35 No

42   M: 35 Mummy wash them

43 2 This is 13 Daddy's socks /
      43 Mum(v)

44   M: 32 Pardon?

45 This is 24 Daddy's sock

Appendix 2

Name: Jane   *Record Number*: 7
Date of Birth: 8.4.1970   *Date of Recording*: 10.1. 1975

Sample number: 8   *Participants*: Mother, Jane
                        Time: 11.57 a.m.
                        Location: Kitchen
                        Activity: Mother preparing lunch, Jane watching

1 Ma(v)   [Radio on]

2 I've got a * cos I didn't – I
  – that make me sick that do

3 Ma(v) can I go out?

4   M: No

5   M: It's cold out now

6   M: One two three four five six
                                               seven eight nine ten (sings)
                                                      [Mother counts before lighting
                                                             the gas stove]

7 Mum(v) what we got?

8 Mum(v) let me have a look
  what's burning

9 Mum(v) that egg's burning in'it?

10   M: What?

11 That egg's burning

. .

12 Oh Mum(v)!(with consternation)
13 Which – where my egg?
14 Mum(v) we both got to have eggs
15　　　　　　　　　　　　M: I'll be a bag of nerves if
　　　　　　　　　　　　　　　you don't shut up (shouts)
16 Mum(v)　　　　　. . .
17 Lift your bag up (command)
18 Oh! what's that?
19 "* * * * * <all the food>"
20 * *
21 Mum(v) we both –　　　　　　　　　　[Mother beating eggs]

Sample number: 9　　　*Participants*: Jane, Mother
　　　　　　　　　　　Time: 12.07 p.m.
　　　　　　　　　　　Location: Kitchen
　　　　　　　　　　　Activity: Mother preparing lunch, Jane watching

1 "Oh"　　　　　　　　　　. .
　　　　　　　　　　　　　. . 4 . .
2　　　　　　　　　　　　M: What you doing?
　　　　　　　　　　　　　. .
3　　　　　　　　　　　　M: You do it the hard way don't you?
　　　　　　　　　　　　　. . 4 . .
4 "Don't fall out"　　　　　　[Jane doesn't seem to
　　　　　　　　　　　　　　　expect any answers]
5 Ah! baked potato!
6 * * * *　　　　　　　　. . 6 . .
7　　　　　　　　　　　　M: Oh God!
　　　　　　　　　　　　　. . 7 . .
8 That egg and chips
9 That egg is dirty Mummy(v)　M: NR
　　　　　　　　　　　　　. . 6 . .
10 Oh! bacon!
11 Now what's this?　　　　　　[Jane mistakes chops for
　　　　　　　　　　　　　　　　　　　　　bacon]
12　　　　　　　　　　　　M: What! (exclamation)
13　　　　　　　　　　　　M: You got bacon on the mind
　　　　　　　　　　　　　　　or summat?
　　　　　　　　　　　　　. . .

14 "Oh"

15   M: Right take a stool in now
                                   ** ready yet
                                . .

16 Mum(v) this is a pancake

17 Pancakes

18   M: It's not a pancake

19   M: It's an omelette (brusquely)

20 Omelette

21 O-o-o-o

22 Omelette omelette

23 I likes omelette

G. THOMAS FOX, Jr

9 Pictures of a Thousand Words: Using Graphics in Classroom Interviews

Implicit in the title of *Uttering, Muttering* is that we don't always say what is on our minds – somehow the articulate becomes lost in the words we use in professional conversation. This is not a criticism but a playful poke at ourselves. We need only to *see* our utterances to realise how much meaning is interpreted in our conversations. Transcripts of our talk, like typed drafts of our writing, leave us nearly speechless as we recognise the incomplete and ambiguous nature of what we thought we said and what we (at one time) knew we meant. Sentences are left incomplete, phrases are only partly stated in dialogue as we think we are understood.

So far I haven't said anything that has not been said in some way or another by each author in this book. What I would like to add, however, is a suggestion of one way of testing more immediately in public the words we use and the meanings we intend, particularly our description of educational actions. I would like to report a method we employed in one project where the attention was on capturing the descriptions of classroom practices *through the use of graphics*. In the project I am about to describe, we recorded detailed descriptions of particular classroom practices *not* by recording the words that were used but by recording pictorial representations of certain intended statements. Our tools were coloured pens and overhead transparencies rather than the tape recorder or the field notebook. Words were still a major source of information, meaning, description, and disagreement – but they were portrayed and aggregated in a graphic rather than a literate style. Contradictions, ambiguities, and misunderstandings about what was done in a school programme became graphically apparent as the interviews were taking place.

I want to describe this process in more detail because there may be some lesson here for us all. Although the project I am referring to was planned in particular instructional contexts, the contribution that graphics brought to the interview process may be more generally applied. The ability of graphics to focus attention, to stimulate recall of details in educational practices and activities, to refine and redirect previous statements, and to test the extent to which the meanings received by the interviewer were similar to the intended meanings of the interviewee, may be relevant to a variety of approaches for gaining accurate descriptions of classroom practices. The use of graphics, which initially was considered an efficient and pleasing way to record a variety of information, may instead have been significant to the probing process itself. Graphics may have touched the different ways in which we understand our work, store our perceptions, and place meaning within the unsensed networks of our minds.

I am getting ahead of myself. First, I would like to describe our project and give some examples of how graphics were used in discourse with teachers to enable us to arrive at a portrayal of their practices and of their intentions. I must also state some of what we missed in these graphic portrayals that were significant in our context and may be significant in capturing other instructional contexts. Next I want to refer our experience with graphics to certain critical issues that have been raised about interviewing professionals about their educational practices and intentions. I will be referring, for example, to ways in which graphics can alleviate the doubts expressed by some investigators that teachers can accurately describe their classroom practices (e.g. Hook and Rosenshine, 1979). I will also refer to the role that graphics may play in the symbiotic influence between belief (or tradition and underlying assumptions) and the perceived action. In short, the mediator's role of graphics when the mind seems to overguide the eye. Finally, as I have said, I will try to take our considerations away from classrooms for a few moments and towards what Hamilton (1980) suggests are the psychological processes which we (all) may use to recall and to understand human action and intent.

THE DESCRIPTOR FOR INDIVIDUALISED INSTRUCTION

Graphics were used in an interview process to stimulate and to record teacher descriptions of what was being meant by stating that their classrooms were 'individualised'. The research project (De Vault *et al.*, 1973) was to investigate the possibility that a generic form of questioning and recording could be used to describe the many meanings being given the term 'individualised instruction' in different school levels (elementary through college) and subject matter areas. The assumption was that many different actions were performed and intended by the phrase 'individualised instruction'. The need was to recognise, respect, and record the significant features of the many actions and intentions referred to by the term. The intent was to describe the actual processes used in instructional programmes and in specific classrooms that were labelling their instruction as being 'individualised'.

In a pre-pilot study performed before the proposal was written, and in the proposal, coloured graphics were suggested as an efficient means to record a range of what seemed to be significant features of classroom practice. The original idea was to observe and interview in such a way that we researchers could provide an accurate and verifiable description in a graphic form that captured specific features of the practices.

During the pilot stage of the study, however, it became apparent that our most accurate and verifiable descriptions were being generated by those interviews where the graphic descriptions could be the common centre of attention. Our data gathering process initially included 1) recording observations and interviews, 2) comparing, contrasting, and synthesising the results, 3) recording the synthesis on graphic descriptor, and 4) taking this synthesis back to be verified and refined. We found this process to be not only time-consuming and cumbersome, but, more important, not as accurate as those cases where we were able to discuss the graphic portrayals initially with the interviewed. Thus, the project turned to developing a procedure for stimulating discussions of classroom practices through the manipulation of graphic displays. Although we also sought to capture significant and generic features of the practices, it is the interview procedure that may be more generally applicable to those interested in continuing to probe for accurate descriptions of classroom actions.

The process of interviewing through manipulative graphics was developed, used, and refined during the fourteen months of the research project, and has been used extensively in a variety of instructional contexts, school settings, and subject matter areas since then. I would like to describe briefly the interview process, and then give four examples of how the graphics were used in teacher interviews.

Figure 1 shows the entire descriptor which was developed (it is about eight times this size when used). Although the category system is not the focus of our attention here, it can be seen that we organised the instructional programme into four distinct categories:

1. the aims of the programme (objectives and learner assessment procedures);
2. the instructional strategies (sequence, rate, programme pattern, media, and grouping);
3. the management (record and use of information);
4. the programme context (e.g. grade level, etc.).

There also is a colour key to show who are making the decisions within these categories (e.g. teacher, student, or neither). Each of the ten subheadings or 'components' on the descriptor (objectives, learner assessment procedures, sequence, etc.) is a separate topic in the interview, supported by its own set of graphic materials. It is through these graphic materials that discourse is stimulated, directed, and recorded, and upon which a portrayal is eventually reached. I will draw examples from four of these ten 'components', but first I will describe the interview process we use.

The interview process

The interview usually takes place with two to four teachers who are teaming together to perform a particular programme of instruction. We begin by introducing the purpose of the descriptor (to describe in some detail the practices of the programme, *not* to evaluate or to judge 'whether one is or is not "individualised"'), the general meanings of the categories, their respective 'components', and the colour key. We then proceed with the interview by focusing on a particular component. The interview process for each component follows a similar course.

Each component has a set of overhead transparencies, one 'clear' transparency of the graphic display as shown in Figure 1 and four 'coloured' transparencies with different versions indicated by the colours used and the ways in which the graphic features are filled in. Before beginning to probe for specific descriptions of the instructional programme, the coloured transparencies are shown and discussed to focus attention and to clarify the terms used on the descriptor with the language of those being interviewed.

After clarification and agreement of what the interviewer and the interviewee mean by the category and the terms within the category, the coloured transparencies are then shown, one at a time, and are described as the graphics portray them. Comparisons and contrasts between the portrayals of the coloured transparencies are included where it is considered helpful. Questions and responses to the transparencies are elicited and considered as the interviewer tries to determine when there is enough understanding of the terms used and of the graphics displayed so that a detailed description of the programme can begin. This preliminary introduction between interviewer and interviewee may last between five and ten minutes for each component (perhaps longer for the first component and less as the discussion goes to later components).

The probing begins after the prototypes on the coloured transparencies are discussed and understood. We return to the 'blank' transparency and ask, 'Now, what does your programme (classroom) look like?' The response may be, 'Why, it looks much like the second transparency you showed us, except for some modifications.' Then they would proceed to describe in detail the actions of their programme, referring their actions to the graphics and to the portrayals of the prototype. (The previous sentence may refer to an hour's discussion among those being interviewed and between them and the interviewer.) The main topic of discussion is how particular activities of the programme operate in a classroom, given the parameters of the component being described. The 'blank' transparency is filled in by the interviewer as the discussion transpires. Occasionally the interviewer may ask, 'Is this a fair way to portray what you are saying?' and direct attention to a particular way of filling in a graphic feature with colour. Other times those being interviewed suggest how to fill in the graphic features. Soluble pens are used in order that the colours and patterns can be erased, refined,

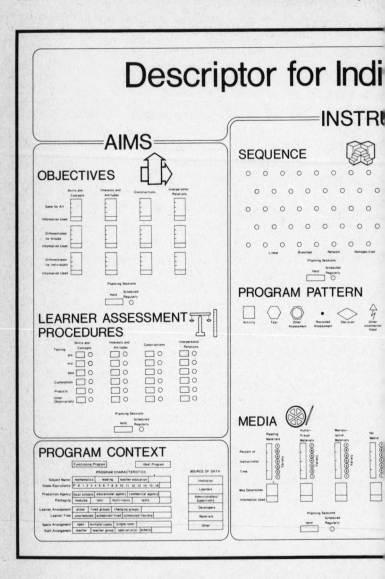

Figure 1: the descriptor is shown much reduced simply to illustrate the layout; individual sections are shown in greater detail in figures 2–14.

dualized Instruction

~ION

ATE

Rate Variability Observed

least
number
Q_1
Mean
Q_3
most
number

1 2 3 4 5 6 7 8 9 10
Number of Units Completed

Planning Sessions

Held   Scheduled
        Regularly

~ROUPING

Self   Grouped   Grouped
        Without Instructor With Instructor

Determines
...tion Used

Planning Sessions
        Scheduled
Held   Regularly

MANAGEMENT

RECORD OF INFORMATION

Information About Learners

	Learner Assessment				Learner Use of Program Options						Instructors		Option Availability				
Storage Form	Skills & Concepts	Attitudes & Interests	Construction Making	Interpersonal Relating	Objectives	Assessment	Sequence	Rate	Media	Grouping	Content Interest	Teaching Style Preference	Objectives	Assessment	Sequence	Rate	Media	Grouping
computer	O	O	O	O	O	O	O	O	O	O	O	O	O	O	O	O	O	O
record file	O	O	O	O	O	O	O	O	O	O	O	O	O	O	O	O	O	O
portfolio	O	O	O	O	O	O	O	O	O	O	O	O	O	O	O	O	O	O
other	O	O	O	O	O	O	O	O	O	O	O	O	O	O	O	O	O	O

Information About Program

USE OF INFORMATION

Who Uses the
Recorded
Information

COLOR KEY

Decision Making   Other Descriptive Features

Learner   Instructor   Program
determined   determined   determined

WISCONSIN CENTER FOR THE ANALYSIS
OF INDIVIDUALIZED INSTRUCTION

School of Education
University of Wisconsin–Madison

M. Vere DeVault
Mary A. Golladay
G. Thomas Fox, Jr.
Karen Skuldt

Visual Design by:
G. F. McVey, C. Priebe & Kathryn Jenkins

changed, and revised if what is portrayed on the descriptor does not reflect what was being described, or if it triggers some additional discussion on what was previously said that alters the previous descriptions. The interviewer probes for more clarity, the describers of the programme order further refinements and changes so that the graphic portrayal more closely represents what begins to become clearer to them as their programme.

Let us take four examples to clarify how graphics are used in this interview process.

Example One: Consider the topic of the sequence of instructional units. As shown in Figure 1, a blank transparency of the sequence would look like a series of empty circles. Each circle would represent a chunk of the content in an instructional programme (some teachers may call these 'units', some 'chapters', some 'major concepts', some 'special projects'). One concern of the probe is whether there is *in practice* a particular linkage between these units of instruction or whether there are alternative linkages. Figure 2, for example, shows a

Figure 2

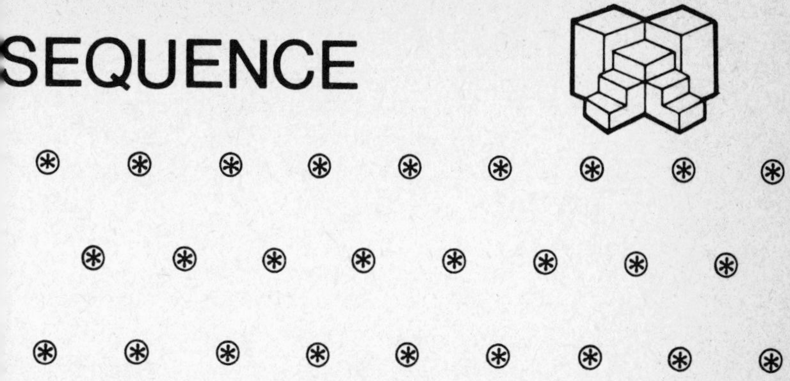

SEQUENCE

❋   ❋   ❋   ❋   ❋   ❋   ❋   ❋   ❋

❋   ❋   ❋   ❋   ❋   ❋   ❋   ❋

❋   ❋   ❋   ❋   ❋   ❋   ❋   ❋

Figure 3

programme with only one linkage between units and no alternatives. We label this a 'linear' sequence, where each unit is ordered and the prerequisites of unit n are all units n-1. The 'colour scheme' (cross-hatching) used in Figure 1 shows that these choices are predetermined by the programme (e.g. by a text series) and not made by either the teacher or the student.

Figure 3 shows a programme where there is no linkage made between units; they can be taken in any order. Furthermore, the cross-hatchings of Figure 3 indicate that the teacher determines what

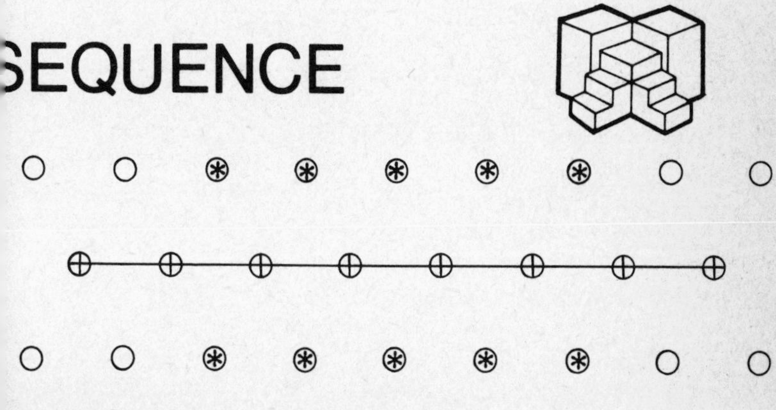

SEQUENCE

○   ○   ❋   ❋   ❋   ❋   ❋   ○   ○

○   ○   ❋   ❋   ❋   ❋   ❋   ○   ○

Figure 4

is to be the next order for any particular student (or group of students). This sequence we label 'nonspecified'.

These two different graphic prototypes may bring the response, 'Well, our programme is basically linear, like the first transparency, but then we have some units that we have created that can be taken at any time.' Thus, the interviewer may draw on the blank transparency what is shown in Figure 4.

The response to Figure 4 may then be, 'No, that's not right, because it is the student who can make the decision; also, we really don't have that many options in comparison with the rest of the units. Come to think of it, all but one of the options are linked to one of the units in the regular sequence.' As more questions probe for details, Figure 5 may represent the next try.

SEQUENCE

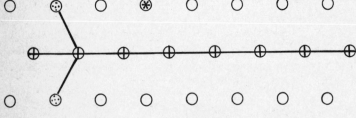

Figure 5

As soon as Figure 5 is pictured on the transparency, some in the small group being interviewed may begin to be satisfied ('Yes, that's it, the alternative units we have in this programme are linked to one, except for the special unit which I decide can be taken sometime in the year'). One may then say, 'Hold it, does that say that some students take all three, because if it does, it's wrong, we give the student an option to choose any one of the three before going on to the next unit.' As Figure 5 is being transformed to Figure 6, someone else may blurt out, 'Say, doesn't that remind you that we have some more options towards the end of the year?' So it goes until a consensus is

SEQUENCE

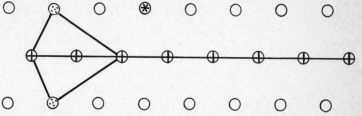

Figure 6

reached on what is the right picture of the sequence of units in the practice of this particular programme.

As I hope is shown in this example, the graphics of the descriptor can be used to help focus attention on the actual sequencing of units of instructional content. The quick comparison, contrasts, and 'recordings' may stimulate recall, point out differences within the group of teachers being interviewed, and call attention to options that may not yet have been considered (for example, who does decide the order of

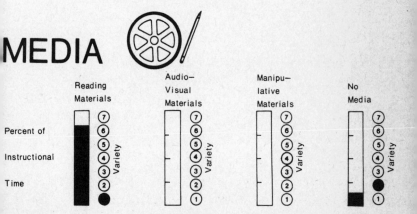

Figure 7

units). Difficulties and complexities are raised at times in the minds of those describing the programme; the difference between necessary prerequisites, and a sequence of units that is done one way, for example, or the difference between an option that is available and one that is actually used.

Example Two: The Media section asks what instructional materials are available and the extent to which they are used (in addition to who makes the choices). As shown in Figure 1, the blank transparency has four long rectangles, a series of circles next to them and a box below. The rectangles represent the approximate percentage of time spent with materials, the circles (with numbers) identify what kind of materials are available, and the boxes indicate who chooses the materials when there is a choice. We will consider the long rectangles and the circles next to them which, taken together, portray the variety of materials used in instruction. Figure 7 shows one prototype. In the programme shown in Figure 7, reading materials are prevalent (over ninety per cent of the time) and consist of a single textbook (circle 1). Audio-visual materials (e.g. tapes, films, etc.) are not used nor are manipulative materials (e.g. games, puzzles, models). What is labelled 'no media' is used and, as is shown by circle 2 being coloured in, these are discussion groups. (Figure 7 may, for example, portray an elementary reading programme.)

A second prototype is shown in Figure 8. This programme has a

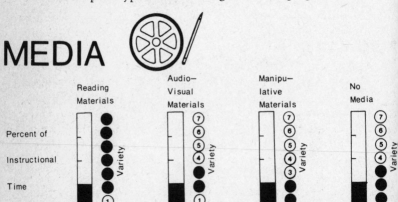

Figure 8

Pictures of a Thousand Words   175

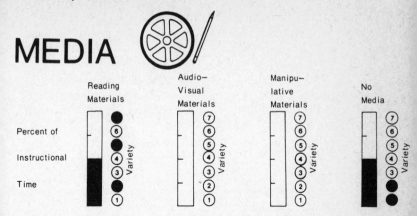

Figure 9

variety of materials, as is shown by the many different circles being 'coloured' in (each numbered circle represents a particular instructional material like textbooks, instructor written materials, library books, etc.). In addition, it is indicated that the four different types of materials (reading, manipulatives, etc.) get used in about equal amounts of time over the life of the programme.

The response to these two prototypes may begin with 'I wish we could approach the second more closely but, in reality, our programme is a variation of the first.' This may be accompanied by 'Yes, but we have more than one text (circle 2), we use some materials we teachers have written ourselves (5), and we use library books (7).' 'Besides,' someone may say, 'we spend much more time in discussions and in lecture-type presentations – maybe 50-50.' In response, Figure 9 may be drawn to portray the use of materials in this programme.

As soon as Figure 9 is drawn, someone may say, 'We also use student written essays as instructional examples' (circle 6 in reading materials). 'Also, I don't think that the students spend an equal amount of time with the materials and in discussions and lectures. I think it's closer to three days of reading and to two days of lecture and discussions.' 'And,' says another, 'some of the students perform a drama in this course and that takes a lot of time, and a few use puzzles and games, remember the ones in the cupboard?' This may trigger some more comments about a film that is used at a certain time of the year or the use of time for special projects (4 in manipulation). Thus, Figure 9 may become transposed to Figure 10 to approximate more closely the programme being described from the view of the teachers (or of the students if they are the ones being interviewed).

This example may show how graphics can stimulate more detail and more unanswered questions than could possibly be transcribed and captured. Questions of how the programme would look to different students (or groups of students), the perhaps unnatural aggregation of average time spent with materials over the duration of a programme, the consideration of active rather than passive modes of behaviour in the classroom for instructional purposes, the possibilities that exist which would *not* necessarily cost more money for materials, or the range of materials that exist which are not used, have all been raised within our interviews, stimulated and directed by the graphics of this comparatively mundane component.

In addition to sometimes unspoken realisations of certain complexities and shortcomings of what is available and what is used, there is a factor in the recall of materials and activities that may be significant. As we begin to fill in the circles, as we try to list the types of materials and activities that are engaged in the programme, one can almost *see* the mental search through the classrooms and into the cupboards of the school. The eyes occasionally focus on the circles, the minds may transfer the meanings of the symbols on the

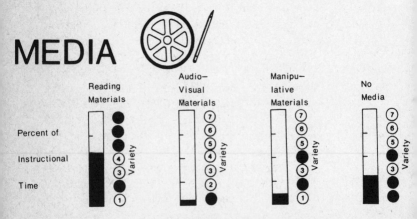

Figure 10

GROUPING

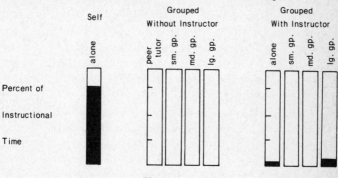

Figure 11

transparency, but even more often, whether the interview takes place in the classroom or not, we can sense the looking that goes on as teachers complete their search for materials. This is a different kind of recall than that used for referring to classroom activities such as discussions or drama.

Example Three: Grouping of students is often a major concern in many programmes that purport to be 'individualised'. As Figure 1 shows, the grouping component in the descriptor is composed of nine thin rectangles, placed in three categories (of one rectangle, and four, and four), and a box under each of the three categories. A major concern of this component is the percentage of time that a student would be expected to be in certain size groups, and whether these groups include the teacher or not. As with media, the rule is that the total time of the various groupings must be a hundred per cent of the student's time – no more, no less. With nine categories and the possibilities that different students in a programme may have participated in different size groups, the juggling game may be a mental challenge.

A simple prototype is shown in Figure 11. As shown in Figure 11, this programme is mainly an independent study programme with nearly all the student's time spent alone. If the student is not alone, then he or she is either in a large group with the instructor (over twenty persons) or alone with the instructor.

Let us stop here for a moment. Without going further, what we often hear is the comment, 'That's not our programme because the student must spend more time with me; there must be, oh, ten per cent of their time spent with me alone. Nearly all I do all day is talk to individual students.' If we then ask how many students are in the class and how many additional instructors there are besides the teacher, and get an answer of thirty and none respectively, then we point out that, on an average, the greatest amount of time that a student could spend with the teacher is three per cent of his or her time. Often this fact alone is shocking, since the question then becomes, what does a student do with the remaining ninety-seven per cent of the time?

To get back to graphics, Figure 12 shows a different programme that has 'individualised' its instruction. In Figure 12, the student spends about the equivalent of a little over one day (period) a week in independent study, about the same amount of time in small groups (two to eight) without the instructor, about a day a week in a large group (more than twenty) with the instructor, and another day in a small group with the instructor. The remaining time is either alone with the instructor or with peer tutors.

The response to these two prototypes may be 'We are a little of both, we have a variety of grouping patterns but mainly the students either do independent study or they are grouped with us in what you call large groups.' As this and similar comments are being made, we return to the blank transparency and begin to fill in the rectangles, usually changing them very quickly as we try to incorporate more responses and work within the rule of a total one hundred per cent of the student's time (e.g. if the estimate of the time in the independent study category seems too much, then some other category must be increased if independent study is to be decreased). Although the discussions are recognised to be far less precise than the reference to 'percentage of time' would suggest, the referral to specific practices and discussions on how they would be aggregated and synthesised into an accurate and fair picture by the descriptor can be extensive. In trying to give a picture of the amount of time that students spend

GROUPING

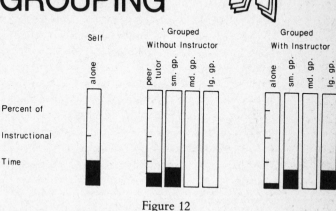

Figure 12

alone and in different size groups with and without the teachers, there are usually a considerable number of contradictions that must be dealt with and resolved in addition to a range of anti-intuitive implications. Nothing quite reaches the initial anti-intuitive shock, however, that with one teacher and thirty-three students, an average of three per cent of the student's time with a teacher would take all the teacher's class time.

Example Four: As is shown in Figure 1, most of the components are not idiosyncratic to the descriptor. They have been part of the literature and language of educators for most of the twentieth century (so, too, has 'individualised instruction', see Fox and DeVault, 1978). During the pilot stage of the project, however, as we were interviewing teachers and students in different programmes and classrooms and trying to arrive at an accurate and fair description of what was being done in the name of 'individualised instruction', we were becoming frustrated with what we were missing. As detailed as we could get in discussions describing the sequence, media, grouping, and the other components shown in Figure 1 (e.g. objectives, rate, and learner assessment procedures), we were missing a central issue of these classrooms.

The issue is that an 'individualised' classroom can look so chaotic to an observer but at the same time be so consistent, comfortable, and known to the students and the teacher. The one common feature of these classrooms was that they had an underlying structure that was not apparent to an observer – and was not being addressed in our interview protocol. We began to realise that this underlying structure was a pattern of activities and decision points within each 'unit' of instruction that left the students and the teachers with an absolute certainty of 'where they were' in the instructional programme. For each instructional unit, we asked, is there a particular pattern of a) instructional activity, b) testing (or other forms of assessment, and c) decisions to go on or do additional work? The thousands of classroom teachers we have introduced to this descriptor have all answered 'yes', they have a particular, often unsensed pattern of activities. As they have described in detail this ordering of activities, it becomes apparent to them that they do have a particular structure that has been (often implicitly) followed. We call this component the 'programme pattern' and, as can be seen in Figure 1, it has a central position on the descriptor. As is also apparent in Figure 1, the component is mostly a blank space except for a few symbols. These symbols are used as building blocks for constructing a pattern of instructional activities, assessment, and decisions.

Figure 13 shows one prototype of a programme pattern. For some readers, it may be apparent that the pattern and the symbols represent a modified systems analysis format (but nothing particularly complex). As shown in Figure 13, instructional activities are represented by a square; a test by a hexagon; some other formal assessment (e.g. a student conference) by a hexagon with a circle inside (if the results are recorded, a dot is placed inside these hexagons); a decision by a diamond; and if other recorded information is referred to in a decision, that is shown by a triangle with a jagged line. Keeping these symbols in mind, you can see that Figure 13 indicates the following pattern of activities.

The teacher makes a decision to enter a unit, a particular activity makes up that instructional unit (e.g. the reading of a chapter), a test follows that activity (the results of the test are recorded), and a

PROGRAM PATTERN

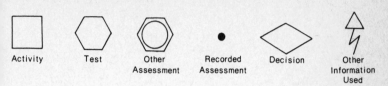

Activity — Test — Other Assessment — Recorded Assessment — Decision — Other Information Used

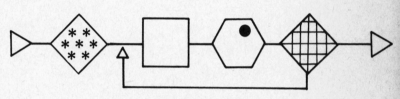

Figure 13

decision is made upon a pre-determined range of scores whether the student is to go on to the next instructional unit or to go back to do the same instructional activity again. This order of activities is the general pattern used *within each instructional unit*.

Figure 14 suggests a more complex pattern but still a consistent pattern within each unit of instructional content. As portrayed in Figure 14, each unit begins with an activity (e.g. a discussion or a unit prospectus), then the student can decide whether to perform this unit or not. If not, he or she goes to the next unit; if so, then there is a unit test given (a 'pre-test') that is not recorded, but which, along with other recorded information, is used to decide what, from a range of instructional activities, to do. This decision is made jointly by the teacher and the student. After the chosen activity is completed, then the student decides when to take a post-test (which is recorded); that is followed by an assessment conference with the teacher (results recorded), and then a joint decision is made by the teacher and student whether the student is ready to go on to the next unit or should return back to participate in some other instructional activities.

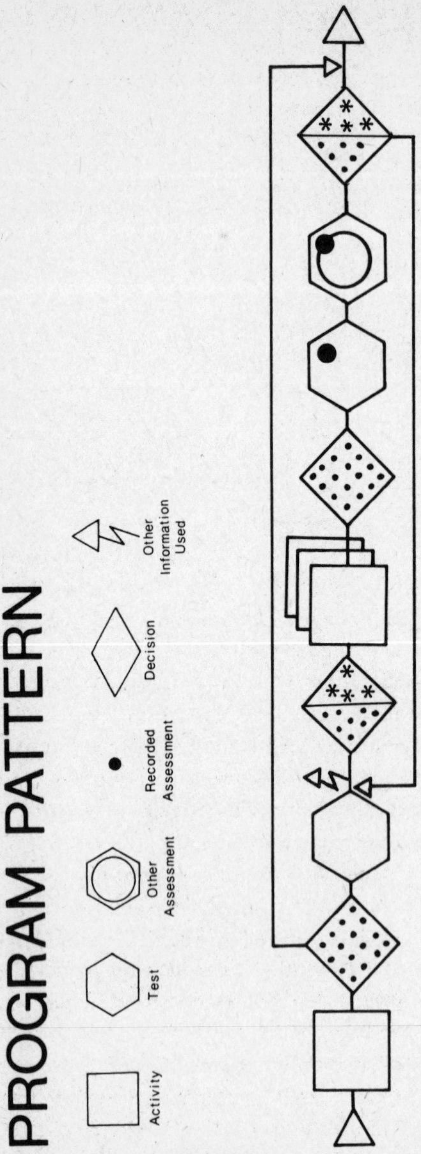

Figure 14

The response to these two prototypes may be 'neither one describes our programme', but as soon as the interviewed understand the symbol system, the probes begin. The resulting discussions are in detail and are often animated. Using the symbols and the colour code for indicating the relationships between instructional activities, assessment, and decisions, the interview becomes nearly a manipulative process where the symbols are placed, moved, arranged, and rearranged as specific activities and their order is recalled by those being interviewed.

One challenge that is apparent in the interview process is the attempt to place what is done and what is said about what is done in classroom instruction onto the symbolic framework provided by the descriptor. It can be surprising, however, how quickly and effortlessly this challenge has been met by those being interviewed. Not only is their attention captured by the graphics and their own manipulation of the graphics to meet their progressive recall of classroom actions, but it seems to stimulate specific examples and cases of what is done and places an unusually intense focus on describing how an instructional unit gets played out from a student's perspective.

Another interesting challenge is that those being interviewed have not considered themselves as having a 'programme pattern'. The order and relationships of the actions represented by the symbols have rarely been raised in their own minds. The consequence of this initial recall, immediate display, focused attention on instructional actions, is often considerable amazement at the structure that they see in their own programmes.

Figure 15, for example, describes the pattern on one mathematics programme for ten years olds which up to then, we must admit, looked very pedestrian and pedantic to us, but was loved by the children. After interviewing the teachers and the students, we arrived at a consistent portrayal of the nature and sequence of instructional actions within each unit of instruction.

In this programme, there was a comparatively detailed prospectus of the unit with objectives and sub-objectives stated, types of problem explained and examples of how to solve the problems included (about twenty pages of introduction). There was also a 'practice pre-test' (actually more than one) that students could try whenever they

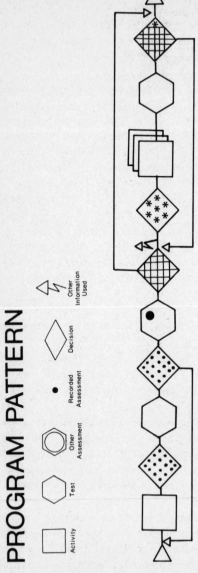

Figure 15

wanted and as many times as they wanted. This practice pre-test was not recorded but could be checked by the student who could then return to the prospectus to re-study it if he or she wanted. Once the actual pre-test was taken, however (and its results recorded), then a student was 'officially' in that unit. From that point, the unit was a domain of the teachers and the programme. Based upon the test score of the pre-test (usually a hundred per cent), the student could test out of the unit and go to the next unit. If the student did not test out of the unit, information on the results of the pre-test, and of the available resources, was used by the teachers to determine the exercises and text pages that the child was to complete. After these activities were completed, a post-test was taken (and recorded) and a decision was made, based upon the test scores (over ninety per cent), whether the child was ready for the next unit or should go back and do some more instructional activities.

The surprise was the extent to which the students emphasised the activities leading to the recorded pre-test. Students would spend up to three weeks going over and over the prospectus. They would take the (unrecorded) 'practice' pre-test, go to older brothers and sisters, to friends who had been in the unit before, or to parents for help in preparing for the actual (recorded) pre-test. The game, to them, was to ace the recorded pre-test (get full marks) so that they could test out of the unit and 'not have to study'. Although this process may take considerable student effort for two or three weeks, it was seen by some students as a way to beat the system.

The graphic portrayal of this programme brought to the teachers' awareness a practice that, although undeniably there, was not so apparent or important to them before the interviews with the students were completed. After the interview, for example, some of the teachers wanted to remove the possibility for students to beat the system by revising the prospectus and the practice pre-tests. The suggestion here is that it was the graphics, the direct and succinct way in which certain activities were portrayed, that began to stimulate reflective judgments *by those being interviewed* about the nature, consequence, and significance of what they were doing. That the teachers modified parts of their programme that we interviewers would not have modified indicates the stimulative nature of an accurate portrayal of a hidden structure.

REFLECTIONS UPON THE USE OF GRAPHICS IN TEACHER INTERVIEWS

Some educators have used graphics. Elliott and Adelman (1976), for example, use branching lines to indicate the range of possible linkages between different actions referred to by the terms 'informal', 'structured', and 'directed' learning (see Elliott, 1976–77). Fromberg (1977) uses lines and enclosed spaces to portray the significant relationships between young children's conceptions and the world(s) around them. Graphics in these cases are used to deliver the wisdom accrued by investigation and analysis. They represent well a synthesis of relationships, they help articulate the complexity of certain educational practices and contexts, they help us to attend to detail while also considering abstracted features of learning and instruction. We support continued use of graphics for these educational purposes, but our use of graphics was for a different purpose.

What makes our use of the descriptor different is that *graphics were used to stimulate recall and to focus initial descriptive discussions.* Graphics were not used to transfer well-articulated conclusions and summaries of thought and analysis; they were used to stimulate the initial thought, to recall, gather, and collect information in order to generate accurate portrayals of long term educational programmes. Portrayals of long term programmes (e.g. programmes lasting the entire school year), we had found in previous experience, were not readily available to observation, nor were they that accessible through verbal probing alone. Similar problems have been noted by Hook and Rosenshine (1979) and by Ironside (1980). Hook and Rosenshine, in particular, question the accuracy and validity of teachers' recall of their own classroom activities, but they reviewed survey instruments and interview data without graphics. It is the focus of graphics on stimulating recall and discourse on classroom actions that may warrant our attention. Graphics, used in interactive dialogue, may improve our assessments of teachers' recall of actual events and the accuracy and validity of their portrayals of classroom actions.

One step in understanding the potential contribution of graphics in the interview process with teachers is to reflect upon our experience with the descriptor. Thus, in this section we will draw upon the lessons we have learned in using the graphics of the descriptor to probe during teacher interviews. We will first raise the limitations we have encountered in using graphics in teacher interviews. We will then discuss what we consider as advantages in our use of graphics in teacher interviews. The final discussion of these reflections on our use of the descriptor will be some suggestions that we have drawn about the type of contexts, problems, and situations where we feel graphics may be most useful to future educational inquiries. The section following this will discuss *why* graphics may have a significant role in stimulating our recall and in delivering some meaning and sense to our actions in educating the young.

Limitations of graphics

There are three limitations that must be recognised as we discuss the difficulties and successes from our experience with the descriptor. These three limitations are:

1. the focus on the descriptor is on actions, not on the underlying assumptions, consciousness, or private beliefs held about education;
2. the descriptor is only one lens for looking at classrooms with a necessarily narrow language system and perspective;
3. the descriptor has the restrictions of a symbol: it is both more and less than it appears to be.

The descriptor's focus on actions should be apparent from the previous examples and from the major categories shown in Figure 1. When one begins to ask what happens in the use of materials, the grouping of students or the ways in which the students are assessed, the probe is into classroom process rather than an unpacking of instructional intent. The descriptor was not formed to probe deeply into the intentions and beliefs that may have led to these practices. Instead, the descriptor was formed, first, to see if significant actions of certain complex programmes could be described, and, second, to see to what extent these actions were an appropriate focus over a range of content areas, grade levels and subject matter areas. This made it necessary and appropriate not to probe deeply into underlying theories of instruction or of the instructional content.

This probe for classroom actions, of course, is not a trivial matter.

There are requests for more attention to procedural features of classroom actions by investigators and curricular theorists such as Schwab (1970) and Goodlad (1977). The descriptor does make classroom process less ambiguous and more publicly acknowledged. It has also been used to request that teachers reflect upon, discuss and project their goals and hopes for future actions and procedures. We have probed, for example, not only for what is done but also for what the teachers would consider an ideal (or more ideal) use of media, or sequencing of units, or who should be choosing if there were certain options available. Still, we do not go further than that; we do not probe into the values and beliefs which may influence the actions performed, the choices made or the vision teachers have of ideal classroom activities and structure. If an inquirer were interested in probing the intentions and hypotheses that underlie the actions performed in classrooms, there could be a more efficient way than through the descriptor.

Not only does the descriptor limit its focus on classroom actions; its perspective on action is limited. In the early construction of the descriptor, for example, it became apparent that we investigators were portraying action in two contrasting and not compatible ways. One was to look at learning as the accumulation, refinement and aggregation of information, where the breaking up of content into chunks made sense. The other was to look at learning as an activity-oriented enterprise, where the learning project and its analysis was the ultimate concern. Both of those approaches, we found later, were linked to individualised instruction from the early twentieth century on (see Fox and DeVault, 1978). It became apparent, however, that the descriptor could efficiently probe and capture significant features of only one approach at a time. Although we began to construct two descriptors with two quite different sets of categories and indicators, we eventually felt it necessary to refine and develop only one. We picked the approach that was most consistent with the classrooms we visited that claimed to be 'individualised'. Since much of what we saw, and have seen labelled 'individualised instruction', has come from a systems orientation, the components of the descriptor reflect a nearly common language and commonly accepted view of classroom action. Nevertheless, it must be noted that the descriptor is but one lens through which to focus on classroom action, and we would expect to have other lenses where they are appropriate.

A third limitation is that, even as a lens, the descriptor is not entirely translucent; it does not capture everything. When we performed the interviews, for example, we had many pages of back-up materials to catch the remaining information that was not portrayed on the descriptor. As the examples discussed earlier indicate, the descriptor leaves much that can be said unrecorded. When we use the descriptor to portray a classroom, we find it necessary to include an additional three- to five-page discursive account to describe some details and contextual information that is not included on the descriptor but which further explicates the programme.

There is some value to limiting the amount of information to be recorded. It reduces the detailed information about classroom activity to a manageable range. The back-up materials, we found, were too much for participants or outside observers to ingest. The detail and depth of information provided by the back-up materials neither drew much attention of interest, nor added much additional sense to the programmes. In short, the descriptor has the limitations of all graphic forms: it is limited by the amount of information that can be transferred through symbols.

In addition to these three limitations, we have encountered other difficulties in using the graphics of the descriptor. One difficulty in our use of graphics in these interview probes is the accompanying feeling of the interviewee and of those looking at the descriptor that we have captured everything. It looks so complete and sounds so convincingly detailed when we refer to the graphics and describe the programme, that many implicitly assume that there is little else to discuss or analyse. The wholeness of the descriptor, like the unity of a photograph or of a painting, suggests completeness when it is very selective. Although this is not a problem shared only by graphics (the same can be said of interview data), the physical attractiveness of the graphics further hides the rough nature of the description.

Another difficulty in using graphics is that the range of the discussion may be restricted by the range of the graphics. We could conceivably have discussed only rate of progress, use of media, and patterns in grouping and left participants (and us) feeling we had described most of the programme. As in verbal interviews, our choice of categories and resulting lines of inquiry set up a context that may narrow rather than expand the possible topics of discussion. Not only is the view of teaching limited by the category system of the graphics (in part by necessity as we stated earlier), but the focus of the discussion may be linked perhaps too closely to the power of the graphics and the creativeness of the graphic artist.

As we use the descriptor in closed, comfortable, professional settings, we have seen a tendency to talk in graphic symbols rather than in everyday commonsense terms. We begin to hear (and to cue ourselves) such phrases as 'I think our programme has too much yellow' rather than saying there are not enough choices here for the teacher or the student to make. Furthermore, the appeal of the graphics may be to solidify the jargon of our educational talk to a degree that is not wanted. Although, as Elliott and Adelman (1976) indicate, it may be necessary to continue to re-define the common terms used in educational discourse if we are to arrive at shared meaning and understanding, nevertheless, the continued focus on words such as 'rate', 'sequence', 'record-keeping' and 'objectives' may restrict rather than stimulate reflective discourse on teaching.

To summarise these disadvantages in using graphics to probe for better understanding of our educational actions, there may be significant and unintended reductions in the range of our probes. From our experience in using the descriptor, we would say that graphics do well in stimulating discussion and recall of instructional actions but not of the values and underlying assumptions supporting these actions. Furthermore, a law of graphics begins to determine what perspectives of educational activities can and cannot be included. Although the descriptor may look and sound complete, it is only one rough accounting of a myriad of activities and procedures that make up classroom instruction. These limitations of graphics, however, also hint at their usefulness in probing into classroom activities. Some of these restrictions may be essential if we are to focus dialogue, stimulate recall, and record and aggregate details of classroom instruction.

Advantages of graphics

The primary advantage in the graphics of the descriptor is its nearly immediate display of what is meant by what is being said. Graphics are not only a quick translator of words into messages, they are also an attractive and accessible form through which these messages can be revised, changed, refined, and re-stated as differing views are compared and contrasted. In short, the graphics of the descriptor, capable of being manipulated and changed in different ways, was an excellent stimulator of dialectical analysis. As statements were placed into colours and positions on the descriptor, the display nearly begged for disagreements, refinements, and alterations. Our primary appreciation of the descriptor is the extent to which it stimulated reflectivity, public analysis, and professional discourse. That this discourse may be considered limited from certain viewpoints of teaching or of educational contexts pales when compared to its contribution to describing, designing, and arriving at portrayals of specific educational practices.

Another advantage to the graphics in the descriptor is that they reinforce and intensify the need for agreement on some basic terminology. As in Elliott and Adelman's branching trees, the pictorial items on the descriptor begged for common understanding. The simple graphics of shapes filled in with colour made it apparent to all that, until the meaning of such terms as 'percentage of time', 'reading materials', and 'who determines' were commonly shared, the care used in drawing these symbols was lost in different translations. For some reason, which we will discuss later, the graphics of the descriptor reinforced the importance of communication, and the value of accurate and valid descriptions of classroom actions. Furthermore, trying to get the graphics 'right' has stimulated animated interest in such issues as the variability of these actions for the group(s) of students being portrayed, the notion of choice and decision-making, the instructional procedures actually being used, and the perspectives of the students as well as the teacher's own perspectives. Parallel interviews with students, for example, were always treated with great interest and respect, and were considered as the basis for additional reinterpretation and re-analysis of their own perspectives in order to arrive at a more accurate description.

Another advantage to the graphics of the descriptor was that they made it more possible to discuss professional actions independent of the personal image created by one's own words. This has been a problem noted by Elliott (1976–77) and, of course, may be seen as a liability by such personal describers of educational action as Jenkins or MacDonald. Nevertheless it appears, from our experience in using the graphics of the descriptor, that an immediate graphic display made it possible for those being interviewed to be interested, detached, and critical of their own utterances, recall, and successive constructs of meaning to a remarkable degree. Like photographs, the identity portrayed in graphics made self-criticism more palatable (see Langer, 1953). Unlike a photograph, however, the symbol used in the descriptor made the process, not the person, the object of public criticism.

Finally, our experience with the descriptor suggests that those involved with the interview process felt that the graphics efficiently captured much of the complexity of their classroom programmes in a relatively small space and a relatively brief time. With the descriptor's cryptic use of terms (e.g. objectives, learner determined, records kept), the occasional reference to numbers (e.g. percentage of time), and its use of some form, colour, and symbol, an interview could probe quickly into procedural details of the classroom. In each separate component as well as in the descriptor as a whole, both the interviewer and the interviewed can grasp the simplicities and complexities of a programme in a comparatively brief time and in a comparatively restricted space.

Thus, our experience with the descriptor suggests that graphics may not only be useful as a protocol for structured interviews, but that the constructive, manipulative, gaming nature of graphics may be a distinct advantage to interviews which are intended to stimulate recall and to encourage dialogue on the occurrence of specific classroom actions. In an area where it has been acknowledged to be difficult to 'get the facts' (a phrase used by Murphy, 1980, and a point made repeatedly by Jackson), graphics may be unusually valuable for focusing reflective inquiry. The descriptor has acted as a stimulant for discourse, calling attention to the give and take of dialogue between participants in order to arrive at an accurate description of what actions are and are not occurring. Triangulation, in the dialectical sense of probing for conflicting views to arrive at an accurate synthesis, is for some reason assumed by the interviewee when faced with the graphics of the descriptor. In addition to supporting a mood of reflective analysis during the interview, the residue of its graphics has helped continue dialogue after the interview is over.

In summary, the graphics of the descriptor seem to be particularly valuable for probing into classroom activities, for making the explicit known, and for encouraging the teachers interviewed to attend to, to analyse, and to plan their own refinements of their classroom actions. Our use of graphics in interviewing teachers was an alternative – an alternative to surveys, to using private field notes, or to using speech transcripts. Like transcripts (or other forms of accessible case data), however, graphics provide a public setting for critical discourse on educational practices. In short, investigative probes into classroom practices may not necessarily be made in words only. The investigative features of the interview as described by Murphy (1980) are included; the respectful tone of the interviewer for the knowledge of the interviewee is kept as Wax (1971) and Elliott (1976–77) suggested is crucial; and the expansion and reduction of focus suggested by Guba (1978) as stages of naturalistic inquiry are collapsed into a single interview process and performed many times during an interview.

Thus it is unfortunate that the potential of graphics is not pursued more in capturing the practices and intentions of teachers. Colour, shape, form, line, and symbol can be as significant as speech in directing attention, focusing and stimulating dialogue, comparing and contrasting practices and viewpoints, and aggregating and synthesising impressions. Our experience with the graphics of the descriptor suggests there are good reasons to continue to try out graphics in a variety of interview approaches, settings and situations. In the next section, some suggestions are offered for those who may wish to build upon our experience and use graphics in their interview probes.

Suggestions

The limitations and the advantages of our use of graphics with the descriptor imply that recommendations for future use of graphics in interview probes should be made cautiously. When the ultimate purpose of the interview is to stimulate reflective discourse in general, and to focus on long-term educational practices in particular, however, our experience with the descriptor suggests that graphics may be valuable. The following are some points to consider if graphics are being considered for interview probes. Reference is made to those situations and educational contexts where graphics may be a penetrating alternative to words (and/or observations) alone.

1. *Use graphics to portray educational programmes that are relatively stable, continuous, complex, ambiguous, and whose descriptions are filled with professional jargon*

These criteria may describe nearly all of our educational programmes except idiosyncratic, short-term interventions. One reason that stable and long-term (up to a year or more) programmes are suggested is that graphics-oriented interviews can be a more direct, accurate, and efficient method for capturing the repetitive and structural features of a classroom than long-term observation. Another reason is that graphics can continue to stimulate dialogue and focus well beyond the interview period. Also the necessary incompleteness of the graphics is not so critical if the portrayals of the continuing programme can be re-verified and tested through replication at any time.

2. *Use graphics to portray instructional actions and processes*

Although graphics are both public and private symbol, they are probably not as useful for probing into 'false-consciousness' and underlying assumptions and beliefs as certain penetrating forms of verbal confrontations. They are, however, an efficient and appro-priate way to make the explicit explicit; to try to tell it like it is when that is a significant challenge. In describing educational practices, that is not a trivial task, as Kemmis (1977) and Walker (1980) remind us. In those situations where inquiry is considered necessary to find what is occurring in classrooms and to bring up for public inspection those actions that do occur there, graphics are particularly appropriate. The potential contribution of graphics as a medium for recalling and accurately portraying classroom actions is significant enough to warrant our attention.

3. *Use graphics when instantaneous triangulation may be useful in gaining a valid understanding of what has occurred*

The abilities of graphics to focus 'simultaneously' on a narrow concern and to expand the witness accounts and associations recalled by that focus are particularly relevant to the purposes and processes of triangulation. The stimulation of recall, attention to accurate description, and corresponding possibility for manipulation, revision, and refinement of the graphic portrayals make graphics an excellent source for reflective discourse and professional dialogue. In an investigative interview, when different perceptions and witness accounts are to be expected because of the complexity of the practice being investigated, graphics can be unusually useful in arranging for directed discussion and analysis.

4. *Use graphics when the investigated practice has a supported tradition and when the language used to describe the practice has been so abstract, idiosyncratic, and imbued with personal meaning that little communication of what has really occurred has been possible*

This is precisely the context in which the descriptor was formed. Individualised instruction was rich in background and tradition with a strong supportive background in professional literature. This made it feasible to refer to certain generic phrases, terms and ideas which had been used to capture the meaning of the practice. At the same time, the terms used to describe what was happening were often ambiguous, referring little to specific actions but rather to intentions, goals and purposes. When one is faced with a practice that has a tradition that is supported by professional literature, but at the same time is difficult to discuss in active words, then graphics can be significant. Examples of these practices other than 'individualised instruction' may be 'open-classroom', 'activity-based learning', 'bilingual education', or 'career-based education'.

5. *Use graphics when the occasion of the interview is a significant (e.g. primary, first) recording of the persons' professional work*

As has been noted by other inquirers (notably Elliott, 1976–77, and MacDonald, 1976), the interviews in our investigation may be nearly the first time that the educator being interviewed has had an opportunity to recall, reflect, analyse, and discuss his or her personal actions. In this circumstance, to the person being interviewed it is not necessarily the story that is of utmost importance but the opportunity to have a listener, to see and hear responses (others' and one's own) to what is being said, to begin to make private understanding a public enterprise. In short, there are many times when we enter an educational setting knowing that the investigation is a beginning of a record of what is happening, an initial step towards public discourse.

Graphics is appropriate when continued reflective inquiry is the intended consequence of the investigation. Moreover, graphics is a particularly powerful stimulant in those contexts where there has been little reflective discourse in the past.

Thus, we suggest that when the focus of the investigation is on processes and actions that have become traditional and laden with jargon, and when instantaneous triangulation and continued reflective dialogue is intended, graphics may be a significant contribution within the investigative process of the interview. Form, colour and the physical manipulation of symbols can be useful for capturing accurate portrayals of what is occurring in classrooms. One possibility that has occurred to us, for example, is that the graphics of the descriptor may be pursued through the manipulation of computer images. As is done by some architects and designers, it may be interesting to see how the manipulation of graphic symbols and images can help a teacher (or group of teachers) arrive at a portrayal that is either accurate about what is occurring or that accurately represents their intentions and hopes for future practice.

In the next section we will briefly raise some questions about *why* graphics may be useful in interview probes. Our attention will be on the probing qualities of graphics – on why graphics may be crucial as we search the reaches of our minds to recall and reconstruct what has occurred in our classrooms over extended periods of time.

WHY MAY GRAPHICS STIMULATE RECALL AND ENCOURAGE REFLECTIVE ANALYSIS?

We cannot miss this opportunity to refer our experience with graphics to recent research in nonlinguistic modes of communication. The major question we raise is, if graphics are valuable for probing educational actions, what may be the reasons? If we can understand the role that graphics may play in probing for past educational actions and in the processes of analytic discourse about these actions, then perhaps others can use graphics in a variety of educational inquiries. In particular, graphics may be significant to educational inquiries that rely upon reflective discourse with teachers and other participants in the educational enterprise. The work of investigators such as Elliott and Adelman; Walker; Lebbett; Bussis, Chittenden, and Amarel;

Ericson and Florio; Ward and Tikunoff; and Carini, for example, may eventually benefit from a better understanding of the role of graphics in the dialectics of human comprehension.

We will be brief, pointing to those who have been interested in understanding the role of graphic representations in human thinking. Initially, philosophers, critics and artists have been attracted to the ways in which we make meaning. Challenges to an overruling assumption that language is the only carrier of meaning, for example, have been made by Wittgenstein (1969) as he points to the shady limits of what can be said. Thoughtful analyses and strong arguments that differences in graphic symbol systems are accompanied by different thought processes have been made by Langer (1953). Merleau-Ponty (1964) sees in films a new psychology 'of behaviour without thought' that is fundamentally existential in its approach to seeing rather than explaining. The themes of meanings constructed by film, photographs and music as well as by words are explored by Barthes (1977). Fascinating examples of the many ways in which graphic symbol systems have captured human imagination and been used to place meaning on human actions are documented in a monumental collection edited by Kepes (1965). Graphic symbols and iconic displays, as has been pointed out repeatedly by Arnheim (1954, 1974), are often what the human mind needs to learn, to understand, to grasp the relevant properties of a situation.

A few cognitive psychologists have heeded the philosophical arguments of Langer, the critical views of Arnheim, the doubts of Wittgenstein, and the celebrations of Kepes. In *Interaction of Media, Cognition and Learning* (1979), for example, Salomon draws together directed inquiries into the relationships between the symbol systems we use and the mental activities we engage in. He refers to the debt of these psychologists to philosophers such as Langer as well as to other cognitive psychologists who argue strongly against their work. It is this work of Salomon's that encourages us to continue to ask our questions about the role of graphics in reflective discourse on teaching. The following will review some of Salomon's views and research along with other investigators such as Levie, Olson and Kennedy who are likewise setting out to understand better the relationships between the iconic image and human thought.

Perhaps unnecessarily restricted by our experience with the

descriptor, we will review these works with two major concerns. The first is the role that graphics may play in the memory and recall of past educational actions. The second concern is the role that graphics may play in encouraging and supporting continued critical analysis of our actions. We believe that the results of continued probes into our recall and critical analyses of our professional actions will begin to illuminate how we do and do not learn from professional experience.

Graphics in recall

Recall and memory is not a trivial process when it comes to drawing understanding from professional experience. The question we raise is what enters into memory from experience and what then can be drawn from that memory using our cues and probes in interviews and in professional dialogue. When we consider much of the work in teacher interviews, we see evidence that most of what enters the professional memory of teachers is unanalysed observations and feelings. This is not unlike the findings of perceptual psychologists such as Tversky (1977) and Palmer (1975) who find that the perceived attributes of everyday realities (such as the façade of the building where one works) are distorted and selected, yet are the basis for judgments of what is and is not real. What this suggests is that our probes should be towards the mental representations of reality, towards the professional memory of the participants, while assuming that there may be significant distortions, instability, incoherence and ambiguities in those memories. This is to be expected and appreciated as the human reality of the participants' perceptions. Given this as the probable state in the memory of experience, what can graphics do? There seems to be more than one answer to this question and all of them are interesting.

First, graphics can stimulate memory and there seems to be some basis for understanding why. Kennedy (1974), for example, reviews as fact that iconic displays (graphic images) can act as memory aids. Both Kennedy and Arnheim refer to studies that indicate the evocative nature of a variety of graphic forms (e.g. pictures, diagrams, line charts) that can arouse memory, stimulate associations, and aid participants to make meaning of previously unanalysed perceptions. In short, it does seem clear to perceptual psychologists that graphics can serve a generative function in recalling significant features in past experience.

There are some reasons given for this generative function of graphics in recalling and evoking memory. One reason given is the novelty of graphics, the interest and attention given by us to a new image. Another reason given is that the nonverbal evokes because there are internal systems used for storage and thought which are not linguistic. Mental orthogonal transformations of abstract geometric objects, for example, seem to follow pictorial patterns rather than verbal patterns (Shepard, 1978). There seems, in short, to be more than one symbolic mode which we use in different thought processes, more than one internal symbol system (Salomon refers to Hatano, Miyake, and Binks, 1977; Flavell, 1977; Shepard, 1978; Furth, 1966). This evocative function of graphics is *not* necessarily related to the fidelity nor to the authenticity of the visual images to the actions they represent (Arnheim, 1974). Rather, it is the link between the structural features of the graphics and the structural features of our internal modes of representation. We may infer from this that the forms, colours and distinctions of the descriptor may have had particular antecedents in some teachers' experiential memories. Colour, for example, seems to be one factor that plays a major role in visual memory (Heider and Olivier, 1972).

When considering the stimulation and evocation of our memories about educational activities, what is most relevant is that what we did is – must be – judged against our personal knowledge of those activities, as selected and distorted as it is. Salomon calls such knowledge our 'internal representations' of our actions, and states 'in the absence of the object, similarity is clearly judged against an internal representation of one kind or another' (p. 46). It is in this sense that the dialectics we fell into when using the descriptor as a memory probe is so important. When there is no edifice to use as the ultimate test of accuracy, when there is no 'object' upon which to judge one's perceptions, then the dialectics in testing one's perceptions with another's is crucial. More than that, the opportunity to probe one's experiential memory in visual as well as linguistic code made it possible with the descriptor to have the dialectics occur in more than one symbolic system. In playing with the images of the descriptor, we had some dialogue without words. (That is why we suggested playing with the graphic images of the descriptor using a display screen and a computer terminal.) In another situation, the graphic branching structures provided by Elliott and Adelman may have been as essential to their continued discourse with teachers as their definitions of terms (see Elliott, 1976–77).

Thus, there seems to be some evidence to suggest that graphics can trigger aspects of tacit knowledge, of unorganised or partly organised experience and past actions that have not yet been recalled, and may not have been if graphics were not used. Some reasons supplied for why this may be so rest upon two important claims: first that there are significant distinctions between external and internal symbolic systems and, second, that there exist *different* internal systems through which we think. These two claims are also essential as we consider the possible contributions of perceptual psychology to our understanding of the role that graphics may play in the critical analysis of our educational actions.

Graphics in thought

As perceptual psychologists such as Salomon deal with their perceptions of the significant differences between the external environment (including knowledge from other humans) and the individual's mental operations, symbols become major signifiers. Most cognitive psychologists, Salomon says, define cognition – thinking and analysis – as the process that enables us to represent and deal symbolically with the external environment. Not only is there the belief that 'all cognition and learning are based on internal symbolic representations' (p. 3), but, in addition, Salmon assumes that a *variety* of these symbolic forms are used in thinking. Levie (1978), for example, identifies two internal symbolic systems: verbal and imaginal. Verbal is temporal, sequential and relatively abstract; imaginal is spatial, simultaneous and relatively concrete. The notion of dual (or multiple) modes of mental processing is, of course, being supported by neuropsychological evidence as well. Gardner (1974a, b) points to some evidence (not conclusive) that different symbolic modes are processed in different parts of the brain. The left hemisphere processes linguistic and notational symbolic modes (e.g. reading), the right processes dense and figured symbolic modes (e.g. map reading).

A focus on mental processing, however, is only one side of the issue raised by Salomon in understanding significant features of symbol systems. In addition to the need to understand the symbolic functions in mental operations, there is the need to understand the symbolic in the environment. It is the link between the symbol systems of the environment (including media) and the symbol systems of the mind that fascinate the mind of Salomon:

> The acquisition of knowledge from a coded message is mediated by skills of information reception and processing. We can entertain the possibility . . . that these skills are significantly affected by the specific nature of each symbol system into which the content of the message is coded. Thus, each medium, using symbol systems, may have its own specific effects on how meanings are arrived at. (1979, p. 27)

This is where the graphics of the descriptor may have been so useful in teacher critical analysis: it presented a different symbol system with its own specific effects on how meanings were arrived at. Before we continue to examine the possible contributions of graphics to critical analysis, however, there is a very useful distinction made by Salomon. Building upon Goodman's (1968) logical theory and analysis of symbol systems, and doubting the significance of resemblance or similarity between external and internal symbol systems, Salomon arrives at the following distinctions. *Symbols* he defines as characters or coding elements. A symbol *scheme* is the set of syntactic rules for ordering these symbols (or coding elements). A symbol *system* is a special kind of symbol scheme. When a symbol scheme (a set of coding elements and their rules) is correlated with a field of reference, then one has a *symbol system*. Salomon uses musical notation (a symbol scheme) and its performance (the referent) as an example of a symbol system. More than that, Salomon makes *notationality* a feature for discriminating crucial differences between systems.

Symbol systems vary with respect to their notationality. A fully notational symbol system occurs when both its symbolic elements *and* their referents need to be disjointed and separated. Another way of saying this is that there can be a one to one correspondence between the symbolic elements and their referents. Language, to Salomon, is only partly notational (Salomon calls language a notational scheme, not a notational system). In contrast, music, to Salomon, is more a notational system, whose elements and referents are more nearly disjoint and separate. Although Salomon's view of music is more simplistic than his view of language (see Meyer, 1967), it is a view that makes it possible to place *something* in the category of a nearly fully notational symbol system (dance notation is another). As symbol systems vary with respect to notationality, Salomon proposes, how one extracts information and the kinds of information one extracts from them vary accordingly.

We are nearly ready to analyse why graphics may have a role in teachers' analysis of classroom activities from the view of Salomon (and some other perceptual psychologists). We can use the two interrelated dimensions proposed by Salomon:

1. *notationality*, an intrinsic quality of symbol systems, independent of who uses them or how;
2. *structural resemblance to internal representations*, which depend to a considerable extent on the user, on his or her purposes, content and context.

These two dimensions are not necessarily related in a simple and direct manner. As an example, dense, non-notational depictions, Salomon points out, 'are often taken to resemble their objects, even if there is no faithfulness, and even if there is no real object, by sharing some *structural* properties with internal representations' (p. 49). Thus, resemblance, realism, iconicity are qualities that result from the interaction between the symbol system and the symbol user.

Now we can return to the descriptor. Clearly different components in the descriptor a) have different degrees of notationality, and b) probably differ in their structural resemblance to internal representations. There is an obvious intent to be notational in the sequence component of the descriptor by representing units of instruction (e.g. chapters of a text) by independent circles (see Figure 1). The autonomy of each instructional unit was selected as a significant feature of instructional programmes; it was meant to represent accurately that feature in its referent. Although there was no intent to have a one to one correspondence between each circle and a referent unit, there was the intent to have a direct correspondence between the *relationships* indicated by the symbolic elements of the descriptor (i.e. the circles and their connecting lines) and the relationships between the instructional units of the referential programme. This makes the sequence component of the descriptor both simple and abstract, with no intended resemblance between the symbolic circles and their referents, but with an intended correspondence between the structure of the symbols and the sequential structure of the instructional programme.

Although we are not at all sure of the resemblance of this symbolic structure to the internal representations of the teachers, we can suggest two possibilities. One possibility is that the graphic structure portrayed in the sequencing of units resembled quite closely the internal representations of the teachers, but that they never considered the implications of that structure before (e.g. units were treated as independent entities but branching possibilities were seldom considered). Another possibility is that the notational features of the symbol system conflict with some teachers' internal representations of instructional content, but that the structure aided them in analysing their views (e.g. instructional content is not represented as autonomous units, but doing so clarifies some features of the way the programme works).

Thus, we are suggesting two reasons why reflective analysis occurred with our use of graphics in the sequence component. One reason is that the component was intentionally notational. Both the symbol scheme used and the referent programmes had elements that were disjoint and separate. This made it possible to symbolise graphically alternative structural relationships that corresponded with possible alternatives in the real settings. The second reason is that this symbol system shared some structural properties with internal representations. In other words, as symbolic and abstract as the circles and lines were, they *appeared* to be real to the teachers. There was a sense in which the graphic symbolic structure of the figures resembled the structural properties of the sequencing of instructional content in the minds of the teachers describing the programme. The combination of these two reasons made it possible for the sequence component to become a new way to analyse the relationships between different units of instruction.

In a very similar way, the programme pattern component was also successful as a stimulant for recall and as a system for encouraging reflective analysis by teachers. The symbol system of the programme pattern was notational, and shared enough structural properties with the internal representations of teachers to appear real to them. The disjoint and separate symbols in the programme pattern corresponded with the disjoint and separated referents in the instructional programme (e.g. instructional activities and student assessments). In addition, the intended notationality of the symbol system of the programme pattern appears to have resembled structural properties of the internal representations of the teachers. This made it possible for the symbol system of the programme pattern to become a new medium for teachers to formulate, discuss and analyse the possible relationships between instructional activities and student assessments. Most important, these discussions did not appear to violate the teachers' sense of the reality of these enterprises. They did not appear to be mere abstractions.

The media and grouping components of the descriptor contain a different story. The media component (Figures 8–10) is only partly notational. The (numbered) circles refer to separate and distinct materials but the rectangles of percentage of time are a symbol scheme with no intent to be notational. The referents (e.g. the actions with materials) are not as distinct as the symbols imply. Furthermore, the internal representations of 'percentage of time' may be far removed from the graphic symbols of the descriptor. It is obvious that we are asking teachers for a number of transformations to refer their sense of classroom activity to graphs of percentage of time within categories of instructional materials.

The grouping component of the descriptor is similarly non-notational. The referents are not so discrete, and the internal representations of percentage of time in the nine grouping categories are not easily transformed into symbolic thought. That our experience with the grouping component was that the logical aspect of the grouping category was its most dramatic feature further emphasises that the graphics of this component were not so captivating.

For these reasons the media and grouping components of the descriptor are not as successful in focusing and continuing critical analysis as the sequence and programme pattern components. They are not as notational and the graphics seem to be well removed from the internal representations of the teachers. There could, perhaps, have been better ways of depicting the use of media and the variety of grouping patterns than that constructed for the descriptor.

The extent to which the media and grouping categories do assist critical analysis, however, depends upon another important feature of graphics. That feature is its public nature. The graphics of the media and grouping components (as well as the other components of the descriptor) become the external referents of the teachers' internal search for accuracy. They are the externalisation of private thought and analysis on selected educational experience. The possibility for public analysis and subsequent revision makes for a kind of external dialogue with internalised experiential referents that, in our view, is the essence of critical and reflective thought. Levie (1978) labels this the productive process in the iconic mode. He, of course, has a diagram of this process (see Figure 16) and emphasises the importance of manipulation and productivity of the external iconic systems in evoking mental imagery. Especially in complex situations, Levie suggests productivity may be an excellent avenue to a richer understanding.

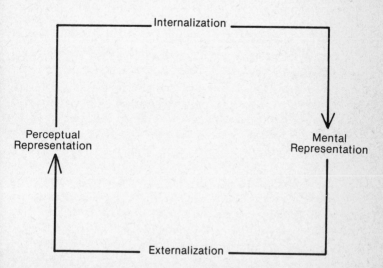

Figure 16. A Model of the Iconic Mode from Levie (1978).

In summary, our experience with the graphics of the descriptor in stimulating teacher recall and encouraging critical analysis and dialogue seems to be supported by some current research and embryonic theories of perceptual psychology. The symbolic selectivity of graphics can lead to better recall and critical analysis of experience when a) the notational features of the symbol system are (or can be) reflected in the teachers' perceptions of their actions, and b) there is the possibility to manipulate and rearrange the graphics as the dialogue between the externalisation of the graphic symbols and the internalisation of experience transpires. In this way, some of the better graphic symbol systems (such as the sequence and programme pattern components of the descriptor) can be used in the teachers' reconstruction of their work. The graphics may become, as Salomon suggests, a new internalised symbol system for capturing the teachers' sense of the reality of educational actions, thus making it possible, as Levie suggests, for them to redirect and to reconstruct that reality. Although graphics are not as rich as language, nor as potentially dense in meaning as photographs, their selective and notational features can have an important role in encouraging thoughtful reflection on professional experience. More than that, we suggest that in some cases graphics may be unusually potent in redirecting future actions.

Earlier we suggested that those who have examined the role of dialogue and reflective inquiry in action research may benefit from a consideration of graphics in this process. We suggested that graphics may be particularly valuable to investigators such as Elliott and Adelman, 1976; Bussis, Chittenden, and Amarel, 1976; Carini, 1979; and Ericson, 1978, to name only a few. There are other views of teaching processes and their relationship to critical thought that may likewise be enriched by a consideration of the symbolic, iconic codes of graphics. We speak here to the emphasis on the unconscious in teaching by Hill (1971), to the call for productivity assessments in 'self-referent research' by Scriven (1980), to the reminder that we engage our thought with the errors in our teaching (Stenhouse, 1979), and, most of all, to the challenges of Whitehead (1980) that the language of most critical analyses by educators misrepresents the referents of classroom teaching.

In conclusion, uttering and muttering are what we do in differing capacities with words, but we have similar difficulties in expressing our thoughts through other symbolic modes. Capturing or recalling what we have done before, constructing meaning within our experience, relating discrete features of that experience, expressing and then critically examining our recall, meaning and drawn relationships, are challenges regardless of the symbolic mode we choose. If we choose a graphic symbolic mode, we can expect similar hesitation, doubt, lack of clarity, ambiguity and contradiction as we have noticed in our verbal utterances.

The point that we have tried to make, however, is that our groping for clarity and focus in the analysis and re-analysis of our educational actions may be significantly aided by graphics. To induce critical analysis through dialogue has usually referred to the dialectics in the words we use to describe our educational actions and intentions. It may also refer to the dialectics in the iconic images of our human thought. Not only does a nearly immediate graphic display of the aggregation, comparison, contradiction and conflict of what we say we did make the need for continued dialogue apparent, but in some cases the dialogue (and internal search) is further enriched by the graphics. We found graphics encouraged teacher dialogue and reflective analysis on educational issues such as: i) the organisation of curricular content, ii) the structure induced in a classroom by repeated relationships between activity and assessment, iii) the time spent between teacher and child, iv) the possibilities in using different instructional media, and v) the range of perspectives for evaluating a student's understanding. Whether we can have thought without words, we can leave for some later discussion. What we are sure of is that graphics, iconic symbols, may help our words describe some very complex actions in a relatively accurate and engaging manner.

REFERENCES

ARNHEIM, R., *Art and Visual Perception*, University of California Press, 1954.

ARNHEIM, R., 'Virtues and vices of the visual media', in D. E. Olson (ed.), *Media and Symbols*, University of Chicago Press, 1974, pp. 180–210.

BARTHES, R., *Image, Music, Text,* Hill and Wang, 1977.

BUSSIS, A., CHITTENDEN, E. & AMAREL, M., *Beyond Surface Curriculum,* Westview Press, 1976.

CARINI, P. F., 'The art of seeing and the visibility of the person', North Dakota Study Group on Evaluation, University of North Dakota, September 1979.

DEVAULT, M. V., GOLLADAY, M., FOX, G. T., Jr. & SKULDT, K., *Descriptor for Individualised Instruction: Development procedures and results,* and *Users manual*; Parts I and II of Final Report to the National Institute of Education, Washington, D.C., Grant No. OEG-0-72-1254, 1973.

ELLIOTT, J., 'Developing hypotheses about classrooms from teachers' practical constructs', *Interchange,* 1976–77, 7(2), 2–22.

ELLIOTT, J. & ADELMAN, C., 'Classroom action research', Ford Teaching Project, Unit 2, *Research Methods,* Centre for Applied Research in Education, University of East Anglia, 1976.

ERICSON, F., 'On standards of descriptive validity in studies of classroom activity', Paper presented at the annual meeting of the American Educational Research Association, Toronto, March 1978.

FLAVELL, J. H., *Cognitive Development,* Prentice-Hall, 1977.

FOX, G. T., Jr. & DEVAULT, M. V., 'An historical perspective on individualised instruction', *Programmed Learning and Educational Technology,* 1978, 15(4), 271–283.

FROMBERG, D. P., *Early Childhood Education: A perceptual models curriculum,* Wiley, 1977.

FURTH, J. G., *Thinking Without Language: Psychological implications of deafness,* Free Press, 1966.

GARDNER, H., 'A psychological investigation of Nelson Goodman's Theory of Symbols', *The Monist,* 1974, 58, 317–326. (a)

GARDNER, H., *The Shattered Mind,* Vantage Books, 1974 (b).

GOODLAD, J., 'What goes on in our schools?', *Educational Researcher,* 1977, 6(3), 3–6.

GOODMAN, N., *The Languages of Art,* Hackett, 1968.

GUBA, E., *Toward a Methodology of Naturalistic Inquiry,* University of California, Center for the Study of Evaluation, 1978.

HAMILTON, D., 'Generalisation in the educational sciences: Problems and purposes', in T. Popkewitz & R. Tabachnick (eds.), *The Study of Schooling: Field-based methodologies in education research,* Praeger, 1980.

HATANO, G., MIYAKE, Y. & BINKS, M. G., 'Performance of expert abacus operators', *Cognition*, 1977, *5*, 57–71.

HEIDER, E. R. & OLIVIER, D., 'The structure of the colour space in naming and memory for two languages', *Cognitive Psychology*, 1972, *3*, 337–355.

HILL, J. C., *Teaching and the Unconscious Mind*, International Universities Press, 1971.

HOOK, C. M. & ROSENSHINE, B. V., 'Accuracy of teacher reports of their classroom behaviour', *Review of Educational Research*, 1979, *49*(1), 1–12.

IRONSIDE, R. A., 'What can be learned from validation of self-report data?', Paper presented at the annual meeting of the American Educational Research Association, Boston, April 1980.

KEMMIS, S., 'Telling it like it is: The problem of making a portrayal of an educational programme', in L. Rubin (ed.), *Handbook of Curriculum*, Allyn & Bacon, 1977.

KENNEDY, J. M., 'Icons and information', in D. E. Olson (ed.), *Media and Symbols*, University of Chicago Press, 1974, pp. 211–240.

KEPES, G. (ed.), *Education of Vision*, George Braziller, 1965.

KEPES, G. (ed.), *Sign, Image, Symbol*, George Braziller, 1966.

LANGER, S. K., *Feeling and Form*, Charles Scribner's Sons, 1953.

LEVIE, W. H., 'A prospectus for instructional research on visual literacy', *Educational Communications Technical Journal*, 1978, *26*(1).

MACDONALD, B., 'The portrayal of persons as evaluation data', Paper presented at the annual meeting of the American Educational Research Association, San Francisco, April 1976.

MERLEAU-PONTY, M., 'The film and the new psychology', *Sense and Non-sense*, Northwestern University Press, 1964, pp. 48–59.

MEYER, L. B., *Music, the Arts, and Ideas*, University of Chicago Press, 1967.

MURPHY, J. T., *Getting The Facts: A fieldwork guide for evaluators and policy analysts*, Goodyear, 1980.

PALMER, S. E., 'Visual perception and world knowledge: Notes on a model of sensory-cognitive interaction', in D. A. Norman & D. E. Rumelhart (eds), *Explorations in Cognition*, W. H. Freeman, 1975.

SALOMON, G., *Interaction of Media, Cognition, and Learning*, Jossey-Bass, 1979.

SCRIVEN, M., 'Self-referent research', Part I, *Educational Researcher,* 1980, *9*(4), 7–11; Part II, *Educational Researcher*, 1980, *9*(6), 11–18.

SCHWAB, J., The Practical: A language for curriculum, Washington, D.C., National Education Association Auxiliary Series, 1970.

SHEPARD, R. N. 'Externalisation of mental images and the act of creation', in B. S. Randhava & W. E. Coffman (eds), *Visual Learning, Thinking, and Communication*, Academic Press, 1978.

STENHOUSE, L., 'Research as a basis for teaching', Inaugural lecture delivered before the University of East Anglia, February 1979.

TVERSKY, A., 'Features of similarity', *Psychological Review*, 1977, *84*, 327–352.

WALKER, R., 'The use of case studies in applied research and evaluation', in A. Harnett (ed.), *Educational Studies and Social Science*, Heinemann Educational, 1980.

WAX, R. H., *Doing Fieldwork: Warnings and advice*, University of Chicago Press, 1971.

WHITEHEAD, J., 'Describing the values in educational practice', Paper presented at the meeting of the British Educational Research Association, Cardiff, September 1980.

WITTGENSTEIN, L., *On Certainty*, Harper and Row, 1969.

ROY TODD

10 Methodology: the Hidden Context of Situation in Studies of Talk

The importance of the 'context of situation' in determining features of talk and the necessity to take it into account in making sense of talk are both now generally accepted. Without reference to the 'context of situation' the interpretation is, at best, inadequate. This point is clarified by Halliday[1] as follows:

> We do not experience language in isolation – if we did we would not recognise it as language – but always in relation to a scenario, some background of persons and actions and events from which the things which are said derive their meaning. This is referred to as the 'situation', so language is said to function in 'contexts of situation' and any account of language which fails to build in the situation as an essential ingredient is likely to be artificial and unrewarding.

The basic concept of the 'context of situation', from its introduction by Malinowski,[2] through its later development by Firth,[3] to its more contemporary usage, has acquired a variety of meanings and considerable breadth of definition. For some, context may extend to a community or social system, while others focus on the interpersonal setting. The context may be determined by objective features or subjective interpretations. It may treat the speaker as a product of the environment or social system or focus upon the individual as an active, reflexive, definer of contexts. The context may also be considered to be determined by linguistic conditions or to be a product mainly of extra-linguistic features of communication.[4]

One of the difficulties of sociolinguistic research derives from the nature of research as a social process. Thus, research which is intended to clarify the significance and consequences of contexts of situation forms, in itself, a context of situation. The social interaction which occurs in the processes of locating or establishing a research setting, the processes of data collection, and the presuppositions built into the selection of subjects for the research, combine to produce a complex and intricate context.

A related difficulty in socio-linguistic research concerns the 'theoretical' nature of the research process. Research data is obtained through a series of inferences. Decisions made in the process of research successively delimit the possibilities for the interpretation of data. Moreover these inferences impose a theoretical framework, albeit one which is often complex and which may not be explicitly related to the avowed conceptual framework of research. The general point here is expressed succinctly by Coombs:

> The basic point is that our conclusions, even at the level of measurement and scaling . . . are already a consequence of theory. . . . All knowledge is the result of theory – we buy information with assumptions – 'facts' are inferences, and so also are data and measurement and scales.[5]

Empirical research is thus seen as a theoretical process which yields an image of the world which is determined by the instruments of research.[6] There is no scientific understanding of social reality which is independent of theoretical concepts.

Starting from these two general points concerning the social nature of research into talk and the theoretical nature of the research process, my objective is to make explicit the range of presuppositions built into research into talk with particular reference to the context of situation. The model of the research process underlying this discussion is of research as a series of inferential stages which progressively constrain the data obtained. The complex inter-relationship of theory and method in sociolinguistic research is of direct relevance to this discussion. On the one hand, particular theoretical perspectives commit the investigator, explicitly or implicitly, to specific types of research procedure. This commitment is expressed through the general methodology of the investigation and more narrowly through the chosen methods of data collection and analysis. On the other hand, the use of specific research procedures has theoretical implications, for research procedures may be characterised as theoretical instruments. To view research techniques merely as technical devices is naive and insupportable. It is the theoretical significance of particular research methods in sociolinguistic research which I shall focus upon in an attempt to clarify the qualitative features of the context of situation determined by the research process. Only the general features of the research context can be referred to here. I shall try to indicate some broad characteristics of the theoretical assumptions and socially determined features of research and thus the context of situation defined through research. However, the discussion is necessarily selective, and in its brevity does not penetrate the full complexity of research methods.

The inferences made through the research process may be considered to be relevant to a context of situation through two dimensions: space and time. Taking the first of these, and interpreting it in terms of social space, I suggest that we consider three analytical levels: the model of society, the relationship between the person and a wider group, and the model of the person. Reference to time as a dimension draws us to consider whether assumptions about the effects of time on social interaction (through development, history, ageing, or other socially constructed features) are appropriate. For example, small group interaction is often recorded, analysed, and generalised from with the implicit assumption that behaviour in groups comprised of subjects who have only just met is equivalent to that manifested in groups which have been established for a longer period. To illustrate the consequences of assumptions and inferences made during research I shall examine a number of steps in the conduct of sociolinguistic research, drawing upon procedures of general design, data collection and data analysis. I consider the way in which these procedures determine contexts of situation at these different levels through the research process and suggest some of their general qualitative features. Broadly speaking, the context is a consequence of two aspects of research: it is provided partially by the social interaction which occurs in research and partially by the research instruments which are deployed. In particular, I examine sampling procedures, experimental methods, observational category systems and statistical data analysis in order to develop my argument. The major implication of this line of reasoning is that it is mistaken to interpret talk in research settings without detailed reference to the context of situation embodied in the research procedures.

SELECTION OF UNITS

The boundaries of a 'context of situation' have been drawn very widely in spatial terms. For example, Hymes[7] writes 'One must take as context a community . . .' Also, in a discussion of language as social semiotic, Halliday[8] includes reference to the social system and social structure. The phases of empirical research which have direct relevance to the context of situation as thus defined, occur in the early stages of investigation which are concerned with the selection of units: these decisions of sampling are, naturally, based upon assumptions about communities or the social system.

In much sociolinguistic research the individual is used, at some stage, as a sampling unit: sometimes as the main point of reference for data analysis. Sometimes, however, individuals are selected for inclusion in task groups by the investigator and at other times individuals are selected as a preliminary stage in the elicitation of linguistic data. Although other units of analysis can be, and are, used to good effect, I shall consider the selection of individuals at this point.

The dominant model employed in sampling for social research is that of random sampling, for there are sound statistical reasons for using a random sampling strategy and the method holds the promise of accurate estimation of results and assured generalisability of findings. The assumptions of random sampling include that the units are considered to be equal and have an equal probability of selection for the sample. These assumptions are of theoretical significance for research into talk if we define the context in terms as general as the social system.

In a discussion of cross-cultural survey research Scheuch makes the following comments:

An important implication of survey research is that all members of a population matter, are largely interchangeable as units (i.e. as carriers of attributes) and exhibit the properties under investigation. That all units matter, and that individuals are the relevant units for the purpose of a study – this is by no means self-evident.[9]

We could extend part of this argument to the study of language and social context. Selecting individuals for research on the basis of a random sampling model involves a process of taking them out of their social context and presuming that they may be treated as equivalent for research purposes. But to assume, with reference to social contexts, that each individual may be treated as the same, fills an equal social position or role, has an identical social and cultural history, or brings to bear similar expectations of the research requirement, is to make very dubious assumptions. The grouping of individuals thus selected for experimental tasks, while disregarding their formal and informal positions in the social structures from which they have been drawn, is equally questionable.

Sometimes the investigator, despite having drawn a sample which assumes representativeness and equivalence of subjects, finds that the research results suggest that these assumptions are mistaken. An ad hoc account of differences between subjects which provides an explanation of unanticipated patterns in the data then becomes necessary. An example of this can be found in Whitehead's[10] interpretation of differences in children's descriptions of a game where he speculates about previous experience with the game. The 'hidden' context of sampling procedures may also have contributed to the differences between the talk obtained in the 'participatory phase' and the 'experimental phase' of the work described in this volume by Barnes and Todd.[11] The subjects in one phase were working in friendship groups, whereas those in the other phase were grouped at random. The social contexts of these two settings seem very different: one a group of friends, used to working together, with an established informal structure, and the other a group of people not used to cooperating, with different qualities of relationships, and with power and status dimensions being worked out in the process of the experiment.

There are alternative approaches to sampling which may be more appropriate for sociolinguistic research. Some of these remain under the general heading of probability sampling, such as stratified sampling procedures. These provide the opportunity for incorporating theoretical dimensions in the design based upon our awareness of social structural and other variables while still offering the inferential power of probability sampling. The work of Wells,[12] in this volume, may be taken as illustrative here, for his sample incorporated equal representation of sexes, four classes of family background, and four seasons of birth. This complexity of design draws attention to other variables which may also be considered relevant to the study, such as the number of siblings, birth order, and the sex of the eldest sibling. These possibilities are mentioned, not to detract from a study which is both complex and meticulously designed, but to underline the necessity to adopt complex sampling designs for sociolinguistic research.

This complexity in sampling may be developed, in a manner which explicitly depicts the context of situation in research, through what has been referred to as theoretically directed sampling. Theoretically directed sampling, sometimes referred to as scope sampling, has been distinguished from representational sampling and proposed for both quantitative and qualitative styles of social research. Theoretical sampling is sampling which is based upon criteria of theoretical purpose and relevance. Thus it differs in principle from the representational purpose which underlies simple probability sampling. Within the tradition of qualitative research, sampling on a flexible, theoretically directed basis, rather than on pre-arranged criteria, has been proposed by Glaser and Strauss.[13] The notion of theoretical development through theory construction by systematic comparative analysis is central to this strategy. Somewhat similar goals, but within the context of quantitative modes of research, have led Finifter[14] to discuss a variety of theoretical sampling procedures under the collective name of 'random subsample replication'.

Theoretically directed sampling should not be simply equated with naive subjective sampling, nor be presumed to follow the vagaries of individual judgmental sampling which have contributed so often to what Lazerwitz[15] describes scathingly as 'the junkyard' of subjective sampling. Rather it may be seen as providing valid and rigorous options in research. In particular it avoids the imposition of inappropriate models of the social context and provides the opportunity for focused development of theoretical understanding. An example of its use in a sociolinguistic study is found in a study by

Cook-Gumperz and Corsaro.[16] Their analysis of episodes in a nursery school is based upon theoretical sampling of video-taped recordings. However, the problem of replication, which is hinted at by the phrase of Finifter mentioned above, becomes apparent here. Unless the concepts employed and the selection and exclusion procedures utilised are clearly defined and illustrated in studies based on theoretical sampling, other investigators are prevented from checking the work independently or replicating it. The danger arises that theoretical sampling may be employed as a slogan concealing arbitrary, inconsistent, or ill-defined selection of units.

This discussion has been based primarily upon the selection of individuals as the unit of analysis in sociolinguistic research. However, it is evident that other units are appropriate and some of these have found their place in a number of projects. Alternative approaches to sampling for the study of talk include the following: the location of individuals precisely within a social context prior to sampling; the sampling of informal social groups; the sampling of social episodes; the sampling of segments of discourse. General questions of the context from which such units are taken for analysis remain. They pose specific technical and theoretical problems which are beyond the scope of this paper. Nevertheless, I would argue that they need to be incorporated in any analysis of the context of situation embodied in research.

COLLECTION OF DATA IN EXPERIMENTAL SETTINGS

The early phases of the empirical research process – concerned as they are with the selection of units – raise problems about the underlying model of society and of the latent conception of the relationship between the person and society. Later stages of research involve inferences at other levels. In the processes of data collection, presuppositions are made about the individual subject of the research, or, at a more abstract level, the underlying model of the person. This is also relevant to our interpretation of the research process as a context of situation, for in the process of data collection the structures and dynamics of social interaction as well as the research instruments employed impose restraints upon the subjects of the research. Moreover, it is to these analytical levels that some sociolinguists refer for their interpretation of language. Bloom, for example, in her study of language development, writes: 'Non-linguistic information from context and behaviour in relation to linguistic performance' provides additional information clarifying the semantics of children's sentences.[17] Ericson and Schultz, in a paper concerned with theoretical and methodological issues in the study of context, write: 'Contexts are not simply given in the physical setting . . . rather contexts are constituted by what people are doing and where and when they are doing it.'[18] I am thus concerned here with the underlying model of the person and, derived from this, assumptions about modes of interaction between persons which are an intrinsic part of research methodology. I shall focus upon the experimental setting to illustrate these underlying preconceptions as they relate to features of the context of situation.

Experimental studies have often been criticised for their artificiality. They are viewed as sources of invalidity in research as a result of the unnatural settings or peculiar tasks which so often form a part of experimental designs. However, I am not concerned with any departure from 'natural' social settings, nor to argue in terms of 'error' introduced through the use of the experimental paradigm. My objective is to begin to analyse the qualities of the context provided by experimental research methods. I suggest that, in the interpretation of sociolinguistic data derived from experimental research, these qualities should be considered as attributes of a context of situation determined by the research. Thus I am considering the experiment in the light of its constraints or theoretical implications, not with reference to an idealised view of an undefined 'reality'.

There are numerous alternative approaches to the design of experimental studies which incorporate considerable variations in the experimental task and in the social interaction prior to, throughout, and after, this mode of data collection. There are also a number of studies of the social-psychological aspects of experimental method-ology.[19] This discussion, therefore, is necessarily selective. I shall take as a starting point the experimental method in its most restrictive form, while recognising that less restrictive options are available to those engaged in sociolinguistic research. Features of the classical psychophysical experiments are described and the extent to which they are analogous with sociolinguistic experiments is considered.

This section is derived from the work of Harré and Secord.[20] Harré and Secord point out that the traditional perception experiment places the subject in a setting where he or she is physically restrained (e.g. the head may be held in a clamp) and for which attention is directed to a simple stimulus with limited dimensions (e.g. pure tones). The responses open to the subject in this form of experiment are similarly limited to a narrow range of options (provided that the subject cooperates fully with the experimenter: eccentric responses such as falling asleep between the presentation of stimuli are normally excluded from the data analysis). Taking the work of Gibson[21] as a contrast to the traditional perceptual investigation, an alternative to this traditional psychophysical view of perception is presented. It is argued that simple sensations have little connection with how the world is normally perceived, for complex behaviour is not derived in any elementary functional way from simple judgments, and perception is achieved by active exploration of the world.

Although restriction in sociolinguistic studies may not involve the physical restraint referred to above as typical of psychophysical experiments, in social terms they can be equally limiting. In a number of experimentally presented tasks in sociolinguistic studies the subject is isolated from others, in a setting with the experimenter which restricts non-verbal cues and channels of communication and establishes a pre-determined relationship with the experimenter in proxemic terms. From this basis the experimenter directs the subject to respond to a task which may be elementary in its nature, and specifies the mode of the response. Harré and Secord claim of this type of experiment:'Common to all types of overly-restrictive experiments is the conception of people as information-processing machines rather than information seeking and information generating agents. Thus information is deliberately restricted and inter-action prevented.' This underlying behaviouristic model of the person responding somewhat mechanically to the stimuli of the experimental setting is easily carried through in the discussion of the results, where the 'in-put' is specified in terms of social variables, the 'out-put' in enumerated linguistic categories of utterances, and no possibilities for internal processing are offered save those, if any, which are deterministically implied by the operational definitions of the variables.

Another feature of the experimental setting which is relevant to the discussion is that typically the experiment is a special kind of social situation in which the interaction occurs between strangers, albeit strangers who adduce clues to the social identities of each other from the restricted contacts and definitions of role relationships which are inevitable components of the research. Nevertheless communication in the experimental setting does not inevitably result in a standardised understanding by the subjects. The implicit demands of the experimental setting, the assumptions about relationships between subject and researcher, the subjects' understanding of the general framework and purposes of experiments and their willing compliance with the experimenter's requests, all frame the experiment as a distinctive communication setting. A substantial number of studies of communication in experimental settings are reviewed in a paper by Orne.[22] He challenges common assumptions about consonance between experimenter and subject perceptions of experimental tasks, as well as about the uniformity of subject's interpretations. He also discusses their significance for the interpretation of experimental findings. Clearly, even the most restrictive and simple experimental settings are deceptive, for they conceal qualitative features of perceptions, behaviour and interpretation which are extremely complex.

The qualities of the experimental paradigm as a context of situation can be clarified by reference to, and in contrast with, a study of language in a natural social setting. In the study referred to above, Cook-Gumperz and Corsaro[23] investigated the conversations and communicative strategies of children in a nursery school. The study was conducted with an awareness of the research contexts and assumptions about the subjects which are incompatible with those referred to by Harré and Secord and thus serves as a useful illustration. The communicative strategies of children were recorded as they participated in interactive episodes. At the same time the contexts were noted in terms of linguistic phenomena and the social-physical setting. The contexts of situation in the study were not assumed to be neutral, insignificant or minimal; attempts were made to analyse them and incorporate them in the discussion of results. This was achieved by relating transcriptions of children's speech to the socio-ecological context via descriptive analysis and interpretation.

The subjects of the research were treated as active and significant definers of the context, not as passive responders to a context provided by the investigators. The authors assert that 'the interpretation of a series of utterances depends upon the interactant's definition of context as it is communicated in the course of interaction.'[24] For these researchers' purposes the mode of communication is not restricted to verbal utterances; paralinguistic and other cues were noted and referred to as parts of the communication process. 'Language is considered as part of a total communication system, in which the system itself generates certain particular understandings during the course of interaction.'[25] An outcome of the results which links with the comment above about the relationship of simple behaviour to complex behaviour is that the children showed a greater range of communicative competence than is sometimes revealed by other methodologies. Cook–Gumperz and Corsaro write: 'Our analysis ... revealed the children's employment of communicative devices which are often overlooked in studies of child language.'[26]

This example is set against my earlier depiction of experimental settings to indicate contrasts in assumptions about the subjects and the interaction of subjects. I have also used it to identify an approach which takes note of the research context and to illustrate one way of approaching the description and analysis of contexts. It is important to note that I am not arguing that sociolinguistic research should be conducted entirely and exclusively by observation of natural social settings. Restrictive control of social interaction, manipulation of the setting, mechanistic models of the subjects of research, can become as much a part of research in non-experimental settings. They are the outcome of decisions made by the investigator. Indeed, some uses of interviews and questionnaires in sociolinguistic research may be said to be quasi-experimental in that they are modelled on similar constraints: interaction with the subjects may be restricted, explanations are limited, paralinguistic cues are controlled, the subjects' responses can be coded within a pre-determined framework.[27] This approach is derived from a general methodology which is based upon similar philosophical assumptions to those which support experimentation and, for better or worse, achieves similar ends.

OBSERVATIONAL CATEGORY SYSTEMS

Having considered the selection of units for research, and the structuring of the research setting for data collection, I want to continue the sequence by examining aspects of the interpretation and analysis of data. First, I shall refer to the use of category systems for summarising and interpreting talk, drawing attention to the specific theoretical constraints which they embody and the kinds of context of situation which they thus define.

There are a number of category systems for coding talk and paralinguistic features of communication. These may be used singly, together with other systems, or as a component of multiple strategies of data analysis. [28] Each category system, inevitably, is based upon a theoretical orientation which it manifests in its content through its definition of the categories. For example, the early scheme for Interaction Process Analysis developed by Bales[29] and his associates has twelve categories which focus almost wholly on instrumental activities, minimising the expression of affect, and separating affective and instrumental behaviour. These categories enable the recording of talk which is concerned with the giving of, or asking for, orientation, opinion, suggestion, agreement and disagreement. Thus they are based upon and are appropriate for interaction in a context of general agreement about goals, purposes, ends and the means of achieving these ends. This category system is somewhat inappropriate for the recording of groups such as negotiating sessions where there are conflicting objectives, the display and use of power, hard bargaining and threats. Whereas the context of an integrative social system is assumed in Interaction Process Analysis, a context of fundamental conflict cannot be adequately recorded with the scheme.

A category scheme which may be contrasted with Interaction Process Analysis in a different way is that developed by Freedman and his colleagues which focuses entirely upon affective features of behaviour, recording the socio-emotional context on a 'wheel' which reduces neatly to two orthogonal dimensions, love/hate and dominance/submission, and allows for the recording of degrees of emotional intensity.

Other questions can be raised about category systems at a different level of analysis, independently of both the content of the categories and the definition of the unit of interaction. To what extent does the use of categories, i.e. the *form* of the analysis of interaction, define a context of situation? The answer to this question can be framed through a consideration of a limitation of category systems, namely their clumsiness in coping with sequences of interaction. Although, as Bales has demonstrated, phases of interaction can be analysed by the use of time segments and frequency counts, nevertheless the impression conveyed by category systems is of stable patterns of interaction with a high degree of order and uniformity, and with clearly specified messages. Thus they cannot adequately represent a context which is marked by disturbances in interaction, rapid and marked transition and change, or especially those critical incidents or crises where radical qualitative changes in the situation occur. Moreover, ambiguous messages and contradictions which are the hallmark of some roles and social structural conditions pose particular technical problems for category systems and, for the moment, can be said to mark out types of context of situation which elude them. In a number of specific ways, therefore, the use of category systems in the interpretation of language can be said to define contexts of situation with reference to, and independently of, their content.

An approach to the observation of social interaction which, although systematic, does not depend upon category systems has been used by Reiss[30] in sociological studies of interaction between juveniles and police. Although not yet, to my knowledge, adopted in socio-linguistic research, the approach may prove useful for the complex description and analysis of contexts of situation, especially when tied in with recordings of interaction. The observers in the research directed by Reiss were required to complete detailed questionnaires about the episodes they witnessed. These questionnaires were partly compiled with closed questions but also included open-ended questions. Such an approach to noting details of observation can potentially incorporate diversity, complex description, and rigour in accounts of context of situation.

STATISTICAL ANALYSIS

This final stage in the sequence, the statistical analysis of data, is necessarily selective, just as earlier discussion has been selective. Statistical analysis of sociolinguistic data, however, has used few of the many statistical procedures available. Although some elementary descriptive statistics and a range of inferential statistics have been used in studies of talk (especially in studies comparing 'working class' and 'middle class' speech) it seems that many statistical resources are ignored. Perhaps the use of a wider range of sensitive statistical methods would yield advantages in the development of our understanding of features of talk. However, statistical procedures also bring us further problems of inference.

Statistical models are based on assumptions which vary in their number and strength and whose theoretical implications may be complex and not readily apparent. The use of statistical procedures is also linked with methodologies which incorporate an underlying model of the person through the process of operational definitions, through the specification of variables and by norms of data interpretation. In very general terms therefore it is possible to identify approaches to statistical analysis which introduce different contexts of situation through the combined assumptions of statistical models and statistical practices.

Within a paper discussing the use of statistics in the social sciences, Boudon[31] refers to three types of image of the person ('homo sociologicus' in his phrase) which underly the use of statistics. In the first of these, explanations of social behaviour are sought in the environment. In the second, social structures are seen as the major determinant of social behaviour. Boudon suggests that these first two approaches are common in that they introduce a determinist vision of the person, although this determinism is considered to be probabilistic. The third approach does not depict the person in a deterministic way, but does acknowledge that behaviour is subject to constraints. Rather than emphasising social or environmental antecedents of behaviour, however, it gives a central place to action, choice and decision. In this context statistics are considered useful for descriptive purposes when they are supplemented by other analyses: interpretation of results does not rest solely upon the automatic application of a statistical procedure.

Analyses of talk which account for variations in patterns of speech entirely in terms of social structural variables would be located in

Boudon's categories which are based on deterministic models. Accounts of flexibility in talk which involves adaptability and decision through the choice of a range of codes, registers, or other markers according to changes in context show a close fit with Boudon's third category.

Like other instruments of research, statistics give a representation of social context which depends upon how they are conceived and employed. Whereas their use in sociolinguistics may convey a deterministic image of the person in a social or environmental context, this is not inevitable: there are also statistical options, primarily descriptive, which if used in conjunction with other forms of analysis convey a social context which is qualitatively different.

CONCLUSIONS

It is now apparent that no sociolinguistic research can be 'context-free'. Even those approaches to research which attempt to present a 'neutral' or simplified setting are based upon presuppositions which both impose a context and seriously underestimate its complexity. The process of sociolinguistic research inevitably incorporates a social context which ranges across conceptions of society, models of the individual, images of the relationships between the individual and society, and notions of human interaction. Since each component of the research process introduces such presuppositions, there is an accumulation of dimensions to the implicit context of situation as research progresses from beginning to end.

These features of context often remain wholly implicit in the study of talk. At best they are only partially analysed, more often they are given a passing nod of recognition or presumed insignificant. I would suggest that the context of situation carried by the research process needs more attention than this: if only to prevent the construction of complex theories from being undermined by deterministic, mechanistic and structureless conceptions of people and society which form the methodological foundations of some empirical studies. If I may take this constructional metaphor further, I suggest that the methodological foundations of sociolinguistics form a base, with which any conceptual or theoretical structure must be compatible if it is to have any hope of permanence.

NOTES

1 HALLIDAY, M. A. K., *Language as Social Semiotic,* Edward Arnold, 1978, pp. 28–29.

2 MALINOWSKI, B., 'The problem of meaning in primitive languages' in Ogden, C. K. & Richards, I. A. (eds), *The Meaning of Meaning*, Kegan Paul, 1923.

3 FIRTH, J. R., *Papers in Linguistics 1934–1951*, Oxford University Press, 1957.

4 See HALLIDAY, M. A. K., 1978, *op. cit*; HYMES, D., *Foundations in Sociolinguistics*, Tavistock, 1974.

5 COOMBS, C. H., *A Theory of Data*, Wiley, 1964.

6 For discussions of the philosophical issues underlying conceptions of social science see BENTON, T., *Philosophical Foundations of the Three Sociologies*, Routledge and Kegan Paul, 1977 and KEAT, R. & URRY, J., *Social Theory as Science*, Routledge and Kegan Paul, 1975.

7 HYMES, D., *op. cit.* p. 4.

8 HALLIDAY, M. A. K., *op. cit.* see p. 69.

9 SCHEUCH, E. K., 'The cross-cultural use of sample surveys: problems of comparability' in Rokkan, S. (ed.), *Comparative Research across Cultures and Nations*, Mouton, 1968.

10 WHITEHEAD, M., 'Analysis of conversations between pairs of children'; Paper presented to SSRC conference on collecting, using and reporting talk for research in education, Reading University, 1976.

11 BARNES, D. & TODD, F. E., this volume.

12 WELLS, G., this volume.

13 GLASER, B. & STRAUSS, A., *The Discovery of Grounded Theory; Strategies for Qualitative Research*, Aldine 1967.

14 FINIFTER, B. M., 'The generation of confidence: evaluating research findings by random subsample replication' in Costner, H. L. (ed.), *Sociological Methodology*, Jossey Bass, 1972.

15 LAZERWITZ, B., 'Sampling theory and procedures' in Blalock, H. M. & Blalock, A. (eds), *Methodology in Social Research*, McGraw-Hill, 1968.

16 COOK-GUMPERZ, J. & CORSARO, W. A. 'Social-ecological constraints on children's communicative strategies', *Sociology*, 11 iii, September 1977, pp. 412–434.

17 BLOOM, L., *Language Development*, M.I.T. Press, 1970.

18 ERICSON, F. & SCHULTZ, F., 'When is a context? Some issues and methods in the analysis of social competence', *Quarterly Newsletter of the Institute for Comparative Human Development*, February 1977, 1 ii, pp. 5–10.

19 For experimental design see: CAMPBELL, D. T. & STANLEY, J. C., *Experimental and Quasi-experimental Designs for Research*, Rand McNally, 1966; and COOK, T. D. & CAMPBELL, D. T., *Quasi-Experimentation, Design and Analysis Issues for Field Settings*, Rand McNally, 1979. Social-psychological aspects of experiments are discussed in ROSENTHAL R. & ROSNOW, R. L., *Artifact in Behavioral Research*, Academic Press, 1969; and ROSENTHAL, *Experimenter Effects in Research*, Appleton-Century-Crofts, 1966.

20 HARRÉ, R. & SECORD, P. F., *The Explanation of Social Behaviour*, Basil Blackwell, 1972.

21 GIBSON, J. J., *The Senses Considered as Perceptual Systems*, George Allen and Unwin, 1966.

22 ORNE, M. T., 'Communication by the total experimental situation' in Pliner, P., Krames, L. & Alloway, T. (eds.), *Communication and Affect*, Academic Press, 1973.

23 COOK-GUMPERZ, J. & CORSARO, W. A., op. cit.

24 *ibid.*, p. 413.

25 *ibid.*, p. 414.

26 *ibid.*, p. 432.

27 For discussion of options in interview design *see* CANNELL, C. F. & KAHN, R. L., 'Interviewing' in Lindzey, G. & Aronson, E. (eds)., *The Handbook of Social Psychology*, Addison-Wesley, 1968.

28 Multiple strategies of data analysis and their problems are usefully discussed in Denzin, N., *The Research Act*, Butterworth, 1970.

29 See WEICK, K. E., 'Systematic observational methods' in Lindzey, G. & Aronson, E., op. cit., for discussion of systematic observation including reference to Bales and Freedman discussed here.

30 REISS, A. J., 'Systematic observation of natural social phenomena' in H. L. Costner (ed.), *Sociological Methodology*, Jossey Bass, 1971.

31 BOUDON, R., 'Les statistiques peuvent-elles donner une image réelle de la réalité sociale?, *Sociologie et Sociétés*, 8 ii, October 1976, pp. 141–156.

Notes on Contributors

CLEM ADELMAN has a science degree, several saxophones, and teaching experience in schools, polytechnics and universities. He discovered his inclination towards social and educational research in the late 1960s whilst worrying about ways of analysing classroom activities that had been recorded on film and tape. There followed twelve years' work on projects concerned with pedagogy, fostering teachers' action research, institutional and curriculum evaluation and, most recently, a case study of bilingual schooling in the USA. From this research numerous articles in journals and books have emerged.

PAUL ATKINSON is a lecturer in sociology at University College, Cardiff. After taking a degree in social anthropology at Cambridge he completed his doctoral research in the Centre for Research in the Educational Sciences, University of Edinburgh. That research was an ethnographic study of medical students in their first year of clinical studies. Since then he has maintained a teaching and research interest in the sociology of medicine and the sociology of education. His publications include *The Clinical Experience: The Construction and Reconstruction of Medical Reality, Prospects for the National Health* (ed. with Robert Dingwall and Anne Murcott) and *Medical Work: Realities and Routines* (ed. with Christian Heath). His current research includes an investigation of industrial training units for the educationally subnormal. He is editor of *The Sociology of Health and Illness: A Journal of Medical Sociology*.

DOUGLAS BARNES is Senior Lecturer in the University of Leeds School of Education, having moved to this post in 1966 after teaching English in secondary schools for seventeen years. He lectures in Curriculum Theory, and his research has been mainly directed towards understanding the part played by teachers' and pupils' talk in classroom learning. This has led to the publication of *From*

Communication to Curriculum and (with co-authors) of *Language, the Learner and the School* and *Communication and Learning in Small Groups*. At present he is engaged in a study of English teaching from 15 to 17 in schools and further education colleges.

G. THOMAS FOX, Jr is a project associate at the University of Wisconsin-Madison. He was an elementary school teacher for seven years and received his Ph.D. at the University of Wisconsin-Madison in 1972. His Ph.D. work in child language was the basis for a '1973 Promising Researcher' award from the National Council of Teachers of English. Since 1972 his work has included analysing individualised instruction in schools and classrooms, performing evaluation studies of federal intervention programmes, and making critiques of evaluation strategies at the federal and international levels, particularly evaluations of staff development and in-service programmes. Since 1975 he has been a consultant to the Teacher Corps Programme on such topics as evaluation, documentation, demonstration and dissemination.

HELEN SIMONS was educated in New Zealand and Australia, where she was involved in curriculum development before emigrating to England in the late sixties. Here she has specialised increasingly in educational evaluation and currently holds a lectureship in that field at the University of London Institute of Education. In evaluating innovatory curriculum projects and policy initiatives she has undertaken extensive fieldwork in primary, secondary and higher education institutions. Her publications include papers on school self-evaluation, case-study research and student learning.

MICHAEL STUBBS is Lecturer in Linguistics at the University of Nottingham. His first degree was in French, German and Linguistics (Cambridge 1970) and his Ph.D. was on language in the classroom (Edinburgh 1975). His publications include *Explorations in Classroom Observation* (co-editor), *Language, Schools and Classrooms, Language and Literacy*, and articles and reviews on language in education, English language teaching and discourse analysis. His current teaching and research interests include the history and general principles of linguistics, sociolinguistics and discourse analysis. He has taught in France, Australia and China.

FRANKIE TODD followed a degree in Psychology and Sociology with teaching and research experience in various institutions of further and higher education. After the research with Douglas Barnes reported in this volume, she taught applied psychology to health science students at Leeds Polytechnic. Her published work is mainly concerned with collaborative learning and she has recently been applying this interest to the design of continuing education for professional groups. She is currently employed as Research Fellow in the NHS Continuing Education Unit in the Institute of Advanced Architectural Studies at the University of York.

ROY TODD has a degree in Psychology and Sociology and has teaching and research experience in both these fields. He has published papers on adult reading skills, teaching methods in higher education and social policy. He has taught at Leeds University and at Trinity and All Saints College, and during 1980–81 is Honorary Research Fellow in the Department of Sociology, University of Leeds. He is currently engaged in research into theoretical and quantitative aspects of sociological methodology.

GORDON WELLS studied at Cambridge (English) and Edinburgh (Linguistics). He has taught in schools in England, France and Ghana, and in a College of Education in England. Since 1969 he has been Director of the research programme 'Language at Home and at School' based at the University of Bristol School of Education. The results of the research are to be published in a series of books by Cambridge University Press. His other publications include journal articles on language development, discourse analysis and early education.

MARY WILLES has experience in teaching English in schools, and turned aside from her interest in literary and art-historical research, when her experience in teacher education in the 1960s convinced her of the centrality of language to the educational process, and the need for a serious component of language study in teacher education. From her doctoral studies on children's learning of the rules of classroom discourse, carried out in close association with English Language Research at Birmingham, have come several contributions to books and periodicals and to materials prepared by the Open University. She is currently Subject Leader in English Language Studies at West Midlands College of Higher Education.

PETER WOODS is Senior Lecturer in the Sociology of Education at the

Open University, where he has been for nine years. Before that, he taught in primary and secondary schools in Norfolk, London and Yorkshire. Dr Woods has written and edited numerous books and articles on education, the most recent being *The Divided School* and *Teacher* and *Pupil Strategies*. He is currently engaged in research into pupil adaptation to secondary school.

Index

Grant McIntyre Limited specializes in social behavioural and medical science, and publishes books of all kinds – introductory and advanced texts, handbooks and reference works, practical manuals, and important research. The aim is to make a continuing wealth of new work available to all readers for whom it has value.

Look for our books at your local bookshop, or write for a catalogue or to order direct. Simply fill in the form below, and list the books you want.

GRANT McINTYRE LIMITED, Sales Office,
39 Great Russell Street, London WC1B 3PY.

Please send me your latest catalogue/and also/the books on the attached list. I enclose a cheque, postal or money order (no currency) for the purchase price of the books plus 10% for those living outside the UK) to cover postage and packing. (Catalogues and their postage are free.)

NAME (Block letters please):

....

ADDRESS:

....

....

....

....